The Making and Shaping of the Victorian Teacher

The Making and Shaping of the Victorian Teacher

A Comparative New Cultural History

Marianne A. Larsen
Assistant Professor, Faculty of Education, University of Western Ontario, Canada

First published 2011 by
PALGRAVE MACMILLAN

Palgrave Macmillan in the UK is an imprint of Macmillan Publishers Limited, registered in England, company number 785998, of Houndmills, Basingstoke, Hampshire RG21 6XS.

Palgrave Macmillan in the US is a division of St Martin's Press LLC, 175 Fifth Avenue, New York, NY 10010.

Palgrave Macmillan is the global academic imprint of the above companies and has companies and representatives throughout the world.

Palgrave® and Macmillan® are registered trademarks in the United States, the United Kingdom, Europe and other countries

ISBN 978-0-230-24128-2   hardback

This book is printed on paper suitable for recycling and made from fully managed and sustained forest sources. Logging, pulping and manufacturing processes are expected to conform to the environmental regulations of the country of origin.

A catalogue record for this book is available from the British Library.

Library of Congress Cataloging-in-Publication Data

Larsen, Marianne A.
  The making and shaping of the Victorian teacher / Marianne A. Larsen.
      p. cm.
  Includes index.   25046438
  ISBN 978-0-230-24128-2 (alk. paper)
    1. Education–England–History–19th century. 2. Education–Aims and objectives–England–History–19th century. 3. Education, Elementary–England–History–19th century. 4. Education and state–England–History–19th century. 5. Elementary school teachers–England–History–19th century. 6. Education–Social aspects–England–History–19th century. 7. Educational change–England–History–19th century. 8. Educational change–History. I. Title.

LA631.7.L37 2011
379.41–dc22   2011012059

10   9   8   7   6   5   4   3   2   1
20 19 18 17 16 15 14 13 12 11

Printed and bound in Great Britain by
CPI Antony Rowe, Chippenham and Eastbourne

I dedicate this book to all of the good teachers I have had in my life who have inspired me through their knowledge, passion for teaching, love and commitment to their students.

Contents

Acknowledgements

This book is based on the work I completed for my PhD thesis at the Institute of Education, University of London. That thesis (and this book) would not have been possible without the support of my supervisors Dr. Robert Cowen and Dr. Andrew Brown, who gently prodded and pushed me to go far beyond what I ever considered my own intellectual limits to be. I thank Dr. Cowen for encouraging me to develop my own arguments and through them new ways of reading and seeing the world. Dr. Brown urged me to be confident in developing my own language and theoretical framework for making sense of my data. Without their honest and humorous criticism, I would not have experienced the breakthroughs in my thinking that led to the key ideas in this book.

I extend a special thank you to my friends Bev Dalys, Dianne Gereluk, Claudia Lapping, Hiroko Fujikane, and Jason Beech for the emotional and intellectual support to complete this work, including our wonderful conversations, time together in London, and general support throughout my doctoral studies. I also acknowledge the ongoing support from my parents, Susan and Bent Larsen, who encouraged me to persevere to see my thesis and now this book to completion. This book would not be completed without the tiresome and meticulous work of my research assistant, Kelly Crowley. Thank you, Kelly!

I end with a loving thank you to Zach Wilson for supporting me in ever so many ways through the final stages of writing and editing this book. Thank you all for making this book possible.

Part I

Contemporary, Comparative and Historical Contexts

1
Making and Shaping Good Teachers: Contemporary and Historical Contexts

The twenty-first century background

Having all been students at one time or another in our lives, we all have opinions on what makes a good teacher. Some recall their favourite teachers for inspiring and motivating them in their studies. Others claim that subject expertise and enthusiasm for teaching were the most important qualities of their favourite teachers. For others, humour and passion for teaching are the marks of a memorable teacher.

This book is about good teachers, but it is neither a blueprint for how to become an excellent educator, nor can it be situated within the realm of teacher effectiveness research. Rather, this study, which began initially in the present and ended up in the past, is about the making and shaping of good teachers. Before embarking upon the research that led to this book, I had spent almost ten years as a secondary school teacher in Canada, the United States, and England. Over the course of that period, I noticed what I considered a troubling trend: the increasing regulation and control over teachers' work. I found myself spending more and more time and energy fulfilling accountability-based bureaucratic demands that seemed to me to have little to do with good teaching practice, and more to do with *demonstrating*, for external evaluation, that I was a 'good' teacher. To me, teaching had become an instrumental and technical activity that was tightly regulated in minute and continuous ways.

As I attempted to strike a balance between maintaining my own high standards for teaching and fulfilling these new accountability demands, I began to ask myself questions about the nature and effects of these reforms. Why were so many new forms of regulation over the teaching profession being established in these countries where I taught? How could I understand these new modes of control that no longer stemmed directly from the state, but rather involved a whole host of players, including teachers' councils, unions, the government, principals, and teachers themselves? Finally, what were the short term and long term effects of these types of regulatory reforms on teachers and teaching?

One big question grounded all of the others and can be viewed as providing the key to the beginnings of this book. What did these reforms say about the type of teachers we want for our schools? In other words, according to these new policies and practices, who would now be considered a good teacher, and who would not? Broadly speaking then, there were two themes that motivated me to write this book. One involved trying to understand the reforms aimed at regulating the teaching profession, and the second focused on ideas about the good teacher.

Initially, the book began as a contemporary comparison of education reforms related to the teaching profession. Today there is so much emphasis on the twin notions of 'quality teaching' and 'teacher quality'. A Google search under those two headings yields over a million hits. Improving teacher and teaching quality is now viewed as the 'common-sense' key to improving student learning, school efficiency and effectiveness, and as a result governments across a wide variety of jurisdictions have brought in numerous policies to improve teachers and teaching. These policy reforms have included the development of professional teaching councils, as well as standardised professional and ethical teaching standards. A whole range of mechanisms for evaluating and monitoring teachers such as inspections, threshold assessments, teacher testing, performance-based appraisals and other new accountability procedures have also been established over the last ten years or so. Finally, there have been programme (and accreditation) reforms at the pre-service (initial) and in-service (continuing) teacher education levels.

Through my initial reading of the critical research on these reforms, I came to see that my experiences were not unlike the majority of teachers who were the targets of these policy changes. The research I read indicated that overall these policy reforms have contributed to work intensification and exhaustion for teachers. Rather than improve performance, teacher evaluation and monitoring reforms have led to exacerbated levels of stress, anxiety, vulnerability, uncertainty and frustration within the profession. Contemporary teacher policy reforms have also operated to reduce opportunities for autonomy, innovation and creativity in the classroom and collaboration between educators. Indeed, as many have concluded, they demoralise, de-motivate and deprofessionalise teachers (Ball, 2003; Helsby and McCulloch, 1997; Jeffrey and Woods, 1998; Mahony and Hextall, 2000; Troman and Woods, 2001).

I realised, however, that although there is no shortage of research on the impact of contemporary educational reforms on teachers, very little of it has been situated within an historical context. I concluded that I could gain a much richer and complex understanding of the contemporary situation by locating my research within an historical context. However, since my initial training as a historian, I had developed some reservations about the nature of traditional historical research. Reading some of the work of the French social-philosopher Michel Foucault both reinforced and reflected some of those initial reservations. Other literature from new cultural historians provided me with alternative ways to engage in historical research, and offered a means by which to think outside of old limits. In particular, I decided that I would engage in a history of the present, drawing upon the past as a lens through which to understand contemporary notions of the good teacher. For reasons that I will outline below, my focus became the Victorian era, to which we now turn.

The Victorian era background

Contemporary policy-makers are not unlike the English Victorians who looked to the school as the solution to the problems of society. As one contemporary writer claimed, 'The panacea for every social and national evil is to be found only in universal education' (Workman, 1840). With their attention fixed on the school, the Victorians began to consider exactly how an education system could be constructed to address the troubles of their era. Over the course of the nineteenth century, the answer became clear: the only real security for a good school was a good teacher. Lord Brougham, recognising the importance of the teacher in the spread of popular education, declared in 1828 before the House of Commons:

> Let the soldier be abroad if he will, he can do nothing in this age. There is another personage – a personage less imposing in the eyes of some, perhaps insignificant. The schoolmaster is abroad, and I trust to him, armed with his primer, against the soldier, in full military array (Brougham, 1828).

And if the schoolmaster were abroad, then abroad the reformers would look for clues to the reform of their schools and teachers. Some reformers turned their attention to countries such as France where Francois Guizot, the Minister of Public Instruction, had introduced new school legislation in 1833, claiming that all of the provisions for the organisation of compulsory instruction would be of no effect if pains were not taken to procure for the public school 'an able master worthy of the high vocation of instructing the people. It cannot be too often repeated that it is the master that makes the school' (Quoted in Jones, 1924).

This claim 'the master makes the school' was echoed as the reform mantra in England and abroad over the next half-century. Educational promoters argued that the only true guarantee of a good school was a good teacher. They agreed that the best preventive medicine against a bad school was a well-qualified and devoted schoolmaster, and that education reform was dependent upon securing such a good and proper teaching corps. As Henry Dunn, Secretary of the British and Foreign School Society, asserted, 'give me a good teacher, put him anywhere, and he will have a good school; if he be an inferior teacher, put him anywhere, and he will not' (Select Committee on Education, 1835, p. 45). The stage was set. If the teacher made the school, and the school as a panacea to society's ills was in need of reform, then it followed that the teacher must be re-formed as well.

Such thinking went beyond the borders of England and was taken up across a wide range of European and North American settings. In continental Europe, we see some of the discourses and reforms associated with the good teacher implemented earlier in the century. The processes associated with the making and shaping of the good teacher were also played out across North America. 'As is the teacher, so is the school' became the Whig's battle cry in their crusade for public schooling in the United States (Herbst, 1989). School promoters in Canada, where educational reform was closely tied to the nineteenth century construction of the nation-state, also took an active interest in the role of the teacher.

Despite some differences in the timing, nature and pace of educational reform across these nineteenth century settings, there were some common trends. These included the state's increasing involvement in education system building, including the funding and construction of schools, the development of standardised curriculum and examination systems, and state-funded (and controlled) teacher training colleges. Moreover, in all settings an inspectorate was established to inspect local schools and the training colleges. These reforms were a part of the process of building educational systems, but for me their significance lies in the ways that they created or enhanced practices for socially constructing and controlling teachers. Specifically, this book attempts to demonstrate how the formal training, examination and inspection of teachers, all practices established or enhanced as a part of the wider project of Victorian educational system building, operated in such a way to make and shape the good teacher.

Why the Victorian era?

There are a number of reasons why I focus on the Victorian era (the period of Queen Victoria's reign from 1837 until her death in 1901) and on the country of England. My account begins in the late 1830s because this was a period characterised by great interest across England in the role of the teacher in the building of educational systems. By the end of the century, the main processes and practices aimed at con-structing and governing the teacher had been firmly in place for many years and their impact felt on teachers and their work.

Over a hundred years later, politicians continue to evoke Victorian era values to justify their educational reform agenda. The vision of society put forward by political leaders in England since Thatcher has been its justification in terms of a return to 'Victorian values' of per-sonal responsibility, independence and private enterprise (Aldrich, 1995). Indeed, the Victorian era continues to be viewed as particularly significant for an understanding of our contemporary social world. As Birch (2008) writes in the preface to her recent book *Our Victorian Education*:

> Entering the twenty-first century has made the Victorians seem further back in history. But we still live in their light, and in their shadow. Because their legacies are everywhere, we hardly notice them. They built the political, economic and social frameworks that support our lives...They founded great cities, the military and political power and the manufacturing bases that have defined our national identity. They shifted our population density and gave us new jobs. By the end of the nineteenth century, for the first time in history, significantly more people had urban rather than rural homes. *It was the Victorians who invented our world* [emphasis added] (p. vii).

The Victorians also invented the good teacher, a legacy we continue to live with today. While many of the ideas associated with being a good teacher have changed over the last hundred years or so, there still continues to be considerable emphasis on the significance of the teacher in educational reform (Larsen, 2010). Moreover, it was during the Victorian era that the most significant changes related to the making and shaping of the teacher occurred, and these changes are still with us today. To be exact, focusing on the period between the late 1830s and 1880s, there were two significant sets of changes that occurred. The first was a shift in systems of ideas and reasoning about the teacher. The second was the establishment of new mechanisms or practices to control and regulate teachers. These two complementary processes provide the organising framework for this book, which I will describe next.

Book structure

Overall, this book is a study of the effects of educational processes and practices that operated to socially construct and regulate the teacher in Victorian England and a range of other settings in Europe and North America. The main argument is that the Victorian teacher was constructed and governed as a modern and moral subject through educational policies and practices that are referred to in this book as disciplinary technologies. I focus on the elementary school teacher because secondary schooling was not a common feature of the educational landscape until late in the nineteenth century.

The book is divided into three parts. Part I *Contemporary, Comparative and Historical Contexts* is comprised of this introductory chapter, Chapters 2 and 3. In Chapter 2, I present the methodological and theoretical approaches of the book, beginning with a brief overview of relevant histories of teachers and teaching to contextualise this study within the existing literature. I then outline the key components of the new cultural history approach that are adopted in this book. Chapter 3 provides the broader educational, comparative and international contexts to the study. I review Victorian educational reform in England, Europe and North America. I outline and critique some standard academic explanations for nineteenth century educational reform, including state formation, industrialisation and urbanisation, before turning attention to a set of conditions that made possible the global flow of similar educational ideas and practices over such wide ranging, disparate settings.

Part II, *Discourses of the Victorian Teacher*, is made up of Chapters 4 and 5. Chapter 4 describes two popular nineteenth century official discourses. The first, a critique of the poor, immigrant and labouring populations, began early in the century. Reformers and school promoters expressed considerable alarm about the poverty, immorality, criminal behaviour, and ignorance of these populations. In response, attention turned towards the state of existing schools, and a discourse of derision about teachers of the poor developed. The chapter details how teachers were discursively positioned as incapable, immoral, ignorant, and conceited; and their classrooms chaotic places where little learning took place. The teacher was viewed as a problem to be resolved and it is against the idea of the 'bad' or 'abnormal' teacher that the 'good' or 'normal' teacher could be constructed.

Chapter 5 examines the discourse of the good teacher by describing what good teachers were supposed to know and be able to do. Two categories (or ideal types), Modern and Moral, are used to organise the ideas about the knowledge, skills and character traits of the good teacher. The Modern Teacher was expected to be capable of rational, philosophic and scientific study based on an Enlightenment commitment to progress through education. On the other hand, the Moral Teacher was required to uphold Christian moral habits and fulfil the moral purposes of schooling. The chapter explores the contradictions between these two conceptions of the teacher, as well as the gendered and dualistic nature of the discourse of the good teacher.

While attention in this chapter (and all others) is on England, reference is made to similar normalising systems of reasoning about the good teacher that circulated through Europe and North America. These processes were not only about how others came to reason about the teacher, but how teachers came to 'see' and think about themselves and their work. Systems of thought and reasoning are embedded in power relations that made possible the development of regulatory technologies to construct subjects, the topic of Part III of this book.

In Part III, *Making and Shaping the Victorian Teacher*, I analyse the educational processes, practices, and policies that were established or enhanced during the Victorian period to control, regulate, and in effect, *make* the good teacher. Chapters 6 and 7 examine the school and the teacher training institution, respectively, as sites of disciplinary control. In Chapter 6, I review the state of schooling prior to the construction of mass education systems to show the shift that took place in teacher-community-state relations. During the Victorian era, the school was transformed into a disciplinary site infiltrated by school inspectors, trustees, managers, and other visitors who drew upon a variety of strategies to surveil, monitor, and control teachers.

Chapter 6 also reviews the ways that teachers were called upon to inspect themselves. I show how the teacher was transformed and came to recognise him/herself and to be recognised by others as a moral subject through the processes of self-reflection, study, and play. These practices are viewed not only as technologies that constituted the teacher as subject, but techniques of control and regulation. Self-study and self-reflection produced the self-governing teacher, who learned to internalise expectations of the meaning of the good teacher and act accordingly.

The focus in Chapter 7 is the teacher training institution. The chapter begins with an overview of the teacher training colleges that were established during the Victorian era in England and abroad. Chapter 7 addresses the shaping and regulation of the teacher's character and body through admission policies, timetabling, the course of study, institutional rules and regulations, and dress and drill policies. I demonstrate how teacher candidates were shaped as docile inmates of the training college through complex and complete systems of authority. This chapter draws from Foucault's (1977) analysis of disciplinary societies and the techniques of hierarchical observation and normalising judgement through which power is exercised. I show the effects of the constant and careful surveillance of the students in the teacher training institutions, including how male and female bodies were shaped and normalised through a variety of physical exercises, rules, and regulations.

Chapter 8 shows how teacher testing and the publication of documentary information about teachers operated to construct and discipline the teacher. The first part focuses on the constant and continuous ways that teachers (and teachers in training) were examined. The collection and publication of detailed data about the teacher is discussed in the second part of the chapter. The chapter details the ways that teacher testing, the collection and publication of statistical information about the teacher created the conditions for the construction and control of the teaching population. The effects of the examination of the teacher and related collection, compilation and publication of statistical data about the teacher are theorised as significant elements of a power-knowledge apparatus first developed in the Victorian period and still with us today.

Chapter 9 provides a summary of the key arguments advanced in the book. Indeed, the two drawings on the front and back cover of this book illustrate the competing versions associated with the discourse of the good teacher. The Modern Teacher, as reflected by the drawing of the schoolmaster, was a learned, educated philosophic and pedagogic expert. The Moral Teacher, as shown by the drawing of the schoolmistress, was a moral exemplar for her students. She was patient, kind, and nurturing and love pervaded her classroom. I also explore the paradoxical relationship between the making and shaping of the good teacher and the wider tensions and contradictions associated with Victorian society. I reiterate the significance of engaging with this history of the present for understanding contemporary teacher policy reforms.

2
Theoretical and Methodological Perspectives: New Cultural History

This book engages with a form of historical research known as new cultural history. New cultural history, a term that has become increasingly popular since the end of the 1980s, focuses on the construction or production of reality, rather than the idea that texts and images simply reflect social reality. It is in this respect that this book is a new cultural history of the construction of the teacher in Victorian England, with an emphasis on the making and shaping of the good teacher, rather than a traditional historical study of the real lives of Victorian teachers.

In this chapter, I first provide a brief overview of traditional histories of teachers and teaching to contextualise the socio-historical position from which I have conducted the research for this study. I then introduce new cultural history, the conceptual framework upon which this study is based. I review the key concepts associated with new cultural history that have influenced my thinking and writing. In the final part of this chapter, I turn to the work of Foucault and explain how I have used the methodological approaches of archaeology and genealogy to conduct my study. Finally, I outline the primary and secondary source material from Britain, Europe and North America that was used in the research for this book.

Traditional and revisionist histories of education

Up until the 1950s, most professional historians paid little attention to educational history and even less interest to the history of teachers, teacher education and teaching. To fill this gap, educationists took up writing educational histories for trainee teachers in England, first in the Day Training Colleges and then in some new university departments of education. These accounts focused on the continuity and progress of the liberal educational tradition and the significance of the role, status, and formal training of teachers (Jones, 1924; Laurie, 1902; Rich, 1933).

Following the Second World War, the research and writing of educational history increased, but remained situated primarily within departments of education, rather than within history departments. Many of these histories focused on the relationship between industrialisation and urbanisation with the evolutionary development of formal schooling, and celebrated the role of the state in the rise of compulsory education systems. They emphasised control and policy-making at different levels of administration, the provision and structure of emerging education systems, and the beneficial effects of formal, mass education systems (e.g. Armytage, 1965; Barnard, 1947; Curtis and Boultwood, 1961; Jarman, 1951).

These texts were primarily histories of institutions, legislation, committees and commissions involved in education system building. To this end, many of them focused on the work of great education reformers, promoters and legislators such as James Kay-Shuttleworth in England, Egerton Ryerson in Upper Canada, Victor Cousin in France, and Horace Mann and Henry Barnard in the United States, reinforcing the assumption that these individual reformers were responsible for the creation of public education systems (e.g. Bloomfield, 1960–61; Cubberley, 1947; Hubbell, 1910; Judges, 1951; Putnam, 1912; Sissons, 1937–47).

By the 1960s, these histories of education came under attack from revisionist historians. Revisionists criticised these modernist interpretations of universal progress and individual freedom through the evolutionary rise of mass education systems. Revisionists pointed out that most educational historians had focused too heavily on the role of educational 'acts and facts', while ignoring larger social, political, and economic contexts in which education was implicated.

Revisionists pushed for more research on the social history of the working classes, women, children, immigrants and First Nations (in North America), and others 'from below.' They critiqued traditional historians for neglecting the role of the family, the community, and the teacher in education, and early, informal community schooling. To rectify this situation, they took up Bailyn's (1960) redefinition of 'education' to include both formal and informal means of learning. Studies were undertaken on private and community schooling, and other forms of working class and adult education. Focus shifted to elementary and rural education, and in particular, the education of the poor and working classes. Reassessments of educational history that had previously been uncovered, such as informal schooling in pioneer North

America and rural England, were carried out. Much of this new social history was quantitative: analysing trends in the spread of literacy, demography, and social mobility (e.g. Gardner, 1984; Goldstrom, 1977; Curtis, 1981; Gidney, 1975).

Revisionist historians also noted the neglect of research on women's history, including girls' education and the history of female teachers, claiming that they had been 'twice hidden' from traditional history, first as women and then as teachers. 'Women's absence from historical studies', wrote Burstyn (1977), 'has been due to historians' blindness to them, not to a "natural" lack of significance in women's lives' (p. 273). As feminist social historians began to address this gap in the canon, new histories of girls and women's education began to appear (e.g. Bryant, 1979; Gomersall, 1997; Cook and Mitchinson, 1976; Heap and Prentice, 1991).

As interest in the educational histories of women increased, attention was slowly directed towards the lived experiences of teachers, the majority of whom were female. Rousmaniere et al. (1997) noted the historical silence surrounding the daily work of teachers. She contended that by ignoring teacher's accounts of their experiences, traditional historians 'have misread the actual conditions of their work' (p. 7). A number of articles and books on the experiences of schoolmistresses and the feminisation of the teaching profession appeared during the 1980s and 1990s (e.g. Bergen, 1988; Copleman, 1996; Danylewycz and Prentice, 1986; Errington, 1994).

Some of this work focused on teacher training and the professionalisation of teachers. From the 1970s onwards, other revisionist historians revisited these two themes. Numerous articles and books were published on the subject of teacher training and graduate work on individual teacher training institutions was undertaken. In addition, a few survey histories of teacher training appeared in England from the 1970s onwards, chief among these being Dent's (1971, 1977) studies of teacher training. Additionally, a flurry of historical accounts of individual teacher training colleges appeared in England in the 1960s and 1970s, and in the later 1980s and 1990s in North America (e.g. Alexander, 1977; Britton, 1964; Fiorello, 1969; McGregor, 1978; Rose, 1981). Specific studies on the role, status and growth of the teaching profession in England and North America also appeared, this interest continuing through to the present (e.g. Althouse, 1967; Gosden, 1969; Herbst, 1989; Newnham and Nease, 1965; Tropp, 1957).

This work has reflected the wider interest in the rise of professionalism over the nineteenth century, and the influence of sociology in this field of historical studies (e.g. Bledstein, 1976; Gidney and Millar, 1994; Larson, 1977; Perkin, 1990). However, although research on the training and related professionalisation of teachers increased over the past 30 years, in relation to the other areas of historical study, there is still a paucity of published work on Victorian teachers and teaching, pointing to the significance of this study.

Overall, the revisionist histories of education, particularly from within the radical school, provided an alternative perspective to the traditional histories they critiqued. However, much of this revisionist history still reflected many of the modernist assumptions that characterised the work of their predecessors. Revisionist histories, especially those from the moderate school, continued to approach the history of education as an evolutionary story, and remained committed to the emancipatory potential of formal, centralised schooling. In addition, while attempting to include the histories of those who had been previously neglected in the historical record, revisionist historians continue to cling to the dream of objectivity through the application of a social scientific methodology, including the empirical tradition, of their work (Gordon and Szreter, 1989; Miller, 1989; Richardson, 1999a). These were, as much as traditional histories had been, attempts to find the 'truth' about the past, especially through the 'real' lived experiences of students, their families and teachers.

This changed, however, in the 1980s, with the challenges put forward by social theorists who argued that the meta-narrative models upon which the bulk of positivist, social-science research rested were inadequate to make sense of our contemporary condition. These social thinkers questioned the methodological and theoretical underpinnings of traditional and revisionist historical research, and it is their work that has influenced the field of new cultural history. It is to this new paradigm of historical research that I now turn.

New cultural history

New cultural history, the conceptual framework upon which this book is based, first came into use with the 1989 publication of Hunt's *The New Cultural History*. The word 'new' distinguishes it from the longer standing field of cultural history, and the word 'cultural' sets it apart from social history (as outlined above) and intellectual history, with their emphases on mentalities, assumptions or feelings, rather than systems of reasoning and thought. Although new cultural history has been the most successful in the United States, it has also been taken up in France, Germany and the Netherlands, and more recently in Britain (Burke, 2008).

Although the field of new cultural history is growing, there have been relatively few new cultural history studies on education. There are a handful of edited collections with chapters dealing with a range of educational topics from a new cultural (or post-modern) historical perspective (e.g. Popkewitz et al., 2001; Rousmaniere et al., 1997). Some other publications have focused on nineteenth century educational systems and the school reform movement (e.g. Cohen, 1999; Hunter, 1994; Jones and Williamson, 1979), and pedagogy (e.g. Goldstein, 1995; Purvis, 1984; Steedman, 1985). And there have only been a handful of studies about teachers from a new cultural history perspective (e.g. Jones, 1990; Varga, 1991).

New cultural historians challenge the very possibility of a real past being an object of historical knowledge. Much of their thinking has been influenced by the work of post-structuralists, who view language not as a direct reflection of the real world, but as fundamentally constitutive of the world. Far from reflecting the essential nature of the world, language precedes, shapes, and structures the world (Lyotard, 1984). Objects of knowledge are constructed, not only because they are based on texts with meaning that can be deconstructed by the reader, but because the object of study itself is constructed by the historian. Following this line of argument, new cultural historians point out the limitations and arbitrariness of both traditional and revisionist historians attempt to deconstruct texts based on their own strategies that are, like the object of their study, mediated by and through language (Poster, 1997).

Representation is a central concept among new cultural historians who view the past as a construction through the narrative strategies that historians use to communicate their findings. When events or facts come to be incorporated into coherent historical narratives they must, as new cultural historian White asserts, be emplotted in a story that has a beginning, middle and end, which do not necessarily correspond to or represent reality. According to White (1973), 'it's not the unity or coherence of the past that guarantees the unity of a historical narrative; it's the unity of the narrative that guarantees the unity of the past. The past is chaos until from it the historian produces cosmos' (p. 14). History then is a 'narrative discourse the contents of which are as much imagined/invented as found' (Quoted in Jenkins 1995, p. 144). What we have are stories that the historian invents by means of language and rhetoric in order to endow the endless succession of events or facts with some order and meaning.

This builds on the idea that social categories are fluid, flexible and shifting constructions, rather than firm and fixed realities. Class, once viewed as an objective social category by Marxist historians, is now thought of as a cultural or historical construction. Feminists have also encouraged historians and others to view gender this way (Butler, 1990). The revelation that gender and other identity markers such as race are socially and historically constructed has posed additional challenges to historians in thinking about the essentialised and thus historicised nature of taken-for-granted social categories.

These ideas, which have been taken up by new cultural historians over the past 20 years of so, have a longer history. As early as the 1930s, for example, US historians Beard (1983) and Becker (1983), in questioning the idea that history could ever be an objective and scientific account of the past, argued for multiple narratives based upon each individual's imaginative version of history. This debate over the scientific status of the study of history was taken up in North America and Britain throughout the 1940s and 1950s. The English liberal historian, Fisher, for example, questioned the discipline's commitment to objectivity, pointing out the relativity of the historian with respect to his material (Lowe, 1996).[1] And later, historian E. H. Carr (1977) similarly critiqued the historical search for objective truth. Echoes of this debate were heard again with the 1988 publication of *That Noble Dream: The 'Objectivity Question' and the American Historical Profession*, in which Novick concluded that objectivity is not only a delusion, but an essentially confused concept.

If objectivity was indeed a delusion and confused concept, what does this mean for historical research? Some new cultural historians have concluded that we are now facing the end of history. Jenkins' (1998) radical argument that history is 'just one more foundationless, positioned expression in a world of foundationless, positioned expressions' (p. 6) means that history's commitment to provide some kind of true representation and understanding about the past is fatally flawed. Given that historical truth is merely a function of what is possible to write, think and say at a particular place and time, should historians abandon the search for some kind of true representation and understanding of the past? In other words, what purpose is left for the historian if history is only text that can be continually re-interpreted, deconstructed, and never really known? Furthermore, if one goes so far to accept the 'end of history' conclusion drawn by new cultural (or post-modern) historians such as Jenkins, there would be little point to engage in any historical research at all. I do not take that perspective.

Rather, this book is an attempt to strike a middle ground between traditional and new cultural history. Some of the themes and strategies of traditional histories are retained. While principles such as the objective search for truth, the notion of the rational subject as socio-historical actor, and the idea that history unfolds along a linear, evolutionary path, are questioned and problematised in this book, the project of engaging in historical research is not entirely abandoned. What this book does is engage in a new cultural historical 'turn' from the search for the objective truth about the past, towards trying to understand the ways in which meanings and identities have been socially produced through relations of power and knowledge. This shift is not simply a denial of the existence of reality or truth, but recognition of the limitations of traditional strategies and conceptual categories in apprehending the past.

New cultural historians have been influenced by the work of a number of social theorists, including Michel Foucault. The next section describes the new cultural historical strategies known as archaeology and genealogy that have been drawn from the work of Foucault and used in the research for this book.

Archaeological approach

In this book, I use the methodological approach known as archaeology, developed by Foucault in a number of his earlier writings, to understand the socio-historical making of the good teacher. Drawing upon this methodology, the concept of discourse is deployed to describe and understand the ideas, knowledge, and practices towards and about the Victorian teacher. This Foucauldian conception of discourse moves away from a linguistic approach that concentrates solely on language as constitutive of truth, as discussed above, towards an analysis of the relationship between disciplinary practices (technologies) and disciplines (bodies of knowledge) at the level of the statement (Foucault, 1972).

Discourse is conceived as an object of attention rather than a medium of expression. Foucault (1972) defines discourses as 'systems of statements whose organisation is regular and systematic, consisting of all that can be said and thought about a particular topic, as well as who has permission to speak and with what authority' (p. 216). Archaeology involves describing recurrent statements, understood as units or parts of knowledge, found in the archive on any particular topic or theme.

Archaeology, according to Foucault (1972), 'organises the document, divides it up, distributes it, orders, arranges it in levels, establishes series, distinguishing between what is relevant and what is not, discovers elements, defines unities, describes relations' (pp. 6–7). A description of what was written on a topic allows the historian as archaeologist to determine what constitutes a discursive unity. References to the topics of schooling/education and teachers/teaching framed decisions concerning what material was to be read and analysed, and comprise the broad discursive unity of the texts examined for this book.

The process of examining texts for recurrent statements on a particular topic or theme is one aspect of the archaeological method. Archaeological investigation then involves determining whether or not a statement has fulfilled a set of conditions that allow it to be considered an instance of a particular discourse. These conditions consist of the rules, relations, and patterns that connect, relate, and divide what can be said and repeated about a topic. In this way, description can allow the archaeologist to establish an open, theoretical model to understand the rules, relations, and procedures between and amongst statements (Foucault, 1972).

In this study, the focus shifts from how education reformers, politicians, inspectors and others unified their own arguments for education reform, to a close reading of the statements within a group of texts to determine the ways in which statements are organised and related to one another. An examination of the organisation of and relations between statements enabled me to better understand what made a group of statements possible. It is this highlighting of the way that knowledge is organised or systematised that makes discourse an analytic tool.

In analysing a group of statements unified by a common theme, archaeological research does not attempt to smooth over the apparent differences, aberrations, and inconsistencies between statements. Foucault (1972) cautions that the archaeologist should not force unity and coherence on a group of statements. Rather, archaeology involves the process of studying forms of division and dispersion.

Rather than search for continuity, causes, and origins of thought, this book attempts to locate ruptures, breaks, gaps, and interruptions. Discontinuity becomes a problem to be investigated. Foucault (2000a) explains:

> History becomes 'effective' to the degree that it introduces discontinuity into our very being – as it divides our emotions, dramatizes our

instincts, multiplies our body and sets it against itself. Effective history...will uproot its traditional foundations and relentlessly disrupt its pretended continuity (p. 380).

As events, discontinuities are the moments when the normal course of things is interrupted. Unlike the traditional historian that aims to place and order events in a linear, continuous pattern in order to understand historical laws or phenomena, archaeological research leaves these breaks exposed.

Focusing on breaks and discontinuities draws attention towards the reappearance and repeatability of statements on a particular topic. In this book, attention is drawn to the repeatability of statements related to education reform as they were played out across a variety of settings. For example, education reformers across North America, Britain, and Europe quoted one another in their reports. The French educational reformer, Victor Cousin was oftentimes quoted in reports by North American and English education reformers in order to bolster their arguments for reform. Lord Brougham's claim that 'the schoolmaster was abroad' was also taken up outside of England, leading to reforms to produce an educated teaching force.

Archaeological research also entails describing the appearance of new statements on a topic or, in other words, breaks and discontinuities in discourse. This move is especially important in this study given the mid-century shift in how people spoke, wrote, and thought about teachers. Specifically, during the Victorian period, a change can be noted from descriptions of teachers as ignorant, immoral, dregs of society to the teacher as an intellectual, studious, and moral exemplar. What is of significance is this apparent newness in statements about the good teacher, which were fundamentally different from how teachers had been described with derision and scorn.

Archaeology points to the specificity of each moment or period in time. Each historical period is viewed as different from our own, but not necessarily better or worse than the present. The traditional evolutionary history of teaching and teachers as a narrative of uninterrupted progress is challenged here to provide an account constructed from unintended consequences of the interactions between a complex of ideas and actions (Foucault, 1967).[2]

In this book, the subject of teaching and teachers is not considered a clear-cut and unproblematic narrative of continuous progress. Each moment in time is considered within its own specificity, and described without attempting to connect it in a linear, developmental pattern to that which went before and that which followed. This process entails cultivating 'the details and accidents that accompany every beginning' so that the historian can 'recognize the events of history, its jolts, its surprises, its unsteady victories, and unpalatable defeats – the basis of all beginnings, atavisms, and heredities' (Foucault, 2000a, p. 369).

In emphasising the specificity of each moment in time and place, historical events are described as contingent, meaning that the emergence of any particular event was not necessary, but only one possible result of a whole series of complex relations between other events. Thinking causally privileges determinism where the existence of certain factors, in and of themselves, leads directly to or determines certain outcomes. With this type of thinking comes the correlative focus on predictability and inevitability. For if it can be determined that certain events inevitably cause or determine other events to unfold, then the historian, as social scientist, can predict the likelihood or probability of a similar event occurring if the correct conditions are met.

An examination of conditions rather than causes eliminates the inevitable nature of how events unfold over time and place. Understanding how a certain discourse arose out of series of conditions means that there is nothing necessarily inevitable about the unfolding of historical events. This type of new cultural historical research is less certain and predictable, and acknowledges the possibility of a range of different ideas and practices emerging at any one time and place.

In thinking about history in terms of conditions of possibility, the concern is not to explain why people started to think, speak, and write about teachers in a new ways. Rather, the focus of attention shifts to how it became possible for new truths about the teacher to be invented across a range of settings during a particular moment in historical time. In other words, the book examines a set of conditions, some connected, others not, that made education and the teacher objects of attention to the Victorians.

The archaeological method also involves determining who had the right or privilege to speak or write about a certain topic, and the rules and rituals associated with this speaking and writing (Foucault, 1972). Those whose ideas, opinions, suggestions and thoughts were most visible in Victorian educational discourses included middle to upper class, white male politicians and education reformers. These officials who determined the limits of the discourse on education, teachers and teaching, claimed a space for their opinions, ideas and suggestions about the reform of Victorian society through the re-formation of the school and its teacher.

This is not a study of the biography and personality of individual educational reformers, pedagogues, school inspectors, training college principals, or any other 'great' nineteenth century educationists. I am not interested in trying to uncover the underlying hidden origins of thought, attitudes, motives, and intentions of the individuals who were allowed to speak and write about a particular topic. Instead, my focus is studying **how** it became possible for teachers to be thought, written, and spoken about in fundamentally new ways during the Victorian age.

In other words, the key concern is not what caused individual Victorians to think about teachers in a new way, but what were the *conditions that made possible* the emergence of new ways of thinking about the teacher and new practices to be put in place over the Victorian period? This involves stepping back from focusing on individual biographies to examining the ideas and processes related to Victorian education reform. Archaeology, it is argued, does not preclude the use of other, more traditional, historical strategies. Chapter 3 of this book, for example, combines traditional and new cultural historical strategies to understand how education came to be an object of considerable attention to the Victorians. Various processes and patterns are described to show how a similar set of educational ideas and practices were taken up in England, and much of Europe and North America.

Chapter 4 addresses this theme: the positioning of education and the teacher as objects of concern, from a discursive point of view. In describing a set of discourses that brought public attention to schools and teachers, this chapter adopts an archaeological approach. The discourse of the good teacher is described in Chapter 5; where I examine the systems of ideas and reasoning that came to enclose, shape, and construct the good teacher. The ideas, reasoning, or truths that were articulated about the good teacher comprise one part of a discursive analysis. These ideas (disciplinary knowledge) needed to combine with practices (disciplinary technologies) for the construction and governing of the teacher to occur. This process points to the productive or enabling nature of discourse, and it is this particular characteristic of discourse that connects the archaeology to genealogy.

Genealogical approach

The above description of archaeology focused primarily upon the statements, rules and patterns that comprise discourses. Discursive analysis, however, is concerned with more than describing statements and their relations. Discourse cannot be fully understood without taking into consideration *what statements do*. To rephrase this differently, discourse entails analysing the productive capacities of knowledge and power. Discourses, according to Foucault (1972), are comprised of 'practices that systematically form the objects of which they speak...they do not identify objects, they constitute them and in the practice of doing so conceal their own invention' (p. 49).

In describing how the good teacher came to be shaped as subject, the effects of discourse are emphasised. As outlined in the section above on new cultural history, the focus is not on how language (knowledge) constitutes a representation of reality, but on how practices composed of power and knowledge produce subjects. Hence, the productive, and not repressive, nature of power is emphasised. As Foucault (1977) writes: 'power produces; it produces reality; it produces domains of objects and rituals of truth. The individual and the knowledge that may be gained of him belong to this production' (p. 194).

This is not so much an attempt to study the human subject as a rational and purposeful agent of change, but rather to analyse the ways in which the subject has been constructed, produced, or made over time and space. This is what is known as genealogy, that is: 'a form of history which can account for the constitution of knowledges, dis-courses, domains of objects etc. without having to make reference to a subject which is either transcendental in relation to the field of events or runs in its empty sameness throughout the course of history' (Foucault, 1980b, p. 117).

The subject is viewed both as an object of knowledge to oneself and to others, and subject to someone or something else by control and dependence. With respect to the first meaning, I seek to understand the systems of ideas and reasoning that have made it possible for the teacher as subject to become an object of knowledge. With respect to the latter meaning, this book examines the emergence of the subject in conjunction with a set of practices (technologies) enveloped within this system of reasoning about the good teacher. In other words, these disciplinary technologies are constituted by the systems of reasoning about the good teacher.

Technologies are understood in this study as a set of practices, pro-cesses, procedures, methods and tactics used to construct and govern the teacher. These practices possess their own specific regularities, logic, strategy, and forms of reasoning. The task of the genealogist is to analyse the components and interplay between technologies to understand their effects in constructing the subject (Foucault, 1991).

This new cultural history analyses those practices or technologies through which the Victorian teacher was made and shaped. Technologies of government, explains Rose (1999), shape the conduct of others in the hope of producing certain desired effects and avoiding undesirable events. He continues:

> A technology of government…is an assemblage of forms of practical knowledge, with modes of perception, practices of calculation, vocabularies, types of authority, forms of judgement, architectural forms, human capacities, non-human objects and devices, inscription techniques and so forth, traversed and transected [sic] by aspirations to achieve certain outcomes in terms of the conduct of the governed (p. 52).

Two broad types of subject-creating technologies are analysed in this book: external and internal.[3] External technologies are those methods and techniques used by others to shape and make the subject. External technologies act to frame possible modes of behaviour and actions of governed subjects. Generally speaking they include the ways that a variety of authorities, agencies and institutions seek to shape the aspirations, ambitions and self-conceptions of the individual and social body. In this study, external technologies include the means by which school managers, inspectors, politicians, educational reformers, and training institution principals and masters acted upon the lives and behaviour of Victorian teachers, so as to shape the ways that they thought about and conducted themselves.

The norms, values, and expectations that individuals have of themselves comprise internal technologies or techniques of the self. Broadly speaking, technologies of the self are the ways in which an individual turns him or herself into a subject and are constituted by the norms, values, and expectations that individuals have of themselves. They include the intentional or voluntary means by which individuals seek to question, think about and understand themselves, and as a consequence shape and change their own thoughts, bodies, souls and general mode of being to fit a desired norm.

Specifically, this book attempts to understand the ways in which individual men and women who worked in schools came to recognise themselves as good teachers. What were the messages they received from official sources about what it meant to be a good teacher? How then did teachers come to think and act upon themselves in ways to shape themselves as good teachers? In such a way, teachers are not thought of as victims of power, but as vehicles through which power moved. Foucault (1980c) argues that power circulates through the freedom of the human being and not against it: 'not only do individuals circulate between its threads; they are always in the position of simultaneously undergoing and exercising this power. They are not only its inert or consenting target; they are always also the elements of its articulation. Individuals are the vehicles of power, not only its target or point of application' (p. 98).

Power and knowledge circulate through individuals via external and internal technologies. With respect to external technologies, the power is sovereign: visible and possessed by the other, such as the school inspector or the training college principal. This type of power is expressed in recognisable ways through particular and identifiable individuals. It is the type of power on which traditional historical research has focused; power that is viewed in opposition to knowledge. However, this book views sovereign power as working through discourse in conjunction with systems of knowledge.

Power is not only examined in its sovereign, top-down manifestation, but also in an ascending direction, at the level of micro-technologies. Power, as this book demonstrates, also has the capacity to operate in more diffuse, fluid and web-like ways. Hence, attention is directed towards the micro-mechanisms of power and knowledge that shaped the Victorian teacher. This shift challenges the notion that power is solely a repressive, obstructing and negative force. Rather, power is analysed in terms of its productive capacities to understand how it both constrains and enables behaviours, expectations, and actions.

While the above discussion has distinguished between internal and external technologies, the distinction between the two is ambiguous. There was interplay between the productive capacities of these different types of technologies that operated to govern, shape, and constitute a particular type of teacher. While school inspectors and teacher training college instructors, for example, asserted that it was the teacher's responsibility to keep up to date with the latest pedagogical developments, these expectations were also internalised by those teachers seeking to become the sort of teacher valued in Victorian society. Certain expectations, norms, and values concerning what it meant to be a good teacher were therefore internalised by teachers. External technologies became technologies of the self.

Specifically, this new cultural history of the teacher involves analysing three 'macro' external technologies that were all established or entrenched over the course of the Victorian period. The first consisted of formal teacher training which was established by the voluntary societies in England and increasingly managed by the state over the century. The second, a system of regular inspections of teachers, their schools, and the training institutions, was also implemented over the Victorian era. Third, a system of teacher certification following successful completion of standardised examinations was initiated. These three technologies: formal training, inspections and certification, provide the focus of analysis for Part III of this book.

However, as noted above, it is not only at the level of these larger policies and practices that the ways in which the teacher came to be constructed and governed as subject can best be understood, but at the micro-level of the mundane. Within the technological complex of examinations, inspections and training, there was a myriad of micro-technologies through which relations of power and knowledge individualised and normalised the Victorian teacher. Small and ordinary technologies that operated as external and internal disciplinary practices included, for instance, seemingly insignificant details such as the colour of dress considered most appropriate for the female teacher, and the exact time when candidates in teacher training colleges were expected to turn off their gaslights each evening, advice to teachers to study and reflect upon their work, and the precise classification of teachers based on certification examination results.

Finally, there is no assumption underlying this analysis that these disciplinary mechanisms were inherently good or bad. Rather, the deployment of these practices enabled the teacher to be constituted in such a way that power could henceforth function much more efficiently and effectively. This web of practices and processes produced the teacher as subject, and constitutes a salient example of what Foucault (1977) calls a disciplinary society whereby internalised discipline, or surveillance, works to ensure the efficient functioning of power.

Sources and archival research

To carry out this study, I read a wide range of primary sources on Victorian educational reform and teachers and teaching. These documents included official reports on education from statistical societies and government departments, which were carried out to provide an overview of the state of education and rationale for reform. Other documents include articles, speeches, and books written by education reformers, legislators, teacher training institution masters and principals, and other individuals concerned with the role of teachers within the emerging mass education systems. I examined school inspectors reports, as well as the minutes of the two voluntary societies: the National Society and the British and Foreign School Society (BFSS). Additionally, a wide selection of articles from nineteenth century education journals and periodicals were read and analysed.

While this book refers to many of the English training institutions, archival research was completed for four in particular. These are the Borough Road, as representative of the work done by the BFSS. Of the National Society training colleges, two were chosen for being representative of the spectrum of training provided: Battersea which focused on practical training and St. Mark's, which emphasised elevating the status of the teacher. Along with the Borough Road, and the National Society's other training institutions at Chester and York and Ripon, Battersea and St. Mark's were the colleges of the greatest significance, training more students than any of the other smaller diocesan colleges. The fourth college in this sample, Whitelands Training Institution, operated by the National Society for the training of elementary schoolmistresses, was examined to provide a gendered element to this analysis.

Most of the primary sources were from England, although I also conducted archival research on the Normal School of Upper Canada and other aspects of Victorian educational reform in Canada. I relied mainly on secondary literature on education reform, teachers and teaching in Europe and the United States, as well as some primary source material, including reports of common school promoters such as Horace Mann. These primary and secondary sources allowed me to integrate a comparative and international dimension into this study of the making and shaping of the Victorian teacher in England.

Conclusion

This book engages in new cultural history in attempting to understand the ways in which the teacher was made and shaped through relations of power and knowledge. Knowledge and power spread through the daily lives of teachers at the level of macro and micro technologies. These technologies produced the teacher as a modern and moral subject, pointing to the capacity of discourse to produce particular identities. This history of the construction of the good teacher can be viewed as a discontinuous and unstable reversal of previous histories of teachers and teaching. Reversing the evolutionary account of teacher training and professionalisation does not mean that the lives, status, position, and role of teachers is much worse today compared to the past, but that each situation must be fully comprehended within the specificity of the time and place in which it is located.

New cultural history provides the means to understand how what it means to be a teacher changes over time and place, and how identities are constructed through the intertwined intersection of systems of knowledge and power based disciplinary technologies. Rather than think, speak and write about history in the language of causes and progress, this book adopts the view that a whole series of events, practices and processes that were local, national, and international, made possible the development of new ways of thinking about teachers and teaching. This focus on conditions of possibility, rather than on causes, adds a destabilising element to educational history. For it means that out of a set of events, some of which may have seemed wholly insignificant, a particular regime of truth and power emerged. In this case, a complex of discourses about the state of Victorian society, social, and educational reform combined in particularly similar ways across a range of settings to make possible new ways of thinking about the good teacher.

Notes

1   In 1936, H. A. L. Fisher wrote that:
    Men wiser and more learned than I have discerned in history a plot, a rhythm, a predetermined pattern. These harmonies are concealed from me. I can see only one emergency following upon another as wave follows upon wave, only one great fact with respect to which, since it is unique, there can be no generalisations, only one safe rule for the historian: that he should recognize in the development of human destinies *the play of the contingent and the unforeseen* (Quoted in Lowe, 1996, p. 316).

2   Foucault (2000c) demonstrated this in *Madness and Civilization*, reversing the traditional narrative of madness and its treatment and showing how the contemporary situation is neither better nor worse than the past. In his examination of the ways in which the treatment of the mad has changed, he looked not for some original essential meaning of madness, but how the idea of madness was reinvented over specific times and places in history for different purposes. In effect, this book follows this same approach with respect to the teacher.

3   What I refer to as 'external technologies', Foucault names technologies of power, domination, or discipline. Moreover, the term 'internal technologies' is preferred over Foucault's (2000c) use of 'technologies of the self.' The terms 'internal' and 'external' are used in this book to emphasise that both types of technologies (not just technologies of power) are constituted by power and knowledge.

3
Victorian Education Reform: Comparative and International Contexts

During the Victorian era, public education systems were constructed in newly industrialised and urbanised nation-states, and in former colonial societies undergoing these modernising processes, along with the processes associated with new nationhood. The construction of popular, universal education systems was premised on the idea that schooling was to be the cure for the social ills of the time, providing children with the foundation they required to become obedient, moral citizens. While the timing, processes, and practices associated with key educational (political and economic) reforms differed across these settings, the central importance ascribed to mass education did not. Whether reformers called for state funded public education systems, or a system operated in conjunction with religious institutions, local churches or voluntary societies they all subscribed to the general benefits of popular education and, as we will see in the next chapter, the central role of the teacher in education reform.

This chapter provides the reader with background on educational reforms that took place in England and other European and North American countries over the Victorian era with a focus on the period between the late 1830s and 1880s. First I review educational reform in England and then turn attention to reforms that were implemented in continental Europe and North America. While there were differences across these settings, there were also considerable similarities in these reforms. In the second half of this chapter, I take a brief look at three standard academic explanations of nineteenth century education system building: state formation, industrialisation and urbanisation. I point out the limitations of these arguments and then turn to new cultural history to examine some of the conditions that made possible the emergence and spread of similar educational ideas and practices, highlighting the broader productive power of discourse to be taken up across disparate settings.

England: Building an education system

The development of mass education in England over the course of the nineteenth century was a haphazard and hesitant process involving the state and the voluntary societies. During the 1830s, the state made a number of tentative and partial developments in education reform. The first Parliamentary grant of £20,000 was issued in 1833 for building schoolhouses and the education of children of the poorer classes. Although the grant was modest and limited in scope, a precedent had been set and the state would become increasingly involved in educational provision throughout the rest of the century. By 1839, the schoolhouse building grant was increased to £30,000 and the Select Committee of the Privy Council on Education (henceforth, the Committee of Council) was established (Committee of Council, 1840; Anon, 1839).

Although the state was slow to be actively involved in the construction of a mass elementary education system, this did not mean that there was no education system in England to speak of during this period. The voluntary societies were significantly more active than the state in educational provision up until the end of the century, operating the vast majority of schools and teacher training institutions throughout the country. The voluntary school movement was primarily associated with the two religious societies: the non-denominational British and Foreign School Society (hereafter, the BFSS), and the National Society for Promoting the Education of the Poor in the Principles of the Established Church (or the National Society, the term that I use throughout the rest of this book).

Schools associated with the National Society were known as National schools, while those affiliated with the BFSS were called British schools. In addition to these schools, Anglicans, Roman Catholics, and Nonconformists also established their own schools. The National Society was by far the most influential of all of the societies both in terms of the number of schools established and educational expenditures. British and National Schools were not directly owned or managed by the two societies, but rather joined in union with them, receiving funds raised by the local clergy and congregations, in addition to the fees paid by parents and government grants.

By the start of the Victorian era, there were still many gaps in provision and it cannot be said that there was anything close to a comprehensive educational system existing at that time. However, on the heels of rising dissatisfaction with the existing state of educational provision, especially for the poor, there was an increasing realisation that the state ought to adopt greater responsibility for public education. Prime Minister Russell in 1846 recognised this need and promised that the government would pay special attention to education, which they did with the passage of the Education Minutes that year (Committee of Council, 1847).

The 1846 Minutes outlined the regulations to define the qualifications of school teachers and the condition of instruction to be given in schools. A state financed pupil teacher system was established,[1] and the type of teacher required to train the pupil teachers outlined. A system of teacher certification following successful completion of standardised merit examinations, accompanied by state-funded salary augmentations, was also initiated. State financing of the teacher training colleges run by the voluntary societies was implemented. The Minutes also extended a system of regular inspections of teachers, their schools, and the training institutions. As a result, significant changes took place in the state's role in educational provision, teacher certification, examination, inspection and training (Committee of Council, 1847).

Processes associated with constructing a state-funded (and controlled) education system continued, albeit hesitantly, from the 1850s until the 1880s. Government grants for schools and teacher training colleges increased, and changes were made to the pupil-teacher system, inspections, and teacher training. A significant piece of legislation was passed in 1862, the Revised Code, which ushered in a system of payment by results for the elementary schools (Committee of Council, 1861). The Code was hotly contested and criticised by many teachers. Further, after 1864, grants to the teacher training college were dependent upon the number of certificated teachers who had completed two full years of studies at a training college, and had successfully completed their period of probationary teaching.

By the end of the 1860s, there were still gaps in educational provision. The Elementary Education Act of 1870 was intended to fill in those gaps and created, in effect, a national system of education. School boards were established with the power to enforce the attendance of their pupils. The 1870 School Act had tried to repair some of the damage from the 1862 Revised Code. The role and responsibilities of school inspectors and managers were prescribed, including the disbursement of school grants based on the results of examining pupils and their teachers. Teachers' work became more closely regulated with the specification of teaching subjects and the requirement that the teacher regularly maintain a school register and log book (Horn, 1978; Hurt, 1971).

Thus the key nineteenth century education reforms that were implemented in England up until the end of the century had an uneven and protracted pattern. It was only by the 1870s that one could begin to speak of a national education system in England. Up until that point, the system was primarily one of voluntarism with some state support and regulation. Compulsory attendance was not implemented until the 1880s and state secondary schooling had to wait until the 1902 Act. Throughout the Victorian era, education spending by the state remained relatively low, especially in comparison to other European countries, which I turn to next.

Building education systems: Comparative and international contexts

By international comparison, England was slow and partial in constructing a mass, public education system over the Victorian period. Nevertheless, there were other similarities between England and other countries in the processes and patterns associated with education system building. State schooling, as a formal process, arose first in the absolutist monarchies of eighteenth century Europe. There were differences, however, in the forms of national education within absolutist states in continental Europe. Prussia took the lead in the construction of state schooling, first establishing a national, compulsory education system and taxing citizens to pay for public education during the late eighteenth century. Universal enrolment was largely achieved there by the 1830s. On the other hand, the French absolutist state never tried to impose compulsory education on the peasantry as did the Prussian state (Green, 1990; Maynes, 1985).

Throughout the nineteenth century, the state across a variety of European nations extended its role over education, including teacher training and school inspections. Steps were taken to establish state-financed public education systems in Scotland, Scandinavian countries such as Denmark and Sweden, and in France, Holland and Switzerland before mid-century, and in countries such as Italy and Finland in the 1860s. Although taxation for public education was first promoted in France in 1848, the Ferry laws of the 1880s formalised this system, and made public instruction there compulsory, secular and free (Coppa, 1995; Dahlmann-Hanse, 1961; Green, 1990; Maynes, 1985).

Across many European countries, state funded and controlled education came to be associated with the economic and political development of the nation, constructing national identities and national cultures, and inculcating in the population a sense of moral discipline. As Green (1990) has argued, the major impetus for the construction of national education systems in Europe was to forge a national identity through the education system and provide the state with trained administrators, engineers and military personnel.

Furthermore, in many European countries, struggles were fought over the role of the Church and state in educational provision. As in England, the origins of formal schooling in continental Europe lay with the churches and religious societies, which were the vehicles of early educational expansion and systematic forms of teaching. However, over time, secularisation occurred as the state became increasingly involved in setting policies concerning national curriculum, inspections and teacher certification. Teacher training institutions, for example, were established with state funding (and regulation) across Europe in countries such as Prussia, France, and Finland (Cook, 1974; Coppa, 1995; Gillis, 1994).

Similar developments took place in North America. Constructing a public education system across the United States developed rapidly after the 1830s during the period known as the 'Age of the Common School'. However, these processes occurred at different times and speed across various states, and there were extreme racial and regional disparities across the country. New York was the first state to create a Board of Regents to govern education (in the late eighteenth century), and established the first state superintendent of common schools and state-supported teacher training early in the nineteenth century. Over the late 1830s, Pennsylvania, Ohio, Massachusetts and Michigan laid the foundations for mass elementary education. However, the principle of a tax-supported, free public education system had not spread much further beyond the northern New England states before the 1840s (Cubberley, 1947; Katz, 1975; Tyack, 1974).

During mid-century, the public (or common) school movement expanded across the United States from New England and New York westward and southward after the Civil War. This expansion of public education systems did not occur, however, without bitter struggles between supporters of the non-sectarian common school movement and those opposed to extending government control over education. Other struggles concerning the role of the central authority and compulsory school taxation took place, as well as debates over the assimilationist aims of public schooling (Binder, 1974; Button and Provenzo, 1983).

After the Civil War the movement to extend elementary education expanded and there was considerable growth in educational provision, although this varied considerably from region to region. In the South, there was really no public education system to speak of until much later in the century. However, by 1865, systems of common schooling had been established throughout the northern, mid-western and western states. In these areas, there was also an increase in state-supported normal schools following demands for trained teachers to work in elementary schools (Binder, 1974; Cubberley, 1947).

A similar pattern of state involvement in education system building was played out across the British North American colonies. Ironically, the colonial state was far more active in the construction of a public education system in Canada than in Britain. Education legislation in Nova Scotia in 1811, New Brunswick and Upper Canada in 1816, Prince Edward Island in 1825, and Newfoundland in 1836 initiated some of the basic features of public education systems, including state funding for schools and elected school boards. Local rates and non-denominationalism were already entrenched in Canadian schooling systems many decades before they were introduced even as partial measures in England. As in many of the United States, public schooling was also supported through land grants in many of the Canadian colonies (MacNaughton, 1947; Rowe, 1964; Gidney, 1980).

Throughout the 1830s–1850s, the British colonial state gained further control of the education system. In Upper Canada, a Department of Education and District Councils were established; roles of trustees, school commissioners and district superintendents specified; a system of formal teacher training was initiated; and rules and regulations for the hiring, dismissing and paying teachers were outlined. Many of these same processes took place in Lower Canada, New Brunswick, Nova Scotia and Prince Edward Island. Corresponding with the processes associated with constructing the colonial state, education reforms continued throughout the 1860s and 1870s to increase state control. Government grants increased, the curriculum was centralised, schooling attendance made compulsory between the ages of seven and 12, and further reforms made to the role of trustees and school boards. By the time of Confederation in 1867, public education systems were well on their way to being constructed across the provinces that comprised the new nation of Canada (Hodgins, 1894; Curtis, 1988; Careless, 1967).

Building education systems: Standard academic explanations

The above has shown the various trajectories involved in the development of education systems across Britain, Europe and North America over the course of the nineteenth century. In some cases, such as France and Prussia, the state was far more interventionist compared to others where voluntary, religious based societies played a much more active role in educational provision. Debates were played out across most settings about the role of the state, Church and voluntary societies in educational funding, the construction and maintenance of schools, curriculum, teacher training, certification and inspections. However, despite the many differences between established nation-states in Europe, the new US nation, and colonies in Canada undergoing processes associated with nation-state building, a similar set of ideas and practices associated with building education systems emerged. In this section I review some of the standard academic accounts of the development of mass education systems. These include the relationship between educational system building, state formation, industrialisation and urbanisation.

Green's work exemplifies the stance that the development of popular education systems cannot be understood apart from the wider processes of state formation. The emergence of the modern capitalist state, Green (1990) argues, was the key social factor in explaining the timing and form of development of mass education systems. The intervention of the state was the major impetus and directly affected the formation of national education systems across countries such England, France, and the United States. With respect to Canada, Curtis (1988) develops a similar argument, drawing out the relationship between political processes of the nineteenth century state building and the construction of an education system in Canada West.

The second argument relates the construction of educational systems to the process of industrialisation and urbanisation. This social control historical analysis develops a causal link between the emergence of industrial capitalism and the development of mass elementary education systems. West (1975), for example, viewed industrialisation as directly causing the development of the English educational system. Cubberley's (1947) classic account of the history of education in the United States shows clearly the relationship between urbanisation and mass schooling.

While both West and Cubberley generally view these processes as positive ones, other historians have critiqued the connection between industrialisation, urbanisation and the rise of popular education. These revisionist historians have posited a causal link between the establishment of mass education and the inter-related processes of urbanisation, bureaucratisation and the proletarianisation of the masses. According to many of these Marxist scholars, during the nineteenth century, schools became ideological apparatuses of the capitalist state (Bowles and Gintis, 1976; Johnson, 1970; Katz, 1976; Tyack, 1967).

Limitations of standard academic explanations

There are a number of limitations of the arguments presented above that link education system building to wider processes associated with state formation, industrialisation, and urbanisation. In his book *Education and State Formation*, Green (1990) outlines three factors associated with the process of state formation: the existence of external military threats or territorial conflicts; major internal transformations; and the need to escape from relative economic underdevelopment. These factors were present to varying degrees in various European countries and some British North American colonies during the late eighteenth and early nineteenth centuries. However, while England was undergoing a process of state reform during the Victorian period, the state was not being constructed according to the terms that Green presents. The development of mass education in England was not linked to the formation of the state, which had occurred much earlier, but was a much more haphazard and hesitant process connected to the voluntary system.

There are also a number of limitations with the arguments that posit a direct link between the development of mass education systems and industrialisation, urbanisation and the proletarianisation of labour. By the beginning of the Victorian period, industrialisation was well under way in England, having, as some have argued, its roots in eighteenth century economic changes. In terms of urbanisation, by 1850, over half of the population of England lived in places with more than 2500 people (Briggs, 1984; Porter, 2000).

On the other hand, large scale urbanisation came much later in Europe and North America than in England. By the early Victorian period only 5 per cent of the population lived in cities in the United States, and there were only a handful of cities in the British North American colonies where the population was more than one thousand (Careless, 1967). While industrial economic development and urbanisation occurred more rapidly in the north-eastern United States compared to the Canadian provinces, there were still many regions, especially in the south and west that remained rural until later in the century (Naylor, 1987). Although it has been argued that education reform occurred most rapidly in the urbanised United States, it is also worth pointing out the pace and extent of education system building that occurred in European nations and colonies such as Upper Canada over the nineteenth century, which largely remained rural (Green, 1990).

It is difficult then to sustain an argument that links education system building over the nineteenth century to the processes of industrialisation and urbanisation. Moreover, it is ironic that the process of constructing an educational system was significantly slower, more tenuous and haphazard in industrial, urban England compared to other rural, colonial settings. This shows the flaws in the argument linking industrialisation and urbanisation to the development of compulsory education systems (Kaestle and Vinovskis, 1980).

An examination of educational ideas, policies, and practices taken up in England, Europe and North America reveals that a different approach is needed to understand the flow of educational policies and practices. The movement of educational ideas and corresponding practices was not a direct or linear one. Infusing a comparative and international dimension into this study demonstrates that the processes of state formation, industrialisation, and urbanisation cannot be evoked to explain completely the historical causes or conditions for the emergence of mass education systems. Furthermore, while the concepts such as state formation, industrialisation, and urbanisation are used in this chapter and in the next, they are evoked in a limited and non-totalising way. This is not to say that these processes were insignificant for understanding nineteenth century educational reform, but that they are de-centred in order to see how other processes, outlined next, provided the socio-historical conditions that made a similar educational reform discourse possible.

The spread of educational ideas and practices: Global connections

In the above section, I outlined some of the standard explanations for the development of popular education systems over the course of the Victorian era. However, these arguments do not help us to understand how particular systems of reasoning about education *spread* across such a wide range of settings over this period. In this section I examine the conditions that made possible the movement of similar educational ideas and practices across a variety of nineteenth century settings. Four sets of patterns and processes that had a direct bearing on the spread of similar educational reforms across Britain, Europe and North America are examined. The first concerns the efforts of social, political and colonial reformers. The second focuses on the educational study tour, which was undertaken by these reformers, as well as other teachers, pedagogues, and school promoters. Pedagogical ideas and practices were also spread through the publication and dissemination of educational journals, books, reports, and speeches across these settings. Finally, the spread of educational practices to North America through immigration are described. These individual and institutional patterns and processes operated in such a way to enable the appearance and spread of similar discourses related to education reform.

Political, colonial and educational reformers

The beginning of the Victorian era was a period of active political reform in England and other jurisdictions in Europe and North America. Many of those advocating for political reform, for instance, were interested in wider social reform issues, including the state's role in education. This section will draw out some of the connections between the work of the political, social, economic and colonial reformers with respect to education reform in England, Europe and North America. Reformers across these settings equated political reform with social (including educational) reform. However, the advocacy work of these individuals did not cause education reform to occur. Rather, the overlapping, multi-faceted work of political reformers opened up new discursive spaces for the spread of similar systems of educational ideas and practices.

From the late eighteenth century onwards, political, economic and social reformers took up the cause of public education. In Europe, political reformers viewed emerging school systems as central in the processes associated with nation-state building. Primary schools, in particular, were seen by political reformers as essential in inculcating in children the values, norms and beliefs of the new nation-state (Maynes, 1985; Green, 1990).

Within England, throughout the early Victorian period, political reformers were similarly interested in education and other forms of social reform. They lobbied simultaneously for political reform and educational legislation to increase state funding for schools. Moreover, many advocates of political reform in England were also interested in colonial reform, arguing that the national spirit of reform should be extended to the colonies. Canadian colonial legislators, for example, who were frustrated with the political abuses amongst the Tory elite, demanded the right to responsible government. Unsurprisingly, it was granted to Upper Canada in 1846 at precisely the same time that education reform was at the top of the political agenda. Indeed, educational reforms in that province were shaped, as Curtis (1988) has described, by the more general struggles over responsible government and the form of the colonial state. The linking between political and educational reform is unremarkable given that many of the same individuals who were advocating political reform both within England and the North American colonies were also active educational promoters and reformers (Burroughs, 1969; Careless, 1967).

Political reformers in the United States were also interested in social and educational reform such as the abolition of slavery. The common school movement emerged out of a set of social and economic factors that included humanitarian reform efforts to create a moral and ordered society through schools, a need to create a disciplined and well-trained workforce, and desire for the upper classes to retain their privileges. Whigs, concerned about social and humanitarian issues, took up the cause of public education across the north-eastern and western states. Most of the common school reformers were middle-class, Anglo-American Protestants such as Henry Barnard of Connecticut and Horace Mann, Secretary of the Boston Board of Education who argued that public schooling could solve the major social, economic and political problems of society (Cubberley, 1947; Good and Teller, 1973; Spring, 1990). Their arguments in support of public education were very similar to those articulated by reformers in England and other parts of Europe. One of the reasons for these connections is the movement of these reformers and their ideas through travel, the topic I explore next.

The educational study tour

The phenomenon of the educational study tour, whereby reformers and teachers went abroad to study foreign educational systems, contributed to the spread of similar set of educational reforms across Europe, Britain and North America. A number of factors facilitated the movement of educational ideas and practices from one country or region to another during this period. Part of this can be attributed to technological developments which made long distance transportation easier. Educational study tours became increasingly popular, along with the corresponding notion that there was much to learn from the study of foreign educational systems.

Prussia, the first modern state to establish a national, compulsory school system, was of great interest to reformers. In particular, the work of Pestalozzi and his followers in Europe attracted considerable attention.[2] After his death in 1827, travels to and within Europe to study his progressive educational practices continued throughout the century, generating tremendous interest from British, European and North American reformers. British parliamentary reformers such as J. A. Roebuck and Sir Thomas Wyse were particularly impressed with the humanistic pedagogy that they witnessed in Prussian schools and advocated for the establishment of an educational system based on the Prussian model (Biber, 1831; Johnson, 1977; Silber, 1960).

Kay-Shuttleworth, one of the most influential educational reformers in Victorian England, undertook a study of schools in Scotland and Europe in the 1830s, in his capacity as Poor Law Commissioner. In his follow up report, he expressed great interest in the agricultural work undertaken by the pauper children at the Pestalozzian-inspired Swiss school, established by Phillipe Emanuel de Fellenberg (Kay-Shuttleworth, 1841).

North American educational promoters also looked to Prussia and Pestalozzian schools in particular for ideas in establishing their common schools. One of the earliest US visitors to Europe was the social and educational reformer, John Griscom, who spent a year in Europe from 1818–1819. In his subsequent two volume book, he described European educational institutions favourably, especially Pestalozzian schools in Prussia. Over the next two decades, US education reformers such as Calvin E. Stowe, Horace Mann, Alexander D. Bache, and later Henry Barnard all took advantage of improved modes of travel to visit Europe and Great Britain in order to study education systems there. These study tours resulted in reports submitted to their various jurisdictions, advocating Pestolozzian teaching methods, state-supported education and inspectorate, and the establishment of normal schools for the training of teachers (Cubberley, 1947; Herbst, 1989; Knight, 1930; Mann, 1846; Spring, 1990).

Education promoters in Canada also embarked on study tours to study educational practices abroad. Egerton Ryerson, the Assistant Superintendent of Common Schools in Upper Canada, spent almost a year travelling through Europe and Britain. His plan for education, based upon what he considered the best educational practices that he had seen on his trip, was outlined in his 1846 *Report on a System of Public Elementary Instruction for Upper Canada*. Ryerson was following in the footsteps of another Canadian education promoter, Charles Duncombe who had undertaken an educational study tour to the United States ten years previously. In his report, Duncombe (1836) claimed that the 'spirit of reform is upon us; Scotland has taken the lead, England is not far behind, Germany, Prussia and France follow close in their wake [and] then the United States' (p. vii).

School promoters were not the only individuals to embark on educational study tours. Some teachers were sent abroad to learn about progressive pedagogical practices. Following the adoption of Scottish educationist David Stow's training system in the Battersea Training Institution in London, teachers from England were sent to the Edinburgh Sessional School to learn the system themselves. English and North American reformers also studied in Scotland where Common Sense philosophers such as Duguld Stewart lectured on the science of the mind from a metaphysical perspective (Jones, 1963; Curtis, 1967).

As well, normal school principals, masters, and other educationists went abroad to study teacher training with an aim to improving their own institutions. In 1858, for example, the Michigan Normal School principal travelled to Europe to study normal schools there. Edward A. Sheldon superintendent of schools in Oswego, New York, was inspired by the Pestalozzian principles of object teaching he saw during his tour of the Toronto National Museum, and used these in the development of the Oswego Normal School in 1866. And to assist him with this work, he brought in a teacher from Canada to work at the normal school (Herbst, 1989; Thornburg, 2004).

The flow of ideas was not only from Europe and Britain to North America. Earlier in the century, educationists from Prussia had sent school commissioners to other European countries to collect educational information. British educational reformers were also interested in researching educational practices in North America. Horace Mann's 12 annual reports were widely circulated abroad. In England, the Newcastle Commission 1861 report included reports on the state of education in foreign countries (including Canada, Germany, France, Switzerland and Holland). A few years later, England's James Fraser was appointed to inquire into education in Scotland, the United States, Upper and Lower Canada (Fraser, 1866).

Educational promoters drew their conclusions about foreign educational ideas and practices not only from their own observations, but also from the observations of other reformers who had studied abroad. The practice of basing their reform arguments on quotations from foreign reformers, politicians, and pedagogues was common amongst them. Ryerson, for example, took up this practice to justify his support for the development of a public elementary school system, a state inspectorate and normal school. He quoted from Victor Cousin (on normal schools in

Prussia and Holland), Francois Guizot (on training teachers in France), Horace Mann (on Prussian teaching seminaries) and Doctors Bache and Young (on teacher training in the United States) (Houston, 1975). Repeatability, or quoting other educationists, within reform documents was a common strategy deployed by these reformers, and helps to explain the dispersion of a similar education reforms across the nineteenth century western world. It was also possible given the explosion in educational publications over the course of the nineteenth century.

The spread of educational publications

The publishing industry played a key role in contributing to the circulation of particular pedagogical ideas and teaching practices throughout many nineteenth century western societies. The growth of the printing industry made it possible for Parliamentarians and other school promoters to read similar educational ideas and systems. For instance, books outlining Pestalozzi's experiences and pedagogical principles were published and disseminated throughout the English speaking world and remained very popular amongst teachers and those working in the teacher training institutions. Diesterweg, the principal of the Prussian normal school, for example, wrote numerous articles in teachers' journals about Pestalozzian theories, which were translated and available for English speaking readers (Barnard, 1859; Biber, 1831; Jones, 1860; Thornburg, 2004).

The translation of European educational reformers' reports into English provided another mechanism to spread continental pedagogical practices and ideas. In England, Sarah Austin played a prominent role in translating into English foreign educational reports, including Victor Cousin's 1831 favourable report on the Prussian school system. Excerpts from Cousin's report also appeared in English and North America educational journals, and were quoted in education reformers' reports (e.g. Mann, 1843; Ryerson, 1846b). The availability of these educational reports provided a stimulus to education reform. England's Prime Minister Russell's interest in education, for example, was said to be related to the publication of Horace Mann's account of European education in 1843, in which he asserted that England was behind all civilised countries in the provision of a national education system.

As we have seen above, Scotland played a prominent role in the dissemination of educational ideas and practices. Scottish educationists and philosophers throughout the century wrote many books on the science and art of teaching and learning that spread throughout the British Empire. These were either re-published and/or copies made available to English and North American populations. For example, various headmasters of the High School of Edinburgh wrote pedagogical texts which were republished in London, referred to in English and other North American educational journals, and in the writings and speeches of reformers across Britain, Europe and North America (Bain, 1896; Donaldson, 1876; Pillans, 1829; Tate, 1857). In addition, Stow's 1853 book *The Training System*, which went through ten editions, proved to be of considerable influence in the establishment of teacher training in England and North America.

Common Sense philosophy, with its pedagogical emphasis on the science of the mind, was spread through the publication of Duguld Stewart's books, which had been enormously popular in nineteenth century Britain and North America. According to one contemporary, the first volume of Stewart's *Elements of the Philosophy of the Human Mind* had 'been more read than any other modern book on such subjects' (Quoted in Tannoch-Bland, 2000, p. 12). Many of the books by philosophers from the Common Sense school were published in Britain and North America, and excerpted in educational journals. The study of phrenology and education remained popular throughout the English speaking world, the result of Combe's writings, lectures, and travels, as well as the publication of articles and book reviews on the topic in education journals (Hodgson, 1839; Warne, 1843; Tomlinson, 1997).

Pedagogical ideas and practices circulated broadly between and within Europe, Britain and North America through these texts and their writers. Dr. Forrestor and Hugo Reid, two educationists who immigrated to Nova Scotia from England and became school principals, both published pedagogical textbooks, which were read by Canadian school teachers. Teachers across England and North America were also encouraged to read other pedagogical texts such as Thomas Tate's 1857 *The Philosophy of Education; or the Principles and Practice of Teaching*, and Henry Dunn's 1837 *Principles of Teaching; or the Normal School Manual*.

Many school textbooks, 'how-to' teach texts, pedagogical and philosophical books were reviewed and excerpted in education journals and periodicals that were published (and cross-published) in North America and Britain. Prior to 1870, more than 90 British periodicals were published, which were concerned with education. Between 1850 and 1860 alone, there were over a dozen periodicals dealing specifically with education and the teacher. A few were weeklies while most others were published on a monthly basis. For instance, the Society for the Diffusion of Useful Knowledge published the *Quarterly Journal of*

Education from 1831 to 1835, which described foreign educational systems, and included regular updates of educational changes throughout the western world. Other successful education periodicals included the *Education Magazine* and the *Journal of Education*. Many were addressed to some organisation or specific group of teachers such as those working in National Society schools (Fletcher, 1970; Sturt, 1967).

Education reformers in North America also disseminated their ideas through the publication of popular journals and magazines. By 1850, there were 60 educational journals in the United States (Herbst, 1989). Some were journals of state teachers' associations (e.g. *The Michigan Teacher*), and others intended for those who worked in the normal schools (e.g. *The American Schoolmaster*) (Thornburg, 2004). Reformers such as Barnard and Mann published the *Connecticut Common School Journal* and *Common School Journal* respectively to promote the common school cause. In 1855, Barnard began publishing the *American Journal of Education*, which became the most comprehensive journal on the subject of education. In addition to republishing important documents related to the history of education in the United States and abroad, it also included reports of education in other countries. It was widely available in major libraries, school systems, colleges and normal schools, and enjoyed wide international circulation to Canada, South America, England, and throughout Europe. According to Button and Provenzo (1983), the impact of the *American Journal of Education* in disseminating and promoting new educational ideas was enormous (p. 114).

In Canada, *The Journal of Education of Upper Canada* (JEUC) was published by the Department of Education on a monthly basis between 1848 and 1870. In the attempt to address the deficiency of domestically published material, the JEUC and other educational journals published later in the century, reprinted articles on pedagogy from the United States, Britain, and Europe. In addition, the JEUC regularly included accounts of systems of public instruction in Europe and the United States in order to diffuse more widely information about popular education. From the 1860s onwards, many other education periodicals appeared in Canada. The *Education Advocate* and the *Ontario Teacher*, for example, included articles of practical value for teachers. Speciality educational periodicals also appeared from the late 1860s, including the *Home and School Supplement* and the *Sunday School Banner*. The 1870s and 1880s were the 'hey-day' of the teachers' periodicals across North America with the spread of education publications across the provinces and states (Althouse, 1967; Butcher, 1886).

The growth of the publishing industry through the nineteenth century facilitated the spread of educational ideas and practices. The increasing availability of printed educational material ranging from reports, articles, books and journals, meant that certain ways of thinking about schooling and the teacher could circulate more freely and widely. Themes such as the science of the mind, and the benefits of progressive, humanistic pedagogy were taken up across a wide variety of printed material. In this way, a similar system of reasoning about education and the role of the teacher was made possible through the availability and circulation of this printed material. This was yet another one of the conditions that made particular circuits of pedagogical knowledge production possible across a wide variety of nineteenth century settings.

The spread of educational practices through immigration

Over the course of the nineteenth century, North American populations became increasingly diversified with the arrival of immigrants from a variety of countries. There were two broad ways that immigrants influenced educational reform. The first is that common school promoters argued for the development of mass education in order to assimilate minorities into the dominant Protestant culture and prepare obedient citizens. Therefore the existence of immigrants in North America was used to promote the common school movement and in the case of the United States, the Americanisation of new citizens (Cubberley, 1947; Spring, 1990).

However, there was another way that immigrants influenced Victorian educational reform. Immigrants to North America carried with them their own values and assumptions about education and the role of the teacher. Throughout the Victorian period, the foreign-born population of the United States increased considerably, reflecting large-scale immigration from Europe over most of the century. Immigrants to the United States numbered almost 600,000 in the 1830s and 1.7 million in the 1950s. Up until the 1880s, the majority of immigrants were largely English, Scotch, Irish, German, and Scandinavian (Cubberley, 1947; Green, 1990).

In English-speaking Canada, immigrants included those from Ireland, England and Scotland. There were also United Empire Loyalists who had settled in the British provinces following the American Revolution, other 'late' non-Loyalist Americans, including Blacks escaping slavery in the south, and immigrants from continental Europe (Morton, 1964).

The migration of these immigrants influenced educational reform in profound ways. Immigrants brought with them their cultural baggage, including sets of norms, values, and attitudes about education. Irish immigration, in particular, heavily influenced Canadian and American educational practices. This influence was manifest in a number of ways, including the establishment of schools in the 1840s to deal with the influx of Irish immigrants. North American educational reformers also turned to Ireland for advice on the organisation of normal schools and elementary schools. This was, as one historian has pointed out, 'the Irish decade' with respect to educational matters (Love, 1978, p. 115).

North American common schools bore the influence of the Scottish immigrant as well. Scotland had advanced England in its efforts to establish government grants for common schools since the end of the eighteenth century. Early in the nineteenth century, Scottish immigrants to North America, committed to publicly funded education, similarly advocated for government grants for the common schools (Burnet, 1972).

Canadian common schools were also influenced by the Loyalist population from the United States, who brought to the colonies a belief in the need and potential for widespread and non-denominational education. Loyalists, like the Scottish and Irish immigrants, were uninterested in replicating the aristocratic traditions of English society. Notions of rank and class background that early settlers brought with them from the mother country began to disappear with the influx of immigrants from a wider variety of countries and class backgrounds. Loyalists carried with them the American commitment to democracy and egalitarianism. Moreover, mixing amongst North American immigrants from different ethnic, class, and religious backgrounds was the norm. The levelling influence of egalitarian life, the democratic values, Protestant work ethic, and assumptions about class that the broad range of immigrants brought with them, worked towards breaking down class exclusiveness, and contributed towards the drive to establish compulsory, state-funded education systems in North America (Careless, 1967; Morrison, 1971; Bailyn, 1960).

Conclusion

In this chapter I provided a brief outline of some of the key aspects of education reform in England and other western countries over the Victorian period. While the speed, pace, and nature of those reforms, as well as the role of the state, voluntary and other religious societies in educational provision differed across these settings, there were some broad similarities. Over the course of the century, there developed a general sense of the importance of providing free (and eventually compulsory) education to the masses. Attention was paid to the structure and function of these emerging educational systems, including the role of the state in educational financing, administration and inspections of schools, teacher training and certification, and control over the curriculum.

These processes were played out in settings that were very different from one another. On the one hand, education reform emerged in many of the well-established monarchist states of Europe in the late eighteenth/early nineteenth century. England, like most other European countries at that time, was a fully formed nation-state, the biggest unit of a large political creation, the United Kingdom of Great Britain and Ireland, and a powerful and rich Empire with colonial possessions in all corners of the world. These included, up until 1867, the British North American colonies, which were engaging in various struggles associated with nation-state building. By 1876, the United States was celebrating its own centennial as a nation-state, and had emerged as a new social, political and economic power.

State formation, industrialisation and urbanisation, as we have seen above, occurred at different times across the settings studied here. It is surprising then that a similar set of educational ideas and practices were taken up over the course of the Victorian period given the diversity of settings studied here. In all of these jurisdictions, considerable attention was directed towards constructing popular education systems and establishing mechanisms such as public taxation and local governance, and formal processes to train, certify and inspect teachers. Some have posited a causal link between the construction of mass, compulsory education systems and processes such as state formation, industrialisation and urbanisation. Introducing comparative and international contexts into this book illustrates the limitations, however, to positing a causal connection between these processes and the construction of mass, compulsory education systems.

Rather, one could look to the work of individual educational reformers and promoters to understand how a similar set of pedagogical practices and ideas were taken up across these settings, However, this new cultural history is not concerned with the history of individual thought, but ways to think about the conditions that made possible the emergence and circulation of particular systems of reasoning about education over the Victorian period. The reform processes, practices, and relations that have been described in this chapter help to shed some light on the emergence and circulation of particular ways of thinking about education. The combination of improved modes of travel, consequent popularity of the educational study tour, growth of educational publications, and practice of quoting from speeches and reports of other educational reformers and promoters contributed to the circulation of a similar set of educational ideas and practices. The fact that most educational reformers directed their attention towards the same progressive Prussian pedagogical models adds to our understanding about the circulation of particular ways of thinking about the role of the elementary school and its teacher. Immigration to North America from Europe and Britain also contributed to the spread of similar educational ideas and practices. Together, the inter-relations and interconnections between these processes help to explain how it became possible for a particular regime of pedagogical truth to develop and move through a wide variety of settings, from and within Europe, Britain and North America.

Rather than search for deterministic, causal explanations to understand Victorian educational reform, I have presented a set of conditions that made it possible for a similar system of educational reasoning and practices to be taken up. Different social, cultural, political and economic characteristics of a variety of western societies were translated into similar patterns of power and knowledge. Comparison, in this respect, allows one to see that while education reforms are mediated by divergent local contexts, similar processes and practices can be taken up across dissimilar settings. The next chapter continues this analysis by drawing upon new cultural history to understand *how*, not why, education and the teacher became objects of attention to the Victorians. This approach provides a richer, more complex, and comprehensive means by which to understand the multiple conditions, which made possible the socio-historical construction and regulation of the Victorian teacher.

Notes

1   The pupil teacher system provided a means to bridge the gap between individuals leaving (elementary) school and training in the colleges to become teachers. For five years (generally between the ages of 13 and 18), senior selected pupils could practice teaching in elementary schools and study the subjects necessary to becoming a teacher under the supervision of a schoolmaster or mistress. To qualify for apprenticeship, they were examined by the local inspector in reading, writing, arithmetic, grammar, geography, and in Church of England schools, in religious knowledge. If the inspector was

satisfied with the results, he would sign the indenture and see that annual grants were paid to the pupil-teacher and the teacher if their work continued to be satisfactory (Committee of Council, 1847).

2 Johann Heinrich Pestalozzi (1746–1827) was a progressive Swiss educator who promoted the idea that children should learn through activity, pursue their own interests, and come to their own conclusions. Inspired by Rousseau, he spent the early part of his life serving the poor and later working out his theory and method of instruction based on the natural development of the child. His pedagogical ideas were very influential during the Victorian period, both within and outside of Europe. They are explored further in Chapter 5 of this book.

Part II

Discourses of the Victorian Teacher

4
Discourses of Crisis and Derision: Targeting the Poor and the Teacher

The Victorians were both optimistic about the times they lived in and terribly anxious about the great promises that modernity held for them. This chapter takes a look at what caused Victorian reformers great concern and worry by examining two discourses, one concerning the general state of society and the other about the teacher. The first, a discourse of moral crisis, was constituted by the fears, worries, anxieties and insecurities that middle-class Victorians felts towards the poor, labouring and immigrant populations. This discourse of crisis provided the conditions for attention to be directed towards education, which came to be posited as a panacea to the ills of the age. As education was formulated as an object of concern, a discourse of derision, targeted at the informal network of Victorian schools and their teachers, developed.[1] These dual, related discourses set the stage for the construction of popular education systems and the related making and shaping of the good teacher in England and abroad.

Crisis discourse: Targeting poor, labouring and immigrant populations

The Victorians, while profoundly optimistic about their times, were also extremely anxious about the rapid changes they witnessed around them. In England, nineteenth century education and social reformers such as James Kay-Shuttleworth, Henry Brougham and Arthur Roebuck expressed considerable concern about the state of the poor in their speeches, reports and other writings. They noted the existence of problems such as the decrepit state of housing, lack of proper sanitation, disease, intemperate and idle habits, and other 'evils' found amongst the urban poor. Statistical, public health and educational reports described the terrible state of health of the poor, brought on by poor diets, sickness, disease and unsanitary living conditions. In particular, attention was paid to the predominance of urban Irish migrants, where the wretched state of their habitations, lack of proper sanitation and close proximity of tanneries, kennels, and cemeteries did little to ward off the threat of cholera and other diseases (Kay, 1862; Select Committee, 1816).

Social reformers were especially concerned with the spreading poverty amongst urban children. Street children made urban poverty a visible problem. Poorly clothed, undisciplined and ignorant children who lived on English urban streets evoked disturbing and heart-rending emotions in the eyes of reformers. Poor parents were criticised for taking their children out of school to work either at home or outside of the home to contribute to the family economy. Concern was also expressed about children being sent out to work at too young an age, and the conditions under which they were expected to work. In their reports, reformers were deeply critical about practices associated with child labour as deterrents to the general improvement of the poor and hindering educational improvement (Committee of Council, 1840; Kay, 1862).

Reformers were especially dismayed with the idle and dissolute ways of the poor. Immoral habits, it was argued, were both the natural products and causes of popular ignorance and immorality. Reference was made to the bad habits of pauper children, ranging from vile language to begging, thieving, gambling and riotous behaviour. Attention was also directed to the immoral behaviour of poor parents who were blamed for their children's mischievous and criminal behaviour. Such parents, so the argument went, had neglected their responsibility to teach their children proper values such as virtue, honesty, duty and respect, and other moral principles. They were considered inappropriate role models for their own children. The result of exposing children to immoral activities such as fighting and drinking was that they grew up predisposed to 'evil influences', the guaranteed prelude to the child's progress to infamy, vice and crime (*Report on the Training of Pauper Children*, 1838 in Johnson, 1970).

Not only were the poor criticised for their immoral habits, but many were said to be idle and lazy. This line of attack was directed most forcefully towards the urban Irish immigrant population, many who arrived in England (and North America) following the potato famine in 1847. It was alleged that the majority were lacking in skills, possessing wretched habits, and with no inclination to work. Other non-immigrant paupers were also said to spend their days involved in idle pursuits and engaging in dissolute activities such as drinking and gambling (Careless, 1967; Kay-Shuttleworth, 1862d).

The fear of the spread of poverty and its immoral, barbarous and ignorant effects caused reformers considerable alarm. To some, pauperism (poverty) and its associated vices were considered to be like a contagious disease that could be spread easily to the working and poorer classes. Lord Macaulay in his 1847 speech before the House of Commons defended the State's responsibility to educate England's poor by comparing ignorance, spread through the lower classes, to 'a leprosy, or some other fearful disease' (House of Commons, 1847, p. 1008).

The likening of poverty and its immoral effects to a disease infecting the body politic suggests a dual concern with the outer (body) and inner (character) disposition of the citizen. Poverty and its associated bad habits, such as drinking, fighting and laziness were viewed as the effects of an immoral and irresolute character. In particular, poverty was considered a sort of moral contamination transmitted through the parent. Reform would entail changing not simply the bad habits of the child, but his/her inner nature in order to rid the social body of the diseased individual body. This was to become the dual reshaping of the individual body and the body politic, through education, in order to stop the spread of the disease-like problem of poverty and its immoral effects.

Education promoters also argued that the poor threatened to undermine the social harmony of society. Reformers feared that the immoral and uncivilised habits that destitute, uncivilised newcomers brought to the towns would spread amongst the rest of the urban population. Kay-Shuttleworth (1862d), in his study of the poor immigrant population of Manchester, had no doubt that 'the moral influence of the immigrants of semi-barbarous masses is prejudicial, by example, and personal intercourse, to the habits of the population with which they mingle' (pp. 151–2).

While general urban disorder and crime captured the attention of reformers, the plight of juvenile delinquents troubled Victorian social conscience even more. By the 1830s, the problem of urban youth came to be distinguished from other crimes. The homeless urban child was sometimes viewed as poor, waif like and blameless and other times as a sinful and delinquent criminal. Both were of great concern to reformers who sought to address these problems through social welfare and public education.

Crime, a result of immoral habits and character, was viewed with considerable concern as a threat to the social fabric, and like immorality, a contagion that could spread to the rest of the susceptible social body. In particular, reformers argued that crime and social agitation threatened to disrupt economic progress and broader social order. Fears about crime were reinforced through statistical studies that were carried out to measure, through quantitative means, the extent and nature of criminal activity, and relationship to schooling. Studies on prisoners in urban centres showed a positive correlation between criminal behaviour and rates of illiteracy, and bolstered reformers claims for popular education (Harris, 1848; Select Committee of the House of Lords, 1847).

Crime and social disorder, it was argued, were spreading because of the immorality and ignorance of the general population. Criminality and ignorance were therefore viewed as moral problems, leading reformers to claim that rates of crime would decrease through improving the moral state of the population, with popular education positioned as the solution. This line of thinking and associated concerns about the immorality and ignorance of the poor was not isolated amongst English reformers, but articulated across a wider range of settings as we will now see.

Crisis discourse: Comparative and international contexts

Issues about poverty, immorality, crime, disease and public health became the subject of public debate outside of England too. Reformers in North America also expressed concern about the immoral and irreligious nature of the poor, and the relationship between ignorance, illiteracy, and rising rates of crime. There was great alarm about the physical, moral and mental state of the poor and decrepit. An 1846 survey revealed that Canada already had a larger percentage of 'idiots and invalids, of mentally and physically handicapped' compared to anywhere else in North America or Europe where comparable data was available (Naylor, 1987, p. 207).

In particular, there was considerable panic about the impoverished state of certain new immigrant groups, such as the Irish, who were without family ties and often unable to understand the English language. In Canada, Ryerson (1848) wrote: 'The physical disease and death which has accompanied their influx among us may be the worst pestilence of social insubordination and disorder' (pp. 299–300). In the United States, reformers also claimed that there was a connection between immigration, delinquency and crime. Poor immigrants, especially those from Ireland, were said to be of an inferior stock and therefore prone to poverty and vice (Katz, 1968).

North American reformers directed their attacks towards poor families, blaming them for the mix of immorality, ignorance, poverty and criminal behaviour of young people, especially in urban areas. According to these reformers, family life had disintegrated, resulting in the corresponding breakdown of social order and control. The main concern amongst reformers was the immoral state of poor and immigrant children and youth. As in England, poor parents were considered unsuitable role models for their children. They were targeted for engaging in immoral activities such as swearing and drinking, and exposing their children to this kind of behaviour (Durham, 1839; Mann, 1846; Ryerson, 1848). As the chaplain of a Massachusetts reform school explained in 1859, a 'family whose parental instructors are ignorant, inefficient and immoral is quite sure to make a disastrous failure of the education of the little ones committed to its care' (Quoted in Katz, 1968, p. 174).

Although urbanisation was not occurring at nearly the same pace as in England, North American social reformers also directed their attention at the problems of the city (or semi-urban areas), demonstrating their fears about the perils of progress. They aimed their attacks towards the visible problems of the city, including youthful vagrants, petty criminals, orphaned and homeless children. As in England, the poor and the immigrant were seen as the most vulnerable to the corrupting influences of the city. Moreover, there was great fear about the threats posed by the poor to orderly civic life. Vice and crime, according to Massachusetts reformer Mann (1846) were 'not only prodigals and spendthrifts of their own, but defrauders and plunderers of the means of others'.

Reformers in continental Europe were also alarmed about the state of the poor. In France, for example, liberal reformers such as Comte and Dunoyer felt that the development of civilisation was hindered by the related problems of ignorance and violence (Weinburg, 1978). The changing nature of rural-urban social relations over the course of the eighteenth century had contributed towards weakening traditional forms of patriarchal authority. Anxiety about the decline of more well established forms of social control in rural areas were also heightened by frequent peasant uprisings, which caused considerable alarm amongst reformers (Green, 1990).

Such fears were taken up in England. Concern about the social unrest, and related radical and revolutionary ideas circulating in Europe led reformers to fear that agitation among the working classes could spill over into revolutionary anarchy, threatening the stability of the state. This was, as the historian E. P. Thompson (1980) has argued, a period of rising class consciousness and the making of the working class. Education reformers worried about international and domestic social unrest and fears that the poor were most vulnerable to revolutionary ideas. Kay-Shuttleworth (1862b), in expressing such concerns, cautioned that he was being neither an alarmist, nor writing under the influence of undue fear or the wish to inspire fear in others, but that his opinions were based on careful observations of Chartist speeches, proceedings and actions.

European unrest and Chartist agitation in England sent shockwaves across North America too. News of political and social upheaval abroad contributed to rising fears about social disorder. In Canada, combination of memories of the 1837 rebellions, racial antagonisms and bitterness between the French and English, news of the 1848 European uprisings and later, the Fenian Raids, caused considerable alarm. Many of these concerns were related to civil obligations, patriotism and the loyalty to the British Empire, and were formulated in response to fears and antagonistic relations between Canada and the United States. Anti-Americanism, which had some of its roots in the War of 1812, was firmly rooted in Canada by the 1840s. Indeed, reformers deliberately evoked fears about US republicanism as a means by which to convince the public to support the spread of public education (Love, 1984).

Whig reformers in the United States also evoked images of lawlessness, crime and disorder to build a case for public education. During the Civil War, criminal activity amongst females and young vagrants increased, causing great alarm amongst reformers. Furthermore, they worried that Irish Catholic and German immigrants new to the country might prove dangerous to social order. Common school promoters became increasingly occupied with concerns about the inter-related problems of poverty, public health, crime, insanity, and disease. And like their counterparts in England, they looked to education as a means to prevent social anarchy and construct a nation of obedient, hardworking citizens (Binder, 1974; Katz, 1968, 1976).

Reformers on both sides of the Atlantic built their cases for educational reform by quoting foreign studies on crime and ignorance. MP Thomas Wyse in the British Parliament referred to the 'marked exemption from crimes and violence' in Prussia, brought about by the educational system (Quoted in Ryerson, 1846b, p. 144). In North America, reformers also referred to accounts of poverty; and statistical reports from other countries to prove that ignorance was the source of idleness, intemperance, and improvidence, leading to pauperism and eventually crime (Duncombe, 1836; Katz, 1968; Ryerson, 1846b). Such reformers had no qualms about relaying stories of the squalid 'hovels' of the poor they had seen in their visits abroad, and the related threats of social upheaval, in order to bolster their claims for educational reform (Binder, 1974, p. 29).

Education as the panacea

The purposeful production of fear in order to create a public consensus around the need for educational reform was neither specific to the nineteenth century nor to England. There are many contemporary manifestations of the production of fear in order to justify major educational restructuring. Discourses of crisis and derision, as Ball (1990) and Thorpe (2003) have shown, are common precedents to educational reform. They have been played out in England and the United States since the 1980s and somewhat later in many Canadian provinces (Ball, 1990; Chitty, 2004). As in the Victorian period, we continue to witness a sense of moral panic about rising rates of societal violence, youth crime and youth alienation. Attention has shifted to schools which are blamed not only for falling educational standards, but broader societal problems such as unemployment, economic malaise, crime and violence. The manufactured nature of these discursive crises is clear, especially in the case of Ontario, Canada, where the Minister of Education claimed that if the public did not think there was an educational crisis, at the very least he would manufacture one to justify comprehensive educational reforms (Ryan, 1995).

Whether manufactured or not, similar discourses of fear and crisis were played out in nineteenth century England, Europe and North America. Discourses of fear are bound up with the sense of risk and danger. This sense of danger of the masses reflected deep-seated Victorian fears of their present and future. Poverty, immorality, and crime became real insofar as they could be a measurable characteristic of particular populations (the urban poor and immigrant). The sense of danger against these groups enabled the discursive positioning of education as a solution to the crises of the age.

Forging the link between poverty, immorality, social disorder, ignorance, and education was bound up with the question of blame. First, the attitudes and values of the poor were attacked. Poverty was a result of their ignorance, immorality, intemperance, and idleness. Specifically, poverty, crime, and disease were a result of poor parenting. The parents of poor children, who had practically signed away their parental rights by virtue of moral abdication, were said to be 'disqualified or incapacitated from fulfilling their natural role' (Quoted in Johnson, 1970, p. 112). The answer to this problem lay with shifting the responsibility for raising children from families to public schools. As US reformer Barnard wrote:

> No one at all familiar with the deficient household arrangements and the deranged machinery of domestic life of the extreme poor, and ignorant, to say nothing of the intemperate – of the examples of rude manners, impure and profane language, and all the vicious habits of low-bred idleness which abound in certain sections of all populous districts – can doubt, that it is better for children to be removed as early and as long as possible (Quoted in Katz, 1975, p. 10).

Poor children, so this line of argument went, would find protection from their own families in public schools. Schools would succeed where their families had failed. The answer was mass education, which would serve as the panacea to these 'evils' of society.

Public education, it was argued, would break and prevent the destructive cycle of poverty and neglect, crime and social disorder. Education therefore came to be positioned as the only solution to solve the problems of poverty, crime and preserve order in a chaotic, disorderly world. Educating the individual would create a more stable, socially useful and productive populace. The interests of the individual, in this respect, were subordinated to the requirements of the social body. Hence, claims concerning what education would achieve were made primarily in reference to the positive benefits for the state or society as a whole.

The relations between the potential of education to create social order, drive industrial development, raise the wealth of the nation, and construct a moral population speak to the interwoven connections between education and the crisis discourse. Reformers in England looked abroad to other countries such as Prussia and even the United States where education systems were more advanced, and concluded that educational developments had led to an increase in prosperity, social happiness and national improvement. Social happiness was bound up with economic progress, with education positioned as the means to create more efficient industrious workers (Mann, 1841; Ryerson, 1846b).

Moreover, in response to fears that educating working classes would lead to social agitation, reformers emphasised the positive potential of education in constructing obedient, moral citizens. Challenging arguments that education would make the working classes discontented and disorderly, Ryerson (1846b) quoted the Swiss Poor Law Commissioner who claimed that 'better educated workmen' were distinguished 'by superior moral habits in every respect' (p. 145). Likewise, Inspector Noel in England wrote that education would ensure that all individuals would be able to take 'their proper place as the most intelligent, cultivated, religious, and cheerful working population in the world' (Committee of Council, 1841, p. 78).

Moral education, it was argued, was especially suited for the poor. Poor children were ignorant of the experiences and values of restraint deemed necessary for the development of their own moral character, sustenance and social stability of society. Values such as order, diligence, and obedience, upon which the social fabric depended, would be cultivated in the school. Schools, as the reformers argued, would instil in these young children the principles of virtue, and habits of prudence, industry, and self-control. In this way we can see how the creation of moral subjects entailed creating governable subjects, and public education was the means to that end.

The idea that education could be used as a means to create governable subjects was taken up outside of England as well. Creating governable subjects in North America meant inculcating in pupils a sense of their duties and loyalty. Reformers argued that the welfare and safety of government lay in the hands of a common school system. In effect, as Curtis (1981) has shown, mid-nineteenth century education reform in Canada sought to shape the subjectivity of the body politic and create governable subjects. With the positioning of education as the panacea to the problems of poverty, crime and social unrest, attention was then directed towards the schools currently in operation. Education was therefore formed as an object of concern through the articulation of societal problems.

Education as the solution to society's ills was embedded within the anxieties of the Victorian period. This embedded relationship between problem-solution reflects the relationship between the crisis discourse and the framing of education as a solution to those fears. These fears were entangled within the paradoxical and uncertain attitudes that middle-class Victorians maintained towards the effects of industrialisation, urbanisation, and immigration. While many praised the opportunities that these processes brought, they also pointed to the increasing costs of progress in terms of poverty, immorality, social disorder, and crime. Hence, one social commentator wrote that Britain had exhibited the strangest spectacle ever witnessed. Along with progress came:

so much suffering in one portion of the people, with so much prosperity in another; of unbounded private wealth, with unceasing public penury...of the utmost freedom consistent with order, ever yet existing on earth, with a degree of discontent which keeps the nation constantly on the verge of insurrection (Archibald, 1845, p. 5).

The middle classes had the most to gain (and lose) from the processes associated with nineteenth century progress. While they largely supported the economic progress associated with industrialisation, they became increasingly worried about how resentment and antagonism could easily transform into revolution. Maintaining social control in a society undergoing tremendous change became one of their main fears; the dilemma being how to facilitate industrial and urban progress while at the same time contain social unrest. Fears of crime and social disorder touched them deeply, providing educational reformers with a means by which to encourage the middle classes to support the construction of common or popular school systems.

The merits and costs of progress, such as the increase in both the profits and the proportion of the poor in society were debated at length. At the heart of these debates lay the city, the space where the trials and tribulations of progress could be most visibly identified. The city symbolised what was best and worst about progress to the Victorians in England. Poverty, ignorance and its effects were made visible in the city and viewed as urban problems. And while urbanisation occurred at a slower pace in North America and much of continental Europe, reformers there also evoked fears about the threats to social and moral order arising from the ignorance, immorality and indolence of the urban poor and immigrant populations.

With their minds filled with fears, anxieties, uncertainties and reservations about the costs of progress to society, reformers turned their attention to schools and teachers. They found in the ad hoc mix of dame, charity, pauper, local, village and pioneer schools the problems of society and more. In particular, they began to attack the immoral, ignorant and indolent teacher and the discourse of crisis (about Victorian society in general) shifted to a discourse of derision towards the teachers of the poor.

Discourse of derision: Targeting the teacher

Teaching as a last resort: The poor teacher

During the early Victorian period, teachers came under scrutiny by educational reformers, inspectors, politicians. A discourse of derision developed whereby schools and their teachers were attacked and demonised. This discourse, as we will see, set the stage for the subsequent making and shaping of the good Victorian teacher.

Teaching in England was viewed as a refuge for the destitute individual who, having failed at their previous occupation(s), or had experienced misfortune, misconduct, or indolence took up teaching. Old retired soldiers, sailors, and sea captains and other 'mere and needy adventurers' were said to have taken up school keeping as a last resort (Committee of Council, 1849, p. 119; Newcastle Commission, 1861c).

Teachers were referred to as being aged, ancient or venerable, conveying the impression that teaching was the sole prerogative of the old. The old, sick, crippled, and disordered body of the teacher also became an object of concern to educational reformers, a site on which reform could later be inscribed. Many of those who took up teaching were reputed to be injured, incapacitated, broken down or crippled men. There were also numerous reports of teachers who were deaf, blind, deformed, missing limbs; lame or disabled in one way or another (Committee of Council, 1845, 1846, 1849, 1851, Newcastle Commission, 1861c).

The National Society (1849–55) echoed these concerns, stating that it was well known that any 'poor, lame, deaf, decrepit, or broken fortuned [sic] man who was likely to require a share of the poor-rates, was considered fit for the office of schoolmaster' (p. 191). There were also statements about the 'poor old body' or 'feeble form' of the dame schoolmistresses, again attesting to the interest reformers had in the disabled and decrepit body of the teacher (Manchester Statistical Society 1836; Newcastle Commission, 1861a).

Statements on the aged and broken down body of the teacher were made in relation to their impoverished situations. The least capable and most transient were often the only candidates for teaching positions given the low wages and poor working conditions. Critics decried the poverty that private teachers were forced to endure as a result of their struggles to collect school fees from their pupils' parents. The pay-per-pupil system was criticised harshly. Local communities were attacked for hiring the cheapest and least well-qualified teacher. However, dire financial circumstances were just as often blamed upon the incompetence and other personal deficiencies of schoolteachers, who had become impoverished through their own misconduct and immorality (Committee of Council, 1849; National Society, 1838–47).

One solution was for schoolmasters and mistresses in England to take on small, paid jobs outside of teaching. Some took on additional educational pursuits such as private teaching, keeping an evening school, or delivering an occasional lecture, to supplement to their daytime teaching income. Others engaged in a whole range of non-teaching activities ranging from work as a porter, rate-collector, clerk, post-master, blacksmith, to journeyman, for example. Teachers were criticised and ridiculed for these practices. Engaging in additional remunerative occupations was considered a character flaw. Such an individual, who had failed at all other occupations, was in 'vulgar speech' described as a 'jack of all trades' (Newcastle Commission, 1861c).

Most criticism was reserved for dame school teachers who, having opened schools in their homes, engaged in additional money making schemes on the side, including taking in washing, needlework, and sewing, and the sale of sweets, snacks and toys. Dames were denounced for mixing teaching with their own domestic duties, and in some extreme cases for simply closing up their schools in order to devote time to their other occupations (Newcastle Commission 1861c, 1861d; Select Committee, 1838). Dame schools were also criticised for their 'shifting and changeable character' (Committee of Council, 1859, p. 118). This critique went beyond the dame school, as well to other individual teachers and their schools, which were said to be 'ephemeral'.

The immoral teacher

The crux of the problem, in the eyes of nineteenth century reformers, was that teachers were immoral. The moral purposes of education came be defined against what the Victorians perceived as being evidence of immoral character, behaviour, and habits in both the poorer populations and in their teachers. Accusations of immoral behaviour amongst elementary schoolmasters in England ranged from complaints about ill-mannered habits to acts such as gambling and fighting.

Criticisms of drinking habits of the poorer population mirrored statements on the intemperance of schoolmasters. In England, Lancaster had remarked early in the century that 'the drunkenness of a school-master is almost proverbial' (Quoted in Sturt, 1967, p. 40). Throughout the next half-century, there were numerous critical accounts of intoxicated teachers. Schoolchildren were found in other schools, or playing in the streets of a local garret, while their own schoolmaster was said to be absent due to drinking. Some were dismissed for drunkenness, and if not then local communities were blamed for turning a blind eye to their schoolmaster's state of drunkenness (Manchester Statistical Society, 1836; Newcastle Commission, 1861c, 1861d).

The assortment of these character faults and habits were considered harmful and injurious to students. Immoral teachers were incapable of keeping respectable schools. Such teachers were considered completely inadequate role models, and lacking the capability of improving the mental and moral character of their pupils. Inspectors noted the relationship between teachers who were morally deficient and the lack of moral tone within their classrooms. By mid-century, Inspector Mitchell had found that the lowest class of England's day schools composed of 'persons, broken in character, health, or morals' (Committee of Council, 1851, p. 250). Among the older and untrained schoolmasters that Inspector Fletcher met, the schools were 'more remarkable for the almost military exactitude of their evolutions [sic] than for the intellectual life or moral tone which pervades their classes' (Committee of Council, 1846, p. 303).

In particular, workhouse schoolteachers, who were derided for their own financial and moral deficiencies, were considered poor moral trainers even for pauper children. Monitorial school teachers were also singled out for attack for their flagrant disregard for moral and religious instruction, or for leaving moral and religious education in the hands of young, untrained monitors. One critic charged that these 'national nurseries of vice' had been unable to achieve their goal of reforming the morals of the masses (Brougham, 1828, p. 238).[2]

Especially harsh criticism was reserved for schoolmasters in small, private schools who seldom attended to religious and moral instruction. Many schoolmasters were said to have no idea what the teaching of morals could possibly mean and were surprised when asked if they engaged in moral instruction. On the other hand, some schoolmasters and schoolmistresses falsely pretended that they taught morals and religion to their pupils. Inspectors noted the complete lack of moral instruction in many of the schools where teachers claimed that they taught morals to their pupils. Inspector Mitchell decried this type of pretence, noting that among the lowest class of schools in his district, the teachers 'assume an extra religious tone as a cloke [sic] to their deficiencies' (Committee of Council, 1851, p. 250).

Disorder: The cruel teacher and chaotic classroom

While some teachers may have been overly pretentious with regard to their own capabilities, when it came to teaching many were criticised for lacking the energy and enthusiasm their work required. Teachers were reputedly wanting in spirit, activity, energy, and teaching power. Classroom teaching was said to be hard and heavy, and teachers slow and slovenly in their movements. Such teachers took little care with their teaching and neglected to enforce attendance amongst their pupils.

Children often came and went based on their parents' needs and expectations. While this flexibility may have suited parents, officials criticised the fact that teachers neglected to enforce consistent attendance regulations (Committee of Council, 1842, 1851; Newcastle Commission, 1861c).

Incompetence, laziness and a lack of spirit led to disorder and chaos in the classroom. Want of system and method was a frequently heard charge against many different types of elementary schoolmasters and mistresses. Schoolmasters in large schools (pauper, workhouse, schools of industry and monitorial schools) were singled out for their inability to conduct their schools efficiently. Parochial union inspectors agreed that it was rare to find an untrained pauper teacher able to conduct a workhouse school class satisfactorily. One such schoolmaster: 'though not deficient in ability or information, was without method or steadiness of manner [and] consequently unable to maintain his authority over the boys' (Committee of Council, 1849, p. 133).

The problem was not confined to workhouse schoolmasters though. Among the broader spectrum of masters and mistresses in private day and dame schools in London, it was said that very few of them understood how to teach. Dame and private school teachers were considered to 'have no acquaintances with correct methods of conveying religious and secular instruction and no idea of the proper mode of conducting the moral and industrial training of children' (Select Committee, 1835, p. 3). One Inspector summed up the situation neatly: 'With few exceptions, there is no system of teaching in the schools in my district' (Anon, 1847, p. 29).

Teachers were also criticised for their use of cruel methods to maintain classroom order. The official record in England is replete with reports of schoolmasters who had little idea of progressive schoolkeeping methods, and consequently resorted to the frequent use of corporal punishment. Some pupils were left confined to their beds or under medical supervision after having been beaten by their teachers. Others spent their school days under the fear of their teacher's 'instrument of torture' (Quoted in Horn, 1978, p. 20). Harsh criticism was reserved for monitorial schoolmasters and their use of corporal punishment. While inspectors and other officials tended to sympathise with the demands these teachers faced in trying to maintain order in such large classrooms, they were also quick to reprehend the monitorial teacher for resorting to 'violent and tyrannical' methods to discipline their pupils (Committee of Council, 1846).

English schoolmasters who relied on the severe, cruel and brutal use of corporal punishment were both ridiculed and denounced in the official record. Some inspectors noted that in a few rare situations the teacher might be forced to resort to the measured use of the rod or cane. However, most teachers were viewed as injudicious, hasty, and careless in the manner in which they disciplined their pupils. Critics agreed that deficiency in character and temper, a facile and weak disposition, and gross moral character among schoolmasters were all linked to the use of corporal punishment in the classroom (Committee of Council, 1841, 1846).

In North America, school promoters also attacked teachers for the use of corporal punishment (e.g. Mann, 1843; Ryerson, 1846b). The use of the birch, beech, rod, cane, or the 'taws' to maintain discipline and order in Upper Canadian schools was criticised by reformers and educational writers there. 'No larnin' without lickin' was said to be the creed in early pioneer schools and that anyone could teach if he could prove his claim to be master over the pupils (Canuck, 1905; Lizars and Lizars, 1896). Moreover, it was claimed that most of the teachers who had come from Britain to North America ruled with 'somewhat despotic sway, enforcing their authority with a sometimes pretty free use of the birch' (Briggs, 1896, pp. 178, 183).

This was a gendered critique with attention focused on the abuse of authority by schoolmasters. Few schoolmistresses were criticised for being cruel in the classroom. Some dames (women who operated small, informal schools in their homes) used mental punishments such as placing the children in dark places such as pantry cupboards and coal cellars, or making children sit in a corner with a dunce cap on as a form of social stigma. Otherwise, like some schoolmasters they secured order merely by the threat of the whip or rod that hung by their side. More often than not, however, dames and other schoolmistresses were disparaged for displaying little activity in both instruction and coercion (Select Committee, 1838; Committee of Council, 1846).

The use of corporal punishment in the classroom was viewed as an inefficient, outdated, and cruel means by which to promote order and learning. England's Inspector Moseley provided numerous examples to illustrate the correlation between the use of corporal punishment and disorder in the classroom. In one school, where the teacher was particularly violent, there was little order and learning going on. Moseley concluded that 'severity on the part of the master, and a stern system of discipline [are] found to be perfectly compatible with great inefficiency in the school' (Committee of Council, 1846, p. 96).

Moreover, reformers argued that the demoralising influence of corporal punishment outweighed any amount of knowledge that may have been gained through its use. Such punitive efforts, they concluded, produced neither order, nor efficiency in the classroom.

The ignorant and conceited teacher

The problem was that such teachers did not understand the appropriate teaching methods and the art of school management. They were ignorant and incompetent; their schools as inefficient systems, lacked method and order. The ignorance of teachers was a constant theme running through inspectors' and reformers' reports. Teachers in workhouse or pauper schools were specifically targeted for their incompetence and inability to perform their duties efficiently. Impoverished dames were similarly described as ignorant and inefficient. Such teachers failed to educate their pupils properly due to their general ignorance concerning elementary subject matter. In some cases, pupils outstripped their teachers. However, it was the others who suffered at the hands of incompetent and ignorant teachers that worried educational reformers the most (Committee of Council, 1845, 1851; Select Committee, 1852).

Statistical and school inspection reports contain reports of incompetent teachers who could not spell or write, speak in a proper manner, read out loud without difficulty, or cipher. The Manchester Statistical Society (1836) simply concluded that 'the generality of the Teachers are wholly incompetent to the task of instruction, and their ignorance on the most common topics is lamentable' (pp. 7–8). Teachers were also criticised for being pretentious, conceited and showy, and acting under the pretence of being able to read and write correctly. Inspector Wood found that among the common day school teachers in Birmingham, many established 'in the eyes of the public a false criterion of their qualifications [including] the art of writing' (Select Committee, 1838, p. 291).

For Inspector Moseley the fact that some teachers claimed more knowledge than they actually possessed was highly problematic and disadvantaged the school child (Committee of Council, 1846). For other English educational promoters, the conceit and self-complacency of some teachers was simply beyond reproach. Amongst teachers, it was viewed with derision. In an article entitled 'Educational Quacks; or, the Puffing System in Education' (1838) the author described the various methods of 'puffing' that teachers used to promote themselves and their schools (Anon, 1838).

Such conceited and 'puffed up' teachers were generally unwilling to accept advice or suggestions for improving their teaching. Some showed no interest in improving themselves, learning their subject matter properly or new classroom methods. Such schoolmasters and mistresses seemed:

> to be strongly impressed with the superiority of their own plans to those of any other school, and were very little inclined to listen to any suggestions respecting improvements in the system of education that had been made in other places. 'The old road is the best,' they would sometimes say (Manchester Statistical Society, 1835, p. 10).

The critique of conceit was bound up with the Victorian class-based notion of knowing one's place on the social ladder, and was also evident in the discourse of critique played out in continental Europe (Harp, 1998). Conceit, especially amongst the working classes, was a character trait not to be tolerated. This suggests a theme that arises with the socio-historical construction of the good teacher, an individual who was expected to humbly accept his moral calling. Within the discourse of derision, teachers, and their values, character, habits, and conditions were dismissed as inadequate to meet the new educational needs of the general population. In his place, a new humble, obedient and moral teacher was to be constructed and simultaneously governed.

First, the teacher had to be positioned as a problem to be resolved. Through the discourse of derision, the schoolmaster or mistress was positioned as a bad or 'abnormal' teacher. It is against the idea of the bad teacher, that the good teacher was socio-historically constituted. Bad teachers and their schools were criticised and derided by educational reformers bent on constructing a new system of popular education. Due to their own misconduct and indolence, bad teachers were impoverished. Their bodies were viewed as old, lame, deformed, and sick; and they were devoid of morals and the knowledge required to teach. Mirroring concerns about crime and social disorder characteristic of urban Victorian society, bad teachers were incapable of maintaining order in their schools.

Moral and religious education was neglected, as well as the basic skills and knowledge that they were supposed to convey to their pupils. Their classrooms were either places where nothing happened or where there was complete chaos. If the latter, the bad teacher took needless recourse to corporal punishment to retain order, being ignorant of more up-to-date progressive methods of classroom management as practiced in places such as Prussia. This critique of the teacher was not isolated to England though. Reformers in North America and Europe also turned their attention to teachers operating schools for the poor and found in them many of the same problems. Next we look at how the discourse of derision was played out in western settings outside of England.

Discourse of derision: Comparative and international contexts

Teachers in continental Europe and North America were also attacked and derided by education reformers. Many teachers, it was argued, were lame and lazy. It was said that those who had been failures in Britain immigrated to North America, were forced into subsistence living, and therefore took up odd jobs such as teaching (Durham, 1839; Rolph, 1836, 1839; Herbst, 1989). Some boarded with families in their local communities to make ends meet and/or took on additional odd jobs for which they were derided (Eggleston, 1871).

North American teachers were also criticised for being itinerant drifters, who moved in and out of teaching. Their schools were 'ephemeral' (Duncombe, 1836; Herbst, 1989; Ryerson, 1870). Teaching, much to reformer's dismay, was seen as being seasonal and temporary work, and not the life-long vocation that it ought to be. One Connecticut school board member talked about a schoolmaster who like, 'young man out of work – thinks of turning peddler, or of working at shoe-making. But the one will expose him to storms, the other he fears will inure his chest....He will nevertheless teach school for a meager [sic] compensation' (Quoted in Shultz, 1973 p. 76).

Throughout the Victorian period, American born teachers remained a common feature on the Canadian educational landscape. These 'wandering pedagogues' were attacked for moving in and out of teaching, from one community to the next. Critics decried the unpatriotic and anti-British sentiments of the American teacher and use of American textbooks in Canadian schools (Rolph, 1836).

Teachers in the mix of private, home and community based schools that existed prior to the spread of public education were derided for being rude, lowbred and immoral. Many critical accounts exist of teachers who engaged in immoral pursuits such as drinking, smoking, swearing, cheating, attending parties, dancing, and betting, amongst other immoral activities (Houston and Prentice, 1988; Tyack, 1967; Wilson, 1974).

They were also derided for their low attainments and being ignorant about teaching. As one American educational reformer noted, 'the teachers of the primary summer schools have rarely had any education beyond what they have acquired in the very schools where they begin to teach. Their attainments, to say the least, are usually *very moderate*. But this is not the worst of it. They are often very young, they are constantly changing their employment, and consequently can have but little experience; and what is worse than all, they never have any direct preparation for their employment' (Quoted in Herbst, 1989, p. 24). Similarly, during his inspections of schools in the Western District (Upper Canada), Charles Eliot found 'some of the teachers very deficient, ignorant wholly of Grammar, able indeed only to read & write, & comprehending Arithmetic hardly as far as the rule of Three' (General Correspondence Incoming, 1844–1865).

Criticisms of the general lack of order in the classroom were articulated by North American educational reformers as well. They noted how little learning took place in schools where chaos reigned in the classroom. One Canadian school superintendent wrote that the 'defects of the Teachers both as to acquirements and system are really deplorable' (General Correspondence Incoming, 1844–1865). As in England, it was the lack of understanding of teaching principles and methods that contributed to disorder. Similarly, reformers referred disparagingly to the use of corporal punishment in the classroom and as in England, wondered why schoolmasters were so ignorant about progressive methods of maintaining order in the classroom that were much more widespread in countries such as Prussia (Mann, 1843).

The problem, according to reformers, was that teachers were inexperienced, untrained and unsupervised. Their schools (or homes) were too firmly rooted in the community and lacked the materials and resources necessary for effective teaching. They were ignorant about what and how to teach and as a result resorted to cruel methods to keep their unruly students in line. These criticisms and others formed the basis for educational reforms such as teacher training, certification and inspections, which are addressed in the next couple of chapters. Before addressing reforms to make and shape the good teacher, I will draw out a few concluding comments about the related discourses of fear and derision that were played out in England and other western societies over the early-mid Victorian period.

Conclusion

This chapter has explored conditions that made possible the formation of education generally and the teacher specifically as objects of concern to the Victorians. Two broad discourses were analysed: the crisis discourse that targeted the state of the poor, immigrant and labouring classes; and the discourse of derision that targeted the elementary school teacher. These discourses, as I have noted above, have also served as pre-conditions to contemporary education reform. In recent times, teachers have been accused of being incompetent and ignorant, incapable of maintaining authority in the classroom, as well as conceited and ideologically dogmatic about their roles and responsibilities (Chitty, 2004; Hargreaves and Evans, 1997; Thorpe, 2003).

Victorian fears of social disorder were related to concerns about the ignorant and immoral state of the poor; just as the chaotic state of early Victorian schools was related to the ignorance of the school teacher. Additionally, the discourse of derision was shaped and influenced by the wider crisis discourse about popular society and, in effect, they mirrored one another. We can see how a dispersed set of fears, worries, concerns and anxieties about modern society came to be tightly associated with education. The crisis and derision discourses provided the basis for the formation of strategies for dealing with the poor. Schools, it was repeated, were the cheapest and most effective way of dealing with the problem of poverty, immorality, ignorance, crime and social disorder. Simultaneously, attention turned towards the teacher as key in attempts to construct popular education systems.

All of this was bound up in Victorian middle-class fears, uncertainties and anxieties about their times. Educational reformers reflected this uncertainty and ambivalence towards modernity. They were quick to point to the advances in society through industrialisation and immigration, for example, but also to their disparate social effects. In effect, the attitudes of educational reformers were a reflection of the wider Victorian ambivalent attitude towards modernity, holding to its promise while simultaneously condemning its costs.

The discourses of crisis and derision were embedded within this contradictory stance towards modernity. Thorpe (2003), in tracing the emergence of 'crisis' discourse in public education since the eighteenth century, shows how 'schooling and educational crisis are reflexively intertwined, inextricably, from the moment of their emergences' (p. 15). The linking of education and crisis reflects the Enlightenment commitment to knowledge as the key to progress. The irony is that while progress itself was being critiqued, the principles upon which Western progress have been based (science, empiricism, reason and rationality) were at the very same moment posited as the solution through mass education. The teacher was at the heart of this debate over the individual and societal price of modernity.

The making of the good teacher was not caused by the fears, uncertainties, insecurities, and anxieties articulated in the discourses of crisis and derision. Rather, these concerns reflected and provided the conditions whereby new practices and policies to construct and govern the good teacher could be established. Discourses, in this way, are posited not as truths, but as the socio-historical conditions that make certain regimes of truth possible. Indeed, it was the crisis and derision discourses that enabled the formation of a new system of reasoning about the good teacher, the topic of the next chapter.

Notes

1 I draw upon the idea of discourses of derision and crisis from Ball's (1990) discursive account of education policy in England through the 1970s and 1980s.
2 Monitorial schools were established early in the century to provide moral education to the labouring poor. The method of the monitorial school was to instruct large numbers of children by mechanical means as cheaply as possible. The schoolmaster was responsible for training a group of ten and 11 year old pupils outside of school hours. The schoolmaster would supervise all of the pupils in a single large schoolroom, while the older pupils (monitors) taught groups of younger students. There were usually ten children under each monitor, who drilled the pupils in the way in which he had been previously drilled by the schoolmaster.

5
The Discourse of the Good Victorian Teacher: The Modern and Moral Teacher

In response to their fears, uncertainties and anxieties, Victorians came to believe that the best preventative against the problems of society was a good school. From this followed the idea that the only security of a good school was a good teacher. 'The teacher makes the school' was a clarion call echoed throughout the Victorian period in England and abroad to ensure schools were filled with nothing but the best teachers. With the idea that the good teacher was the only guarantee of a good school planted in the minds of education reformers, a new set of ideas and reasoning about the teacher began to take shape.

With increasing public interest in education, Victorians began to speak, write, and think about the teacher in new ways, and in so doing constructed a discourse about the good teacher. To understand this discourse, I reviewed archival documents relating to notions about the good teacher. Statements referring to what a teacher should or ought to be, the aims and goals of teachers and teaching, praise and commendation for teachers, and any other positive statements about teachers constituted the data that I analysed. I looked at a wide range of articles from education magazines, journals, and periodicals, inspectors' reports, and books on the topic of teachers and teaching from the 1830s through to the 1880s. These statements formed the object of which they spoke – the teacher – and it is in this way that we can think about the making of the good teacher in the Victorian period.

A wide range of knowledge and skills, as well as a set of moral dispositions and habits constituted this discourse of the good teacher. In this chapter I show how the good teacher was constructed to be both a modern and moral individual. The Modern Teacher[1] was discursively constructed as an active, enthusiastic, and dedicated learner, intellectually capable of translating philosophical theories about the science of the mind into practical teaching strategies and methods. He was to be highly knowledgeable and confident about philosophical knowledge, pedagogy, including teaching methods and subjects, and about the children he taught. He was to know these things thoroughly and completely through study and observation. As an individual capable of rational, philosophic and scientific study, the Modern Teacher was informed by and reflected the Enlightenment optimism and faith in scientific knowledge as the key to progress and human happiness. He is the teacher depicted on the back cover of this book, a writer and thinker, teaching his pupils how to read and think for themselves.

The Moral Teacher, on the other hand, was like a humble, kind, and loving mother. She was a Christian role model for her students, cultivating in them moral habits and dispositions such as humility and obedience to maintain social order. She was, in essence, a devout and committed Christian working with the local clergyman to educate God's children in spiritual and moral matters. She is depicted in the picture on the front cover of this book, humble with her head tilted downwards, gathering her pupils as if her own children, and leading them gently into the school house.

Statements about the Moral Teacher focused on the habits and dispositions of schoolmistress, while statements about the Modern Teacher were primarily about the knowledge and skills of the schoolmaster; hence the separate use of the male and female pronouns in this chapter. Both, surprisingly, were considered the qualities that **all** teachers for the schools of the poor should possess. In this we can see the inherent contradiction of the discourse of the good teacher, which I explore at the end of this chapter. First, however, we turn to the discourse of the Modern Teacher.

The Modern Teacher: Knowledge and skills

Philosophical (science of the mind) knowledge

The teacher as a modern subject appears against a philosophical backdrop of Enlightenment-inspired ideas concerning scientific notions of learning and teaching. The duty of the Modern Teacher was to learn from popular and Enlightenment influenced philosophers, metaphysicians, and ethical writers about the relations between physiology, psychology, ethics and pedagogy.

Three philosophical schools of thought were particularly influential in educational circles. These were Common Sense moral philosophy, Associationism, and phrenology. Although differing in their approach and emphases, they all approached the study of learning from a rational, scientific perspective.[2] Common Sense thinkers associated with the University of Edinburgh developed metaphysical theories concerning the science of the mind and the relationship between human nature and learning (Tannoch-Bland, 2000). Associationist thought, which focused on the influence of empirical experience upon the formation of ideas and their connection through repeated associations, was also extremely influential in the development of theories on education. Like Associationist thought, phrenology was decidedly rational and empiricist, based on the Lockian commitment to understanding social phenomena on the basis of human experience. Phrenology retained the most populist edge out of all of these schools of thought, being spread throughout Britain and North America primarily through the work of George Combe who combined phrenology with Pestalozzian methods (Tomlinson, 1997).

Pedagogues, philosophers, politicians, and educational promoters found, to varying degrees, these ideas to be of great interest and promoted their study in educational circles. To think, to read, to study, and to learn: all had become 'fashionable' pursuits in the modern age, and were no longer viewed as the sole prerogative of academics, philosophers, scientists, and the elite. Hence, teachers – even those in elementary schools for the poor and working classes – were urged to take up philosophical study in the pursuit of knowledge about their profession.

It was said that the spirit of rational and scientific investigation had to be awakened in the Victorian teacher, who came to be discursively positioned as a learner, a thinker, and a scholar. True learning would require that the teacher learn how to use all of his intellectual faculties. School inspectors claimed that the teacher should 'be roused from that mental apathy which has grown upon him by the disuse of his faculties, and to be taught the secret of his powers' (Committee of Council, 1849, p. 356). As a scientific and philosophical learner, the good teacher was constructed as an individual who read and studied a wide range of scholarly books by great metaphysical philosophers and moralists on the science of the mind. The teacher was viewed as 'the one to whom we must look, as the practical and experimental philosopher, who will be able...to perfect a true science of mind' (Smith, 1835, p. 432). Following this line of thought, the schoolmaster was to aspire to:

> be a man who has prepared himself for his duties by a general study of the works of Brown, Locke, Dugald Stewart, Abercrombie and

others, masters of the science of mental philosophy, and invaluable guides to a teacher, by the insight they afford him into the operations of the human mind and the phenomena of our moral and physical nature (Dunning, 1854a, p. 173).

To this end, teachers were urged to engage with moral philosophy by reading Stewart's (1792–1827) three-volume *Elements of the Philosophy of the Human Mind*, Thomas Reid's (1810) *Inquiry into the Human Mind*, and Thomas Brown's (1822) *Lectures on the Philosophy of the Human Mind*. In fact, the Council of Committee placed such books on the science of the mind on the official list of books for teachers to read. Teachers were also advised to make time to read Morell's (1853) *Elements of Psychology* and Locke's (1690) *Essay on Human Understanding* (Tate, 1857).

To provide a foundation for this philosophical study, teacher training institutions provided lectures on moral and mental philosophy. At the Borough Road Training Institution in London, students listened to lectures on the philosophy of the human mind as applicable to education, on attention and memory, association, conception, imagination, and on the principal writers on education. 'The Importance of a Knowledge of Mental and Moral Philosophy to an Elementary School Teacher' was included on the 1847 syllabus of the principal's lectures at Battersea Teacher Training Institution (Committee of Council, 1849, p. 357). Student teachers were encouraged to read about mental philosophy and verify their understanding of mental and moral philosophy through careful study of children in the model schools. Training college masters were urged to provide their students with books on the principles of education, logic, the mental faculties, and moral philosophy to help them prepare for their examinations (Committee of Council, 1854–55).

Pedagogic knowledge

In addition to philosophical knowledge about the science of the mind and human nature, teachers were expected to be well versed in pedagogic knowledge. The pedagogic object of elementary education was to understand the nature of children and then develop their faculties to their fullest potential (Tate, 1857). Like lawyers, preachers, gardeners, physicians, jewellers, builders, stone-workers, mechanics and merchants, teachers were expected to understand the requirements, qualities, and capabilities of the materials they worked with (Drew, 1856). Hence, the call went out for the elementary school teacher to 'Know Your Pupils!'

Understanding the nature of the child involved not only philosophical study, but also closely examining the innermost characteristics of the whole child. This was to be an empirical, scientific and rational exercise. As Stow (1853) argued, any educational system would have to be 'applicable not merely to the head of the child, but to the *whole man*' (p. 12).

In his book, *The Philosophy of Education*, Tate (1857) outlined the rational nature of this study, asserting the necessity of teaching based upon a careful, scientific induction of facts about the child's faculties. To begin with, the teacher was expected to study the nature and disposition of each faculty, how they could be distinguished, one from the other, and how they acted upon and reflected one another. Then the order of development of each of the faculties was to be determined through careful empirical study.

Particular attention was directed towards the study and cultivation of the moral and intellectual faculties. While cultivation of the moral faculties was viewed as important for the education of poor and working class children, the teacher was not to ignore the noble work of awakening and exercising the intellectual faculties (Coleridge, 1842a; Dunn, 1837). The Modern Teacher would be well-suited for the task of laying the foundations of the intellect: 'he who holds in his fingers the threads, upon whose right disposition and freedom from entanglement depends upon the complicated but glorious tissue of the human mind' (J. S. G., 1854, p. 203). Specifically, the teacher had to engage in an objective and empirical study of the complex and scientific nature of the mind. The mechanisms, motives and behaviour of the mind, memory, conscience and imagination; the ways in which facts and truth were associated and recalled, the processes of reasoning, and other evidence of the child's character were all to be closely and continuously scrutinised by the teacher (Donaldson, 1876).

To fulfil these expectations, teachers were called upon to read, study, and reflect upon pedagogical books and articles that they could procure. 'No one but a dreamer,' wrote Drew (1856), 'anticipates a successful career in any ordinary pursuit of life without setting before himself the work to be done, and diligently studying, in connexion with its prosecution, the means best adapted to success' (p. 5). Teachers were urged to improve themselves by studying the general principles of learning, the specific methods of teaching and the subject matter to be taught. School inspector Matthew Arnold, for example, contended that a man was only fit to teach as long as he was engaged in daily learning himself (Arnold, 1910).

Acting classroom teachers were encouraged to attend courses offered by the training colleges during the summer or harvest seasons to engage in further professional learning. In 1843, the Borough Road Training College opened during harvest vacations and offered summer courses for BFSS schoolmasters on pedagogical matters. National Society teachers also enrolled in short courses at these summer and harvest schools for self-improvement (Hewlett, 1932; Etherington, 1969).

Didactical (teaching methods) knowledge and skills

Once the Modern Teacher had thoroughly studied and understood the scientific relationship between the properties of the mind and pedagogy, he would be in a position to determine the teaching methods suited to the needs and capabilities of each pupil. The idea that the successful educator understood both the general principles and practical laws of education was reiterated on many occasions throughout the century. Tate, one of the most prolific Victorian writers on the topic, developed a picture of the ideal educator who was thoroughly acquainted with the branches of elementary education, the leading scientific principles of education, and the daily practices of managing a class. He articulated the need for the teacher to let method guide his [sic] practice:

> [H]e must have realised an idea: all that he has seen or experienced, all that he has read, must have assumed the form of a substantial unity – an idea – an all-pervading law, which connects relations apparently the most dissimilar, and gives oneness and harmony to the most heterogeneous mass of facts and conditions...and out of which he must *evolve* his conduct in the future, – which sheds a light over the path that lies behind him, and becomes the polar star to guide him in his voyage on the dark and shoreless [sic] ocean that lies before him (Tate, 1857, p. 21).

Pedagogical principles and practices were to be studied until they resided deep within the minds of thinking and active teachers, guiding them through their teaching. Method could not simply be copied; rather it had to be founded on principles that were grasped and practiced by teachers.

In particular, teaching methods that fostered humanistic principles of self-development and self-instruction were promoted. The faculties, according to the progressive Swiss educator Pestalozzi, had to be cultivated in harmony with one another. Harmonious cultivation of the mind, for example, involved exercising as many of the intellectual faculties as possible; including concentration and abstraction, observation and attention, reasoning, understanding and judgment, memory, imagination and will. Reason and judgment were considered the best means to help cultivate the memory and were the teacher's primary objects of concern. Examples were to be used to analyse the reasoning process, after which pupils would be informed of general rules to assist their understanding. Cultivation of the faculties of invention and imagination, wit and taste would also develop independence of thought. In effect, the teacher was expected to avoid cramming information into their pupils' heads, and instead to harmoniously cultivate, strengthen and develop the intellectual faculties (Drew, 1856; Hamilton, 1838).

This type of teaching necessitated a much more active and lively role in the classroom for the teacher. Teachers were urged to make lessons interesting by using illustrations, anecdotes and objects to awaken pupils' interest in the subject and create in them a desire to learn. Teachers were encouraged to be imaginative, drawing out the latent power within each child by using poetry, prose, drawing and music and didactical methods, such as Stow's simultaneous style of teaching. Teachers were told that they should be lively, keep children in constant activity, and not lecture to them. Lessons were to be in the form of a continual conversation, with teachers telling interesting anecdotes, and questioning their pupils with intelligence, animation, and vivacity. Expectations of all pupils were to remain high. In contrast to the lazy, listless and slovenly teacher, described in the previous chapter, good teachers were viewed as zealous, active, and energetic in their earnest application of these child-centred techniques (Anon, 1848d; Anon, 1851; Ross, 1849; Stow, 1853; Tate, 1857).

Moreover, the inductive (also known as the synthetic or natural) method was considered especially appropriate for teaching younger children. Didactical strategies such as the reproduction and reiteration of lessons, use of examples and concrete applications, teaching from the known to the unknown, facts before causes, and simple principles before rules would enable the teacher to teach each subject thoroughly, ensuring that all pupils completely understood the first example in any lesson before the next began (Drew, 1856; Dunn, 1837; Landon, 1894). To accomplish this, teachers were called upon to adopt thorough and comprehensive teaching methods. One author explained:

A few ideas *thoroughly* mastered are better than a thousand notions which are dim and undetermined. Superficial knowledge is of little account – *thorough* knowledge alone is valuable. Let the work of the school be *thorough* work. Let the watchword be *Thorough!'* (Omricon, 1853, p. 240).

And as school children were to understand their lessons thoroughly before progressing to the next, so their teachers were instructed to aim at completeness in their own studies (Dunn, 1837; Anon, 1850c; Newcastle Commission, 1861d).

School textbooks provided one source of information on teaching methods for the schoolmaster and schoolmistress. These textbooks formed the basis of required reading for teachers, serving a dual purpose as classroom resource and teaching manual. However, many reformers expressed concern about the over-reliance on school textbooks, without consideration of the broader, scientific principles of teaching. Teachers were therefore urged to enrol in one of the teacher training colleges to become more fully versed in child-centred, progressive teaching principles and practises. Pedagogic principles and teaching methods were covered in the teacher training institution syllabi directly and indirectly. Instructors modelled progressive teaching methods and strategies, by using oral lectures for example, in order to prepare teachers in training for their future careers (Arnold, 1910; Committee of Council, 1849; National Society, 1853).

Practice teaching at the local model school also offered training candidates another opportunity to learn the art and science of teaching. The Master of Method, who managed the practising school, often instructed candidates on pedagogical matters.[3] Weekly one-hour lectures on a range of topics, including the general principles of school management, progressive methods of preparing and carrying out lessons, and the characteristics of the successful teacher, were offered at most training colleges across the country (Committee of Council, 1843; Kay-Shuttleworth, 1862a). Students were then assessed on their pedagogic and teaching methods knowledge through annual examinations. Methodology questions in the men's 1856 training college examinations comprised one third of each of the subject papers. First year students answered methodology questions on reading, writing and arithmetic and timetabling; second year on schoolroom organisation and school registers. Moreover, second year students were also expected to write a moralistic essay on the science of the mind (Alexander, 1977).

Subject matter knowledge

The Modern Teacher was not only fully versed in pedagogy and appropriate teaching methods, but also had a thorough understanding of his subject matter. Such teachers, according to inspectors, were intelligent, conscientious, skilful and successful. Teachers who were well versed in the elementary branches of knowledge were commended by inspectors and educational reformers (Committee of Council 1845, 1851; Newcastle Commission, 1861d).

The good teacher understood that the most appropriate education for working class and poor children was a practical one, and adjusted the curriculum and teaching methods accordingly. Scientific knowledge of both the principles of learning and the subject of instruction would enable the teacher to choose the most appropriate subject and teaching method. Teachers were cautioned not to pitch material too high above the comprehension of their pupils. Rather, they were urged to select the most appropriate subject matter and teaching methods to fulfil their teaching aims. In fact, adapting the curriculum to the various circumstances, gender, and class background of pupils was rationalised according to Pestalozzian principles as following the natural order of things by preparing each child for her/his appropriate place in society (Coleridge, 1842a; Donaldson, 1876; Dunning, 1854b; J. S. G., 1854; Tate, 1857).

To ensure that teachers were adequately prepared for their work, the training institutions covered the basic elementary school subjects in their curricula. Generally, the minimum that first year teachers-in-training were expected to cover included: reading, writing and arithmetic, English grammar, Euclid and elementary mechanics, algebra, geography, history, drawing and singing. Second year students studied all of the above, except for Euclid and algebra, which were replaced by physical science and higher mathematics (Warwick, 1966).

These subjects, it is important to note, were the **minimum** content covered in the syllabi. The majority of training institutions offered a much wider range of academic subjects than that taught in the elementary schools. Offering wide ranging, humanistic education to teachers in training reflected the official commitment to construct the teacher as a cultivated, broad-minded intellectual. Many agreed that the schoolmaster should be a well-rounded, educated individual, fully conversant in a wide range of academic studies. Tate (1857) asserted that the schoolmaster ought to be thoroughly acquainted with the leading doctrines and narratives of Scripture, arithmetic, reading, writing, spelling, English history, and the principles of teaching. As well, the teacher should have a fair knowledge of drawing, mensuration, practical geometry, geography, astronomy, elementary grammar, composition, general history, elementary algebra, demonstrative geometry, industrial mechanics, and experimental philosophy.

To this end, the training institutions offered a broad and humanistic education for teachers-in-training, including (but not limited to) the study of literature, classical subjects, Latin, Greek, history, and geography. St. Mark's Training Institution in London stood out for being especially biased in favour of literary and classical subjects (Coleridge, 1842a). However, St. Mark's was not unique in this respect, as the majority of institutions recognised the importance of studying literary and classical subjects. Kay-Shuttleworth (1862d) in his first report on Battersea explained his rationale for including English literature in the syllabus:

> A course on reading in English literature, by which the taste may be refined by an acquaintance with the best models of style, and with those authors whose works have exercised the most beneficial influence on the mind of this nation...forms one of the most important elements in the conception of the objects to be attained in a training school, that the teacher should be inspired with a discriminating but earnest admiration for those gifts of great minds to English literature (p. 217).

Readings in poetry, and works by Shakespeare and Milton were standard content in the teacher training colleges. Inspector Morell commended the addition of classical subjects into the training course at Borough Road, a training college remembered more for its focus on professional work, than on literary and classical studies (Hewlett, 1932). Student teachers were also expected to acquire a thorough acquaintance of the English language through the study of etymology, leading the colleges to offer lessons in Latin and Greek (Coleridge, 1842a; Committee of Council, 1849; Etherington, 1969).

Like the study of Latin, Greek and English literature, the study of history was seen to broaden and improve the intellectual capacities of teachers. Inspector Arnold (1910) asserted that: 'there is nothing so animating, nothing so likely to awaken a man's interest and to stimulate him to active research on definite points, as the broad views over the history of our race and its general course and connection which universal history gives' (pp. 259–60). As a result, the history curriculum in the training colleges was especially broad, covering Scriptural, Ancient, British and colonial history (Baber, 1850; Committee of Council, 1850). All in all, it can be said that the training college curricula was challenging and wide-ranging, with the aim to create humanistic, cultured and cultivated teachers for the elementary schools of the nation

(Committee of Council, 1852–53; Kay-Shuttleworth, 1862c; Coleridge, 1842a).

One reason to explain the wide-ranging and academic nature of the training college syllabi was the background of the training principals and masters. In almost all cases in England, the Headmasters were clergymen, and in the larger colleges, also graduates of universities at Oxford and Cambridge. In 1853, Oxford graduates were in charge at Battersea, Caermarthen, Durham, Highbury, and Exeter male training colleges. Principals of St. Marks, Cheltenham, Chester, Chicester, York and Ripon, were all Cambridge University graduates (Committee of Council, 1852–53).[4]

Kay-Shuttleworth (1862c), founder of Battersea Training Institution, thought that a training college headmaster should be 'a man of Christian earnestness, of intelligence, of experience, of knowledge of the world' (pp. 405–6). The founder and headmaster of St. Mark's Training Institution for Schoolmasters, Reverend Derwent Coleridge, Cambridge graduate and son of the Enlightenment inspired poet and composer Samuel Taylor Coleridge, epitomised this ideal. Coleridge (1862) viewed St. Mark's as a university, with little to distinguish it from schools for the middle and upper classes. He argued that schoolmasters must become cultured and thoroughly educated individuals. The elementary schoolmaster, wrote Coleridge (1842a), 'must himself be *educated* before he can educate others...It may be enough for others to *be* what they are, but a teacher must *know* what he is, and *why* he is so' (p. 6).

The Modern Teacher: Comparative and international contexts

This emphasis on broad, wide-ranging knowledge in the training institutions was also articulated by educational reformers and promoters in Europe and North America. Indeed, there are many similarities between the discourse of the Modern Teacher in England and in other western countries over the course of the Victorian period. 'A good schoolmaster' wrote Guizot, Minister of Public Instruction in France in 1839, 'ought to be a man who knows much more than he is called upon to teach...that he may teach with intelligence and taste' (Quoted in Ryerson, 1846b, p. 199).

Reformers in North America drew upon Guizot's words to bolster their own support for a profession of open-minded teachers well acquainted with a wide range of subjects (Ryerson, 1850b). Hence, according to the *Journal of Education for Upper Canada*, the successful teacher:

> must not only be thoroughly acquainted with all branches which he proposes to teach, teaching principles as well as facts, but he must possess extensive general information, have a good knowledge of human nature, possess good common sense and prudence (Anon, 1850b, p. 52).

Taking their cue from Europe, teachers in North America were encouraged to adopt humanistic child-centred teaching methods. Such pedagogical practices had their roots in the Enlightenment period with the 1762 publication of Rousseau's *Emile*, which had a profound effect amongst German reformers intrigued by the non-coercive theory of teaching espoused by Rousseau. Two European pedagogues stand out as being particularly influential in advancing Rousseau's ideas within pedagogical contexts: Christian Gotthilf Salzmann and Johann Bernhard Basedow. However, it was the progressive teaching methods espoused by Pestalozzi and his adherents such as Fredrich Froebel, which gained the most support in the English-speaking world (Biber, 1831; Silber, 1960).

According to the progressive pedagogues (or what in the United States were called 'soft-line' writers), the child's mind was not viewed so much as a block of marble, but rather a living organism that could be shaped and moulded like clay in the hands of a skilled teacher. The teacher's work was therefore to unlock the innate potential within each child. Underpinning this Lockian assumption was the belief that the environment shaped the person; an idea that connected most of the progressive pedagogical theories throughout the nineteenth century (Katz, 1968).

Teachers in North America were to understand the complex nature of the child through careful study. The study of faculty psychology, phrenology and Associationist thinking were all taken up in North America, and teachers encouraged to engage in scientific study of the principles of the mind (Mann, 1848; Ryerson, 1846b; Spring, 1990). Cyrus Peirce, principal of the normal school at Lexington, Massachusetts, assumed that teaching was a philosophical endeavour, and called upon teachers to study how the 'different branches of knowledge' harmoniously connected to the child's mind (Quoted in Thornburg, 2004, p. 156).

To this end, educational promoters advocated for formal teacher training and called for a comprehensive, broad and humanistic curriculum in the normal schools. As in England, the program in Canadian and American normal schools was wide-ranging and rigorous. Normal school instructors emphasised the importance of the philosophical underpinnings of teaching and need for teachers in training to study an advanced academic curriculum. Teachers in training were expected to have a thorough knowledge of common school subjects, as well as engage in the study of advanced subjects such as logic, geometry, history, physiology, political economy, mental and natural philosophy. School management, pedagogy and the art of teaching were also taught in the normal schools (Herbst, 1989; Katz, 1968, Thornburg, 2004).

At the Normal School for Upper Canada, for instance, courses were offered in reading, writing, arithmetic, English grammar and literature, rhetoric, poetry and oratory, Euclid and mechanics, algebra, geography, history, drawing, singing, book-keeping, and natural philosophy (physical science). The 1870 syllabus included 70 pedagogic and didactic lectures, which bore a remarkable resemblance to the pedagogical lectures in the English teacher training colleges (Sangster, 1871). The curriculum in the US Normal Schools also broke down the division between professional and academic knowledge, as student-teachers were encouraged to read, discuss, and write about the ideas raised by Homer, Virgil, Cicero, Horace and Europides (Thornburg, 2004).

As in England, this emphasis on the intellectual nature of the curriculum at the normal schools can be explained by the academic and international backgrounds of the principals and instructors. The first principal of the Normal School for Upper Canada, Thomas Robertson, was educated in Dublin and had been the Inspector of the National Society in Ireland prior to taking up his position in Canada. The next two principals, John Herbert Sangster and Henry William Davies, were both graduates of the University of Toronto, and held MA and MD degrees. The founders of many of the US normal schools were thoughtful educators and university graduates who studied contemporary educational theories and often published books about these new methods of teaching. Julia King, graduate and later preceptress of the Michigan Normal School, was an accomplished and talented woman, educated in the liberal arts, who presented papers to the faculty and published articles in educational journals for both practising teachers and academic researchers (Herbst, 1989; Hodgins, 1911; Thornburg, 2004).

Moreover, to assist practicing teachers in their daily study, dozens of journals and books that outlined their responsibility to use the tools of science to study the art and science of teaching and learning were published. Many pedagogical books were excerpted in education journals, referred to by education promoters, and cross-referenced by other authors in England and abroad. One of the first publications of this nature was Henry Dunn's 1837 *Principles of Teaching; or the Normal School Manual.* Teachers working in BFSS schools throughout the British Dominions, North America and as far as South America used Dunn's text in their training. Indeed, as Monroe (1952) writes, there was an aggressive demand for foreign pedagogical books, including Bain's *Education as a Science* (1896), the translated version of Rosenkranz's *The Philosophy of Education,* and Tate's (1857) *The Philosophy of Education,* which was first published in United States in 1884.

The spread of pedagogical publications throughout Europe, Britain and North America made possible the development of similar educational reforms across these settings, and correspondingly the possibility of a well-read and studious teacher. As we saw in Chapter 3, dozens of education journals were published throughout the century, many aimed specifically at teachers. The city of Alleghany, Pennsylvania mandated that teachers subscribe to, and presumably read, at least one education periodical annually. Others, simply urged teachers, as rational intellectuals, to take up the task of studying, reading, and thoughtfully reflecting upon the pedagogical principles of their work (Anon, 1850a; Anon, 1850c; Anon, 1857; Le Vaux, 1875; Solo, 1848).

As in England, teachers were encouraged to attend short courses during the summer or harvest seasons through the Teachers' Institutes offered through the normal schools. Three week long Teachers' Institutes were offered to teachers through the Michigan State Normal School with the aim to advance the 'knowledge on all subjects connected with the Teacher's vocation' (Quoted in Thornbug, 2004). Teachers listened to lectures and participated in pedagogical discussions and learned about new methods for teaching. These institutes became increasingly popular throughout the century, both for teachers and normal school instructors (Herbst, 1989).

The Modern Teacher: Conclusion

The first part of this chapter has described a set of ideas, assumptions, and expectations concerning the knowledge and skills considered most appropriate for the Modern Teacher. The word 'Modern' (itself a discursive construction) has been used to capture the connections between the systems of reasoning about the knowledge of the good teacher and the ideas constituting the paradigm of the Enlightenment. The key foundational ideas associated with the Enlightenment legacy can be grouped under the following headings: reason and rationality, empiricism, science, universalism, uniformity of human nature, progress, individualism and secularism.

According to modern thought, reason and rationality are the primary ways of organising knowledge; the thinking being that the universe is fundamentally rational and therefore can be understood through the use of reason alone. This notion of rationalism is allied with the idea of empiricism: that truth about the natural and social world can be arrived at through empirical observation, the use of reason, and systematic doubt. Ideas about the Modern Teacher reflect these assumptions. The Modern Teacher was posited as a reasoning and rational individual capable of engaging in the scientific study of human nature, pedagogy, didactics and a wide range of subjects. Through the rational study of mental and moral philosophy, the teacher would come to understand not only the scientific principles of the mind, but all the laws governing human nature. Moreover, empirical study of the child was viewed as the key to understanding human nature. The call for teachers to study the nature and composition of each of the human faculties was grounded in these modern principles and echoed the Lockian empiricist orientation of phrenological and Associationist thinking.

Moreover, the study of human nature reflected the Enlightenment belief in the uniformity of human nature, which was said to be at all times and places always the same. This idea was in turn connected to the concept that the entire universe was itself governed by general laws that could be known through scientific study. The Enlightenment commitment to universalism suggested that reason and science could be applied to any and every situation and that these principles would always remain constant. Following this, any individual, through the use of his reason and rationality, could in principle come to know and understand the general laws that governed the universe.

Together, these principles were to guide the Modern Teacher's pedagogic study and influenced the development of a universal system of teaching methods that could be applied to all situations. This principle, however, held true only to a point. While universal principles about human nature necessitated the use of progressive teaching methods, educational reformers were less consistent about the universality of school subjects. This explains the argument that the curriculum for poorer, female, working class and rural children was to be of a practical nature, preparing them for their appropriate stations in life.

Nonetheless, these arguments were made based on the assumption that such choices were for the well-being of these children and the stability (and consequently, the happiness) of society. The Enlightenment idea that science and reason would result in increasing happiness for all citizens was taken up in the nineteenth century by Utilitarians such as Bentham who asserted that education was one of the greatest sources of happiness devised by man [sic], and a force for promoting the well-being and safety of the community. The idea that the natural and social condition of human beings could be improved through education underpinned the Victorian reformers' commitment to the spread of education for the masses and for the teacher. While the drive to establish teacher training institutions is discussed in more detail in Chapter 7, it is noted here to illustrate the commitment that reformers had towards establishing and enhancing opportunities for the Modern Teacher to engage in standardised and scientific study.

The Modern Teacher was not only urged to attend sessions at the formal training institutions, but to engage in the rational and empirical study of the child, pedagogy and didactics in their classroom and by reading philosophical and pedagogic books, articles and reports. Underlying such expectations was a focus on the individual as the starting point for all knowledge and action. Individual thought and experience, in this respect, could and should not be subjected to any higher authority. This points to the Enlightenment opposition to traditional religious authority and general scepticism towards religion over empirical, scientific and rational explanations. Religious doctrines, according to Enlightenment thinkers, had no place in the understanding of the physical and human worlds. In this respect, the knowledge associated with the Modern Teacher was to be secular and free of religious orthodoxies.

These ideas were not without their own contradictions though. In contrast to the ideas associated with the knowledge and skills of the Modern Teacher, another set of statements about the character and dispositions of the teacher emerged. These statements formed what I call the Moral Teacher. Against the Enlightenment ideas outlined above, the characteristics of the Moral Teacher appeared traditional (un-modern), and in many ways contradicted assumptions about what the good teacher should be, think, and do. We turn now to the making of the Moral Teacher.

Morality and schooling

Purposes of schooling

To understand the socio-historical construction of the teacher as a moral subject, it is necessary to review nineteenth century ideas concerning the moral purposes of education. Pedagogues and educational promoters in England and abroad argued that education devoid of moral training was a fruitless and vain endeavour. Moral training would provide the child with the principles to direct his or her intellectual power towards the right direction for the formation of character.

The cultivation of the moral faculties would benefit not only the individual child, but society as a whole. Schooling for the masses was to be a moral force, producing character and habits crucial to maintaining social order. Sullivan (1842) made this point clearly:

> [I]f children be not taught the duties of love and obedience to parents, respect and subordination to superiors, the principles of truth and honesty, and, in a word, the precepts and practice of morality, it is better for themselves, and safer for society to leave them entirely uneducated; for bad as ignorance is, education without morality is a thousand times worse (p. 32).

Elementary education was therefore intended to provide the moral training and discipline to prepare children for their future employments and their appropriate place in society. This was the making of the obedient citizen, a self-governing member of the civil community. School was perhaps the only place where poor children could be taught the appropriate habits and principles of moral conduct. Kay-Shuttleworth (1862b) explained that the education of poor children was:

> not merely to inform their minds on their duties to God and to man, but to influence their habits and feelings, so that a sense of the true source of all moral and social obligations, might not only be merely instilled as a precept on the understanding, but be imbibed from every part of the daily routine in such a way as to influence life (p. 251).

Under proper guidance, the teacher would cultivate the moral habits of humility, veneration and faith in the school child. Moral habits also included cleanliness, modesty, good temper, kindness, punctuality, diligence and industry, with order and obedience viewed as being especially important. The sympathies, feelings, and benevolent and selfless habits were to be carefully cultivated in children, so that the principles and motives of moral action and duty would come to reside deep within them. The child would then be automatically guided by these moral principles. Moral training was viewed as religious instruction to enable the will of God to be known to the pupil. The Christian religion, therefore, was to serve as the basis of education, forming the child's character, and pervading the spirit of the teacher's work (Committee of Council, 1847; Charlton, 1856).

Moral exemplar: The Christian teacher

Morality, in England, was equated with Christianity. Given their responsibility for the moral education of their pupils, the teacher had to be committed to the principles and duties of Christianity. For this reason, it was imperative that the teacher be a holy, devout and true Christian. The teacher's mind was to be thoroughly penetrated by a religious principle. Dr. Mayo claimed:

> Oh let him be some man of God, whose heart, warm with the consciousness of God's forgiving heart, delights to dwell on his Redeemer's goodness, and prompts him, with the genuine warmth of actual experience, to be telling of his salvation from day to day. Let him be one who will not tire of that theme, because it is the truth he lives in himself, and which he feels to be fruitful of peace and joy (Quoted in Anon, 1848a, p. 110).

We can see how the language used to describe the teacher was fused with religious metaphors. Descriptions of the moral, Christian teacher were embellished with sentimental and sacred phrases, suggestive of descriptions found in the Bible. The teacher appears as an ethereal, almost beyond-human figure, nobly carrying out his sacred responsibilities.

Ensuring the religious and moral qualifications of the teacher was associated with the teacher's role as moral exemplar. Children, it was said, expected perfection from their teachers. As quick and acute observers, they quickly picked up their teacher's habits and conduct. Like Christ, the good teacher was therefore supposed to be a shepherd among his flock of children. The Christian Lord was presented as the 'Blessed Teacher', 'Ideal Teacher' or the 'Great Exemplar' to whom the teacher on earth should look to as a role model for inspiration, help and reward (Tate, 1854). The teacher was to contemplate upon the life and works of the Lord, and in effect, become 'Christ-like', in order to feel more deeply the dignity of his vocation (W. R., 1861, p. 42).

As an exemplary Christian role model, the teacher was to educate his pupils as 'God's spiritual Children' (Anon, 1840, p. 113). Hence, a frequently repeated maxim was 'He that makes a little child happier for half an hour is a co-worker with God' (Dunn, 1837). Others viewed the teacher as a co-worker with the local clergyman, equally engaged in the work of saving souls. 'Next to the peculiar Functions of [the Clergyman's] sacred Calling, there is no nobler Work in which he can be engaged than the Education of the young' (Committee of Council, 1842, p. 261). Churches viewed the elementary school as their 'nursery', and the elementary school teacher as an extension of the parish minister. One clergyman told the local schoolmistress: 'You are managing my nursery. Look up and believe you are working for eternity' (Hughes, 1936, p. 58).

Some reformers suggested that the position of the teacher was one of the highest and holiest offices that God has established on earth. Their responsibilities were not to be taken lightly or assumptions made about the ease of their work (National Society, 1849–55). The teacher's duty was to save souls by bringing the young to Christ. While the clergyman may have been responsible for ensuring repentance among sinners, the teacher was expected to 'nip it in the bud' (Committee of Council, 1847; Hughes, 1936; Newcastle Commission, 1861d). Indeed, as the Reverend Sanderson Robins claimed in 1850, the importance of the teacher's work could not be overestimated:

> if only it be followed with a single eye and a devoted heart; above all, if it be carried out in the spirit of that Blessed Teacher, who was content to spend years in the midst of a hard and self-willed generation, correctly their mistakes, bearing with their perverseness, and leading them patiently in the way of truth and holiness (Quoted in Ball, 1983, p. 50).

Morality and schooling: Comparative and international contexts

Similar sentiments about the moral purpose of education and the important role of the teacher as a moral exemplar were articulated in Europe and North America. Reformers across those settings focused on the role of public education in cultivating moral habits and principles in school children, and creating useful and obedient citizens (Mann, 1845; Ryerson 1846b). Morality was similarly equated with Christianity amongst many Canadian educational promoters, but within the United States and continental Europe, many reformers advocated for sectarian school systems (Cubberley, 1947; Green, 1990).

Despite different emphases on the role of the Church in educational provision, in all settings, the teacher's mission as a moral exemplar was emphasised. In 1833, Guizot had instructed French public school teachers: 'Do not undervalue the importance of your Mission...Be penetrated then, with the importance of your Mission; let its utility be ever present to your mind in the discharge of the difficult duties which it imposes upon you' (Quoted in Ryerson, 1846b, p. 199). Moreover, Guizot emphasised the 'high vocation' of teaching, comparing the teacher to a priest who sets an example for his parishioners. Similarly, a verse from 'God's Gardener', written for *The Massachusetts Teacher* in 1857, exhorted:

> Magnify your office, teacher!
>   Higher than the kings of earth; –
> Are you not the prophet preacher,
>   To the future giving birth? (Quoted in Katz, 1968, p. 157).

As a missionary like figure, the good teacher was to be pious, faithful and devout, and motivated in his work by a religious sense of duty, having answered a call from God to undertake his or her moral duties. This notion of the 'calling' distinguished the good teacher from the bad one who merely stepped in and out of the profession at whim; a habit criticised at length by reformers, as outlined in the previous chapter. Hence, many reformers and educational writers in England and abroad proclaimed and praised the earnestness, zeal, and missionary spirit in which the teacher was to discharge his life-long duties (Le Vaux, 1875; Kay-Shuttleworth, 1862b).

Common school promoters in Canada and the United States also emphasised the moral influence that school teachers had on their pupils. As in England, the teacher was viewed as God's emissary and responsible for the future of the human race. As a writer in the *Massachusetts Teacher* pointed out in 1853:

> An employment is elevated in dignity in proportion to the importance of its subject, or the materials with which it has to do...Upon this principle, the work of teaching, especially if we include in this term the work of the ministry, surpasses all other occupations in point of dignity...the subject of the teacher's work is the mind, the masterpiece of the great Architect, delicate in structure, transcendent in value, immortal in destiny (Quoted in Katz, 1968, p. 157).

Simply put, the future of society was dependent on the teacher as a noble, dignified and elevated professional. What then were the moral habits and dispositions of this good teacher?

The moral teacher: Habits and dispositions

Moral character, habits and dispositions

The majority of statements concerning the moral character, habits and dispositions of the teacher were made in reference to the school-mistress, although some generic statements about the teacher as moral exemplar, for example, continued to use the male pronoun or refer to schoolmasters directly. The gendered nature of the language reflects the nineteenth century idealisation of women as being innately better suited for the moral training of young children. This point is taken up in further detail below, but is mentioned to explain the emphasis of the female pronoun in this discussion here.

As a moral exemplar to her students, it was of utmost importance that the teacher's moral character be beyond reproach. Hence, teachers were expected to conform to a set of appropriate standards, attitudes, values, habits, and moral qualities that were to be inculcated in their pupils. She was to be someone of unblemished and consistent character and temperament, and the purity of her motives never open to suspicion. Moral habits, it was asserted, could be best cultivated in the pupil through the teacher's display of her own moral habits and behaviours. Children, wrote Edgeworth, ought to be able to look up their school teacher 'as the living personification of sincerity and honour' (Quoted in Anon, 1867, p. 179).

In addition, the teacher as moral exemplar was expected to exhibit truthfulness, honesty, modesty and humility. Unlike the conceited and arrogant teachers criticised by educational reformers, the humble teacher knew when to acknowledge what she did not know and when to apologise for her mistakes. These qualities would allow the teacher to lead her children towards a love of truth, sincerity and just sense of morality (Committee of Council, 1847; Coleridge, 1842a). Indeed, the good teacher was viewed as the embodiment of the upright, moral citizen that was sought by school reformers in the population as a whole. Furthermore, the formation of the moral character of the child depended on the transparency and visibility of the teacher's moral habits and disposition. As Rousmaniere (1997b) has argued in her historical study about New York teachers, it was crucial that the teacher's moral character be *revealed* to the child, and 'enacted' in the very person of the schoolmistress.

The teacher as parent: Nurturing, tender, gentle and kind

Teachers who were patient, tender, and nurturing were considered especially well-suited for the education of children of poor and working class families. These qualities operated in a compensatory manner to make up for the lack of them in the lives of poor children. Knowledge had to be 'poured' into the child gently, and teachers were to safeguard against cramming. Understanding that sympathy was the key to a child's heart, the good teacher showed affection, kindness, and patience towards their young charges (Committee of Council, 1842, p. 102).

Who else but the schoolmistress better embodied these moral characteristics? Victorian society both within and outside of England idealised the role of women as being innately gentle, patient, tender, caring, nurturing, and sympathetic to the special needs of children. Schoolmasters, it was argued, did not possess the required gentleness, patience and perseverance that schoolmistresses had:

> Above all, they are destitute of those delicate arts which are so requisite to win the affections of children, to call forth and direct their earliest aspirations, and to impart the needful impulse to their minds. Cheerfulness and enthusiasm, courtesy and kindness, and the power of easy, quiet, unconscious influence, are requisites indispensable to the attractiveness, order and efficiency of the school (Anon, 1863, p. 104).

Females, the quotation concludes, were especially endowed with these desirable qualities. They epitomised the Moral Teacher sought by educational promoters.

Moreover, the perfect schoolmistress was a mother to her pupils, preparing them by precept and example for the course of life ahead of them. Statements about the mothering qualities of the schoolmistress were often made in reference to the idea of the teacher *in loco parentis*. While home was considered the most appropriate sphere of moral training, teachers were warned that if parents neglected to perform this task, the load would fall upon them. Therefore, the ideal school was supposed to mirror a harmonious and well-functioning family, with the teacher performing the role of the absent or negligent parent. For the children of the immoral poor, the good teacher would provide the loving support and moral guidance that the natural parent could or would not (Kay-Shuttleworth, 1862a, 1862b).[5]

Besides the idea of the teacher as parent, other analogies of the gentle, kind, and nurturing teacher were articulated both in England and abroad. The teacher was likened to a parent bird, standing before her young flock, sympathising with their weakness and wants, dividing the provisions and feeding them until their mental and moral appetites were satisfied (Le Vaux, 1875). Others compared the teacher to a gardener, tenderly nurturing and caring for the growing child. In this sense, education was comparable to the tilling of land and sowing of seed. The Moral Teacher was required to understand the different dispositions of her pupils 'to whose culture is confided the embryo blossoms of the mind; who is carefully to watch their daily growth, and to aid and accelerate their expansion, so that they may yield rich fruit in beauty and abundance' (Ryerson, 1846b, p. 201). Aiding their growth meant that the good teacher prepared the ground upon which the 'plant-child' grew and then nursed and watered her 'tender charge' (Kay, 1862, p. 60).

Moreover, the teacher's role as nurturing gardener was bound up with the larger aim of education, social control through cultivation of the moral sentiments. As the reformer Kay (1862) explained,

> The absence of education is like that of cultivation, the mind untutored becomes a waste, in which prejudices and traditional errors grow as rankly as weeds. In this sphere of labour...prudent and diligent culture is necessary to obtain genial products from the soil; noxious agencies are abroad, and, while we refuse to sow the germs of truth and virtue, the winds of heaven bring the winged seeds of error and vice (p. 60).

In fact, most of the statements about the positive value of the mother-like schoolmistress echoed arguments previously discussed concerning the societal benefits of education. If parents could not fulfil their responsibilities to teach their children appropriate moral conduct, it fell to the schoolmistress as mother to do so. The devoted schoolmistress, it was argued, would not only be a blessing to her pupils, but to society at large.

Love and emotion: The happy, cheerful teacher as the pupil's friend

Social order could best be ensured by first teaching children how to behave in the school classroom. The teacher as a kind and loving gardener or parent understood fully the power of moral suasion in schoolroom governance. Such a teacher was habitually cheerful in the discharge of her duties. A certain spirit of emotion, joyfulness and delight pervaded her classroom. Humour characterised the devoted teacher who had her heart in her work. 'Wit and humour,' wrote Tate (1857), 'like gleams of sunshine, shed gladness and joy over a class of children'

(p. 231). Her cheerful disposition created order in the classroom: 'In a cheerful hour, we are omnipotent among our children. They hang upon us with their whole heart, they let none of our words fall unheard, they obey our slightest hints' (Salzmann, 1852, p. 382).

Moreover, the Moral Teacher cultivated personal and long-lasting relationships with her pupils. She knew how to talk and associate with children and enjoyed seeing them happy in the classroom. Teachers were also urged to take advantage of opportunities outside of the school to become a companion to the child. This could happen through visits to the home and kindly paying attention to them in the community. As a result, her pupils would never forget such a kind and benevolent teacher. She was their friend (Arnold, 1910; Coleridge, 1842a; Committee of Council, 1845; Anon, 1849c).

Love for children and for teaching was a moral qualification, upon which all other principles of teaching were based. The Moral Teacher was called to gain and secure the affections of her students, which she could not take for granted. It had to be won and then pervade the whole school:

> Love, like the light of heaven, irradiates and beautifies whatever it touches; fear, like darkness, invests everything with gloom. Love one another is the precept of the Great Teacher. Love is the most powerful principle in our nature...If this principle were fully developed in a school, the child would perform his duty for the love of it, and not from the fear of punishment or the hope of reward (Tate, 1854, p. 116).

Love, the most powerful influence that the Moral Teacher could wield, was the key to the maintenance of order in the classroom. She exercised discipline in the classroom in a kind and judicious manner, motivated first by duty and then love and affection, recognising that order could be produced by developing a loving, emotional relationship with her pupils. Moreover, the teacher who loved her pupils would in turn, be loved by them, and her love for them would be visible in the classroom.

Women were viewed as being especially adept at using moral suasion in school government. By nature, they were better adapted than men in school discipline. 'A man may keep a difficult school by means of authority and physical force; a woman can do it only by dignity of character, affection, such a superiority in attainment as is too conspicuous to be questioned' (Anon, 1863, p. 104). In this respect, the kind and gentle schoolmistress was considered in innately superior to the schoolmaster in her ability to maintain order and discipline through developing an emotional connection with the child.

The gendered and dualistic nature of the discourse of the good teacher

This emphasis on the especial moral qualities of the gentle, kind, and patient schoolmistress (against the immoral and cruel schoolmaster) illuminates the gendered and dualistic nature of nineteenth century notions of the good teacher. Statements concerning the moral qualities of the schoolmistress reflected wider conceptions of the innate maternal capacities of women. In effect, we can see the Victorian romanticised image of the morally pure female within the discourse of the Moral Teacher (Herbst, 1989; Rousmaniere, 1997b; Welter, 1969).

European pedagogues such as Pestalozzi and Froebel had idealised the role of the mother as teacher. Pestalozzi's books *Leonard and Gertrude* and *How Gertrude Teaches Her Children* presented a sentimental portrait of the mother Gertrude educating her own children, despite her trying and destitute circumstances. Froebel, the Swiss pedagogue and founder of the kindergarten system, agreed with Pestalozzi's contention that there was much to be learned from observing mothers interacting naturally with their children. He suggested that the ideal teacher of young children was like 'a mother made conscious.' The good teacher, according to Froebel, could learn from what the good mother did naturally:

> [W]aken and develop in the Human Being every power, every disposition... Without any Teaching, Reminding or Learning, the true mother does this of herself. But this is not enough: in Addition is needed that being Conscious, and acting upon a Creature that is growing Conscious, she does her part Consciously and Consistently, as in Duty bound to guide the Human Being in its regular development (Quoted in Steedman, 1985, p. 153).

Education reformers having witnessed the practical implementation of such ideas during the course of their European study tours promoted the reification of the female within pedagogical discourses. In addition, with the translation and publication of the works of Pestalozzi and Froebel into English, their ideas gained even more currency in educational reform discourses in the English speaking world. Froebel's system, for example, was publicised in England by Bertha Maria von

Marenholtz-Beulow, who explained how women were much better suited than men for the education of young children. A woman could:

> take upon herself those responsibilities which men cannot always undertake with actual propriety, and look after those interests which nature expressly intended to be committed to her charge. The position of woman, as mother, nurse, and instructress of childhood, embraces the lofty idea of the female sex having been appointed by Providence to be the legitimate support of helpless humanity (Quoted in Steedman, 1985, p. 152).

The naturally nurturing, selfless and caring qualities of women made them especially suitable for the moral role of teaching. Women, education promoters argued, were pre-eminently fitted to cultivate the feelings of generosity, kindness, self-respect and sense of duty amongst school children (Mann, 1845; Ryerson, 1846b). US reformer Woodbridge, in his 1831 report of the Prussian school system, asserted the particular fitness of women for teaching, arguing that:

> there is something in the *maternal spirit*, the *untiring patience*, which are characteristics of the sex, that qualifies them peculiarly for the instruction of children (Quoted in Herbst, 1989, p. 35).

As Herbst (1989) concludes, in the minds of the school reformers, 'to be a woman was to be a teacher' (p. 28). Moreover, this valuing of women's maternal nature corresponded with the emphasis of the moral purposes of schooling, and reformers' efforts (later in the century) to feminise the teaching force (Albisetti, 1993; Bryant, 1979; Harrigan, 1992; Kamm, 1965).[6]

These ideas about the emotional, caring, and nurturing capacities of the female can be contrasted to assumptions about the rational and scientific nature of man. In the history of modern thought, rationality has been defined in masculine terms, irrationality as feminine. The rational/irrational dualism is analogous to the dualism captured in the discourse of the Modern and the Moral Teacher. The Modern Teacher, understood primarily in masculine terms, was defined as a rational knower of the world, committed to the scientific study of human nature, pedagogy, didactics and a wide range of humanistic subject. In comparison, the characteristics of the Moral Teacher: nurturing, caring, kind, patient, and able to develop loving, emotional relationships with her pupils, were values associated with the feminine.

The designation of the masculine with rational thought and the feminine with nurturing, emotional capacities was directly related to the different ways in which female and male teachers were trained. Examples of teacher training courses of study that were outlined in the Modern Teacher section of this chapter were all taken from training institutions for schoolmasters. Course syllabi at the female training institutions did not include higher mathematics, Euclid, Algebra, Latin or Greek, or the Classics, nor did the female training institutions incorporate lectures on the philosophy of the mind. Rather, in place of these subjects, female training candidates studied needlework and domestic economy, including the details of cooking, washing, baking and brewing (Committee of Council, 1859; Rich, 1933).

In some ways, schoolmistresses were thought to be less intellectually capable than their male counterparts. Dunn noted that women did not have the 'same vigour of mind' as men (Select Committee on Education, 1834). Others thought that it was a waste of time and money to send women to the training colleges. The demands of the programme would only result in 'confused ideas' and 'hinder her from forming and working upon a system of her own' (Committee of Council, 1851, p. 265; Newcastle Commission, 1861b). Furthermore, if women were innately caring, nurturing, loving, and emotional – those characteristics deemed most desirable for the Moral Teacher, then (so the argument went) there was actually no need to educate the schoolmistress. As reformers argued, given that the mother naturally provided sympathy and empathy to the child, the schoolmistress would through her own intuitive sense know what the schoolchild naturally required (Steedman, 1985).

Teaching power: Innate or learned?

This directs our attention to the final point in this chapter; that is the issue of whether or not the characteristics, habits and dispositions of the good teacher were innate or could be learned. The complexities of this issue are exemplified by the nineteenth century debate on 'teaching power.' Teaching power, otherwise known as 'the art of teaching' or 'aptness to teach', was considered the most essential qualification of the good teacher. Teachers who possessed this qualification were praised and commended. Thomas Brown of the Common Sense School claimed that teaching power was 'the noblest, and in proportion to its value, the least studied of all the arts' (Dunn, 1837, p. 66).

Despite the importance of teaching power, the concept remained vague and elusive, one of those qualities that was obvious when seen, but difficult to define precisely. Some countered that it was essential to define the term, claiming that:

> we cannot allow the subject to remain in this unphilosophical [sic] condition of mysticism. The aptitude for teaching must undoubtedly be a qualification resulting from the development of certain intellectual and moral faculties of our nature. Let us endeavour to analyse this remarkable qualification...to discover those qualities, intellectual and moral, with which it is invariably associated, or, rate with which it is connected by the constant relation of cause and effect (Tate, 1857, pp. 277–8).

Such calls to define and analyse teaching power so that it could be either improved upon or acquired through careful and diligent study and training were rare. Nonetheless, most nineteenth century reformers, inspectors and educational commentators agreed that teaching power was not solely about superior talents or technical knowledge that could be picked up through self-study or formal training. They argued that no amount of preparation or training could render a morally unfit individual a good teacher (Dunn, 1837).

Teaching power had much more to do with the innate, moral character of the teacher. The concept was derived from the German notion of *Lehrgabe* or *teaching gift*, and in this respect was considered by some gift of nature that only a few possessed. If individuals were not naturally endowed with it, they would never be able to possess it in any great degree (Anon, 1852). These ideas relate back to the contradictions, dualism, and gendered nature of the discourse of the good teacher. Statements referring to the knowledge expected of the good teacher were made in relation to the need for formal training or education, and self-study on behalf of the teacher. The assumption was that through scientific and philosophical study one could learn the knowledge and skills to be a good teacher.

The Modern Teacher, it was argued, was to be 'educated' into his profession, to become a cultivated and cultured individual. This corresponds with the modern belief in the capacities of the reasoning and rational individual, and in progress for the individual and society through education. In contrast, the schoolmistress was positioned as the Moral Teacher. Her innate mothering capacities, enacted and made visible in the classroom, enabled her to provide the moral foundation of education. The moral habits and dispositions deemed requisite in the good teacher: piety, devotion, humility, kindness, patience and love for children, were innately present in women. Women who were considered naturally pure provided the best moral exemplars for their pupils. There was no need to train or educate the Moral Teacher. She was born into her calling, having come into the world possessing the 'teaching gift' from birth (Rousmaniere, 1997b).

Conclusion

Over the course of the Victorian period, education reformers and pro-moters in England, Europe and North America emphasised the central role of the teacher in popular education reform. Good schools, they argued, were the guarantee of an ordered, moral and well-educated society. And good schools depended on being run by good teachers. 'The teacher makes the school' was echoed throughout the century as a reminder of the importance of the teacher. As a writer in the *Journal of Education for Upper Canada* (1848) noted: 'Much depends on the right selection of Teachers. No school can prosper without *good* Teachers. A bad tree may as well bring forth good fruit, as a bad teacher makes a good school' (Anon, 1848b, p. 87).

This chapter has described the discourse of the good teacher. The ideal types, Modern and Moral, were evoked to represent the character-istics of the knowledge and character traits, respectively, of the good teacher. This has been an analysis not about the ontological basis of teachers' lives. Rather, it has been a study of the constitution of new truths about the good teacher. The concern is with understanding how certain truths about what it means to be a teacher came to be invented. The teacher was constituted as a particular object for thought, one that was both Modern and Moral. The Modern Teacher was scientifically and philosophically engaged with the most contemporary pedagogic principles and practices, thoroughly knowledgeable not only of the elementary school subjects but a wide range of classical and literary studies. The Moral Teacher, infused with the Christian principle, was an exemplar to her pupils through the visible display of her moral qual-ities. She was kind, tender, gentle, humble, selfless, and modest. Above all, she loved her pupils and love pervaded her orderly and happy classroom.

Statements referring to the Moral Teacher were overwhelmingly female, reflecting Victorian assumptions about the innate capacities of women as being more moral, nurturing, and emotional than men. Statements about the Modern Teacher were almost always made with reference to schoolmasters or by using the male pronoun. The Modern

Teacher, reflecting the designation of the masculine with rational modern thought, was positioned as an active scientific and philosophical learner. Although the Modern Teacher actively and energetically engaged in progressive pedagogical techniques, he was largely invisible in his classroom. On the other hand, the Moral Teacher was a visible subject. Her habits, dispositions, and total character were on display and enacted in the classroom as a moral exemplar for her pupils.

Focus has shifted in this chapter from the reasoning and rational subject to the systems of knowledge that operated to construct the teacher as subject. Similar ideas about the good teacher were taken up in England, Europe and North America. This is not only about how others came to reason about the teacher, but how teachers came to 'see' and think about themselves and their work. Systems of thought and reasoning are embedded in power relations that make possible the development of technologies to construct subjects. The specific ways in which the good teacher came to be constructed and governed through a set of disciplinary technologies constitutes the topic of the last three chapters of this book.

Notes

1 I capitalise Modern Teacher and Moral Teacher to indicate the sociological use of these categories as ideal types. In this way, they are heuristic devices to assist in understanding the discourse of the good teacher.

2 There were, of course, many other schools of thought that overlapped with the above and influenced educational thinkers and promoters across these settings. The focus here is on statements about philosophical schools of thought or paradigms that were made in relation to the idea of the good teacher.

3 For instance, following each practise session, the Battersea Master of Method noted the strong and weak points in each student's practical teaching, and then based his later lectures on this material (Committee of Council, 1845). The Master of Methods at St. Mark's approached the teaching of methods differently. Rather than discussing practise teaching with each student, he dictated notes on school management, organisation, and method to the students. This was followed by viva-voce examinations on topics prepared beforehand, and students were expected to incorporate their notes from his lectures into essays in the following week (Committee of Council, 1860).

4 Female training colleges were usually directed by a clergyman who acted as chaplain and secretary, living on or near the premises. The domestic life was under the direction of a resident lady superintendent, with several governesses undertaking the tuition (Committee of Council, 1851–52).

5 The theme of parental substitution is a key concept found throughout Kay-Shuttleworth's writings on education. According to Kay-Shuttleworth

(1862a), the teacher of poor children was to act as a foster or second parent, whose welfare was committed to their care.
6 Albisetti's (1993) comparative history illustrates the differences in the feminisation of the teaching profession across a range of western societies, pointing to the difficulties in applying any one model across places and periods.

Part III

Making and Shaping the Victorian Teacher

6
Schools as Sites of Disciplinary Control

> Nor will we wonder if many [schoolmasters] find it to their advantage to leave the elementary school, and take to employ-ments in which they are at once easier working, better paid, less under surveillance, and in a better social position (Anon, 1861, p. 57).

The focus in the next three chapters is on the making of the teacher as a subject in the sense of being subjected to oneself or someone else. This new cultural history of the teacher as subject focuses on various practices, processes, procedures, rules and regulations – or technologies – that were deployed to make and shape the good teacher. As Rose (1989) explains:

> [The self] a heterogeneous and shifting resultant of the social expec-tations targeted upon it, the social duties accorded it, the norms according to which it is judged, the pleasures and pains that entice and coerce it, the forms of self-inspection inculcated in it, the lan-guages according to which it is spoken about which it learns to account for itself in thought and speech. Thus 'belief systems' concerning the self should not be construed as inhabiting a diffuse field of 'culture', but as embodied in institutional and technical practices...through which forms of individuality are specified and governed (p. 218).

There were two sites or spaces of emergence where these technologies operated: teacher training colleges and schools, the latter which is the topic of this chapter. Much has been written about the school as an institution of social control, primarily with respect to the student. This chapter is concerned with how the school was transformed into a site of disciplinary control over the teacher. After the 1840s, the school shifted from a quasi-autonomous informal setting, governed primarily by the teacher in conjunction with the local needs and demands of parents, to a disciplinary site infiltrated by a wide variety of actors, acting in an official capacity to monitor teachers and their schools. Before examining this process, I review the state of schooling in England and abroad prior to the construction of mass, popular education systems to show the shift that took place in teacher-community-state relations over the course of the Victorian period.

Early schooling: Teachers and community relations

What was the state of schooling for the poorer and working classes in England prior to the construction of a mass education system? Prior to 1833, education of the children of the poor was undertaken by endowments and private subscriptions. Endowments were provided for four types of schools: Cathedral, Ward, Grammar, and Charity Schools. Both endowed grammar and charity schools had been in existence from as early as the sixteenth century. However, by the nineteenth century, many poor, working class families had abandoned the grammar schools for private and charity schools which better met their needs (Lawson and Silver, 1973; Sanderson, 1962; Stephens, 1998).

Other than endowments, schools for the working classes included those which were conducted by charity or philanthropy. These included Schools for Afflicted Persons, Sunday Schools, and Ragged schools. Due to the eighteenth century demands of industrialisation, Sunday Schools had been set up to provide a part-time, basic secular and religious education for as large a number of working class children as funds would allow (Purvis, 1984). Over time, as Laquer (1976) has argued, Sunday Schools became a part of working class culture and they remained popular up until the middle of the nineteenth century. By that time, the philanthropic establishment of Ragged or Industrial schools had been well under way. These schools were founded in urban slum areas, and although they taught reading, writing and arithmetic, their emphasis was upon industrial training, and keeping poor, vagrant children from lives of crime (Bartley, 1871; Curtis, 1967; Stephens, 1998).

Despite the availability of free endowed Grammar, Charity and Sunday Schools, and Ragged or Industrial Schools, many working class parents preferred to send their children to one of the many private day schools that emerged in the nineteenth century. These small private schools went by many different names; including common day school; venture, adventure or private enterprise school; and dame or (less frequently) gaffer school (Leinster-Mackay, 1978; Sanderson, 1962). Anyone could establish a school and attempt to make a living by charging fees. The only requirement to establish a school was a room and in some cases, a few educational materials. Dame schools, run by women in their homes, were primarily for small groups of infants and young children (Purvis, 1984).

Gardner's (1984) *The Lost Elementary Schools of Victorian England* challenged previously held ideas about the nature of working class educational provision. His local study of Bristol revealed that there was a much more extensive system of private education run by and for the working classes than had been acknowledged in the literature on Victorian elementary education. As a proportion of the total available provision of nineteenth century schooling, the private sector was large. The 1851 census revealed that these small private schools had provided most of the education for working class children during the first half of the nineteenth century (Gardner, 1984).

Generally, it could be said that these private schools were diverse, served specific local purposes and needs, shifted to meet those needs, and were dependent upon relations between the teacher and local community. Parents and teachers were bound together in a relationship of mutual obligation. Parents needed to have their children educated and teachers had to make a living. If teachers did not ensure that parents' needs were met, pupils would be withdrawn from school and shifted to another. If parents did not pay the school fee, the teacher would be forced to close down the school and move to another more viable locale. Through such arrangements, the teacher and local community came to depend upon one another (Aldrich, 1995; Newcastle Commission, 1861a; Hughes, 1936).

The fact that many parents and elementary school teachers shared common experiences and class background also contributed to the close relationship between them. Working class parents criticised the pretentiousness and conceit of monitorial and state-aided school teachers, preferring dame, and other private school teachers whom they considered 'persons in their own station of life' (Tropp, 1957). There is evidence to suggest that as an integral part of the community, teachers were trusted and well respected by local parents. Dames, for example, were especially well liked for accommodating the needs of parents by receiving and caring for children at various hours during the day (Newcastle Commission, 1861c; Select Committee on Education, 1838).

Trust and confidence tended to develop in situations characterised by close geographical proximity. In villages, towns and cities, early private schools were located within the neighbourhoods that they served. This was particularly important given that English working class parents preferred schools that were close to their homes, so that little time would be spent taking children to and from school (Higginson, 1939; Stewart, 1972). The vast majority of teachers lived in the community where they worked, teaching in a local schoolhouse or opening up their own homes to local children. In the former case, if unmarried, the schoolmaster would reside in part of the school and keep boarders to make ends meet.

This proximity between teacher, parents, and pupils led to close relations and intimate knowledge of one another, with teachers and parents together collaborating and managing the local school. For instance, teachers, along with parents, determined the subject matter covered in the schools. Parents primarily required that teachers cover the basic subjects plus sewing and knitting for girls, and in some cases grammar, geography and other subjects for boys and older children. After that, the teacher was able to decide independently which academic subjects and teaching methods to follow in his or her school (Committee of Council, 1846; Gardner, 1984; Higginson, 1939; Leinster-Mackay, 1983; Wardle, 1976). Such informal arrangements contributed to close relationships that developed between the teacher and local community, and the teacher's sense of autonomy in the classroom. As Gardner (1984) has shown, these schools were an integral part of the community in which they were situated and as a result were trusted by working class parents.

Early schooling: Comparative and international contexts

Educational opportunities for European and North American children also existed prior to the development of formal, state-sponsored education systems. From the sixteenth century onwards, in continental Europe, the churches and religious societies played a role in educational provision for the poorer populations. In France, most private schools were Catholic and established as a backlash against the Republics' push to eliminate the Church from educational provision. Many of these private Catholic schools were forced underground and a so-called 'schooling war' (guerre scholaire) emerged between Catholics and supporters of the Republic (Derycke, 2007).

In North America, the Churches and religious societies such as the 'United Society for the Propagation of the Gospel' continued their work into the eighteenth century operating Charity and Sunday Schools for the poor throughout many of the Canadian and United States colonies. Charity schools offered education to the poorer populations and in many ways were the forerunners of the public school system. Missionaries offered a Christian education to the Aboriginal populations whom also had their own long history of family and community based education in their communities prior to the arrival of the European settlers (Bailyn, 1960; Kaestle, 1983; Rowe, 1964).

Early emigrants to North America brought with them educational traditions from their 'mother' countries. From the late sixteenth through to the nineteenth century, the family had been the most important agency in elementary socialisation. The family was also responsible for early vocational training especially amongst the agricultural labouring population and small tradesmen who comprised the majority of the population in pre-modern times. The family's role in vocational training was extended and formalised with the development of the apprenticeship system. The educational work of the family was complemented by the stable and slowly changing fabric of the local village or town community. According to Bailyn (1960):

> So extensive and intricate was the community's involvement with the family and yet so important was its function as a public agency that the youth moved naturally and gradually across the borderline that separates the personal from the impersonal world of authority (p. 18).

Over time, the roles of both the family as the primary socialisation agent and apprenticeship for the transmission of skills were reduced. As a result, greater interest in other forms of education developed. This new interest was, as Bailyn (1960) writes, 'a pattern woven of the necessities of life in the colonies' (p. 29).

Thus, from the late eighteenth century onwards, within North America many communities established their own local, private school to meet their educational needs. Dutch and German immigrant communities, and religious groups such as the Mennonites and Quakers, operated their own schools in states such as New York and Pennsylvania. As in England, dames and schoolmasters also offered classes for low fees in the rudiments of reading and writing in their own homes (or a local community building) to local children. In the southern United States, however, schooling was largely neglected for the slave and other poorer populations[1] (Green, 1990; Bailyn, 1960; Button and Provenzo, 1983; Rowe, 1964).

In rural communities, it was common in many of the Canadian colonies and mid-western United States for teachers to board with local families. Local teachers often accepted at least a part of their earnings in kind, in the form of room and board, rather than cash. As boarders, teachers were often considered welcome guests in the homes where they stayed, adding interesting conversations, participating in household labour processes and passing on information about domestic skills (Briggs, 1896; Eggleston, 1871; Harkness, 1896; Spring, 1990). Whether teachers boarded with local families or lived in their own quarters in the community, there is evidence to suggest that there were close relations between teachers and the community, especially in rural and pioneer settings. In many cases, teacher and parents managed the local school together, decided what should be taught, and how children were to be disciplined (Graham, 1974; Eggleston, 1871).

In addition, various forms of home schooling continued in North America and Europe well into the nineteenth century. The most informal consisted of parents providing some form of education to their own children, whilst engaging in other household activities. This was due in part to the fact that children were required to contribute to the household economy and distances between rural families often precluded the combination of resources to hire a teacher (Bailyn, 1960).

Over time, these casual and haphazard educational arrangements in North America and Europe became increasingly formalised and structured with the development of formal education systems (Green, 1990; Katz, 1976). As we saw in Chapter 3, the development of mass state-sponsored educational systems occurred unevenly and in different forms across continental Europe, but generally involved the increasing involvement of the state in educational funding, provision and regulation of schools and teachers (Green, 1990).

Even as early as the seventeenth century, laws were passed in a number of north-eastern United States colonies requiring towns to establish elementary schools. Free school laws were also passed in some southern United States in the early nineteenth century for orphans and poor children. These laws, which enforced the establishment of community sponsored schools by the state, were sometimes obeyed and sometimes not. As in England, poorer and working class parents often preferred to continue sending their children to the local, private schools rather than enrol them in the district schools or schools run by the religious societies (Button and Provenzo, 1983; Herbst, 1989).

Education reformers, inspectors and other officials in North America, Europe and England were often dismayed with the overall support shown for the heterogeneous network of informal small, private schools that offered a haphazard curriculum, classes of students of varying ages and abilities, in rough and unsuitable settings. Reformers regretted that parents were prepared to pay higher fees to send their children to these private schools, rather than the cheaper philanthropic and state-aided schools (Gardner, 1984; Green, 1990; Johnson, 1904; Newcastle Commission, 1861b; Young, 1880).

There are a number of reasons to account for the popularity of these small, privately-run schools amongst poorer, working class and pioneer communities. Many parents felt that compared to the voluntary (Church run) and state-aided and controlled schools, a superior education was provided in them. Teachers adjusted the curriculum, hours of school operation, and other aspects of daily school life to meet local needs. Many parents were opposed to the patronising and heavy-handed attitude associated with the philanthropic, monitorial and other state-aided schools. With the development of a state-aided (and voluntary) education system, many poorer, immigrant and working class families in Europe, England and North America actually refused to subject themselves to increasing bureaucratic controls and requirements and continued instead to send their children to their local, private schools. For instance, many immigrant parents were fiercely opposed to the assimilationist aims of the Protestant school promoters, preferring instead to send their children to the independent, private schools developed in and by their communities to serve their cultural and religious needs (Green, 1990). Indeed, perhaps the most significant reason to explain the popularity of these schools was that they had grown out of the needs of poorer, working class and immigrant communities and remained firmly rooted in local community life.

External inspections: Inspectors, trustees/managers, and school visitors

Breaking school-community relations

By the 1840s, the close school-community relations that had characterised the pre-Victorian era had begun to break down. Within England, the involvement of the voluntary societies and later the state was predicated on the idea that the close relations between the local community and teacher were deleterious to both the construction of a popular education system and professional teaching force. As the voluntary societies took a more active role in establishing and running the school system, the school ceased to be a collaborative venture between the local community and the teacher.

Therefore, constructing formal educational systems in England and abroad meant severing the ties between the teacher and community, and in turn opening up the school to the scrutinising eye of outside officials. There were three groups of individuals whose eyes became firmly fixed on the school: inspectors, school managers, and another group known as official school visitors. Together, these individuals took on a new role to monitor and regulate the work of teachers in their schools. While their responsibilities and powers shifted, overlapped and changed throughout the Victorian period, I am concerned here with those specific surveillance practices that had bearing upon teachers and their work, the topic I turn to next.

Inspections: Powers and responsibilities

In England, local clergy had inspected or visited schools prior to 1839. The National Society and BFSS continued this practice, appointing their own inspectors, before and even well after the state became involved in the formation and regulation of an official inspectorate. However, with the disbursement of the Parliamentary grant to the voluntary societies in 1839 for school building expenditures, the government demanded the right of inspection.

Educational reformers considered the role of the inspector as being particularly significant for the emerging educational system. Inspectors were responsible for inspecting schools in districts that had received state building grants, to convey to teachers 'knowledge of all improvements in the art of teaching', and to submit annual reports to the Committee of Council (Ball, 1963, p. 25). In addition, from 1846 onwards, applications from school managers for the apprenticeship of a pupil-teacher would only be considered if the inspector had reported favourably upon the teachers, methods, discipline, apparatus and financial stability of the school (Committee of Council, 1847).

While inspectors attempted to visit each school in their district at least once a year, managers and other 'official' school visitors, a practice established by some voluntary societies, were to inspect and examine the school more frequently. In some cases, the local wealthy patrons or subscribers of endowed school were involved as managers, but in most cases the local clergy managed the school (Ball, 1983). They were responsible for disbursing the salary augmentation grant to their local teachers upon successful completion of the certification examinations, and after 1861, the attendance and proficiency of their pupils. School managers also issued pupil-teacher candidates with certificates of moral character, without which they could not begin their apprenticeship. Finally, they had the power to dismiss or suspend teachers on account of any objection to their teaching, discipline, or conduct (Committee of Council, 1847; Newcastle Commission, 1861b).

Some school reformers and inspectors spoke out against the potential abuse of power from managers, claiming that teachers were subject to the whim, mercy and caprice of 'ignorant' managers. The schoolmaster, as Kay-Shuttleworth (1853) asserted, was 'at the mercy of the clergyman, who may deem it his duty to render his office untenable by repeated suspensions' (p. 18).

Inspections: A collaborative and cooperative affair

Despite these abuses of power, school inspection was intended to be a form of cooperation between the government, managers, inspectors, and teachers. The inspector was not alone in carrying out his duty, as he was to work in collaboration with the managers and other school visitors to ensure the complete surveillance and supervision of the school and teacher.[2] Inspectors were informed that their job was a means of affording assistance to the teacher, and not to be regarded as a means of exercising control. The inspector was instructed that:

> by cheerfulness, affability, anxiety to consult the convenience of all, and such sympathy with [the teacher's] success as is consistent with the impartial discharge of your duties, it is hoped that you will not only leave on their minds the most grateful personal impression, but that you will inspire them with a just confidence that the Government is anxious to recognise every legitimate claim on the public resources for their proper remuneration, and to give the sanction of public authority to every well-qualified schoolmaster (Hughes, 1936, pp. 61–2).

Moreover, teachers were to receive the clear impression from the inspector that together they were joined in a cooperative venture to ensure the fulfilment of national educational objectives.

Inspectors encouraged clergy to be involved in their school responsibilities and commended those who did. Inspectors outlined the advantages of schools that enjoyed the constant visits of local clergymen, arguing that the excellence of some schools could be attributed to the devotion of the clergy. Inspector Allen went so far as to extend the common saying 'As is the teacher so is the school' to 'As are the pains bestowed therein by the clergyman, so is the school' (Committee of Council, 1845, p. 42). Likewise, Inspector Moseley commended the local clergyman for his active interest in the local school, noting that the teacher, pupil teachers, scholars and clergyman were all united in equal and hearty good will in successfully promoting their school (Committee of Council, 1852).

A mutual relationship: Advising and supporting the teacher

In this way, together inspectors, managers, and other school visitors were positioned as the teacher's friend, confidante, and companion. Their relationship was to be one of mutual dependence, working together for a common cause. One English school promoter claimed that there had never been a time 'when the clergyman and schoolmaster needed the mutual strengthening of hands as in the present' (National Society, 1849–55, p. 415). To this end, inspectors and other school visitors were instructed to provide the teacher with advice on teaching. The Home and Colonial Society, for example, recommended that its school visitors observe the routine of the school and then, after giving advice, revisit it to ensure that the advice had been carried out (Ball, 1983).

Rather than lecture or reprimand teachers who were not fulfilling their duties properly, the inspector was to encourage improvement in a kind and supportive manner. Teachers, it was argued, would appreciate the sympathetic and encouraging role of the inspector. Under no circumstance were school managers or official visitors to embarrass, humiliate, speak disparagingly or find any fault with the teacher in front of the pupils. Rather, advice was to be given in private, and then, later reported to the inspector. Inspectors' reports were to be positive, noting any deficiencies in the school in a supportive, understanding and sympathetic way (Committee of Council, 1845).

Inspectors were also expressly obliged to advise the teacher on pedagogic matters, including progressive teaching methods and school management, and to discourage the monitorial system. The Committee of Council instructed them to 'throw light in the particular direction best suited for the instruction of classes; to introduce groups of classes at parallel desks...and encourage the formation of the system of apprenticeship' (Kay-Shuttleworth quoted in Ball, 1983, p. 100). To fulfil this function, inspectors were expected to keep up-to-date in the latest pedagogical and didactical developments. Inspectors were encouraged to give lectures at Teachers' Associations Meetings and participate in courses taught in the summer and harvest schools operated by the training colleges (Hewlett, 1932; Etherington, 1969).

By providing teachers with pedagogic, didactical and subject matter advice, inspections aimed to incite the teacher to improvement. They were to operate as a stimulus to teachers, encouraging them to greater exertion and the promotion of the general welfare and efficiency of their schools. Teachers, it was argued, would welcome such sound and solid advice to assist them with school teaching (Manchester Statistical Society, 1836). School inspections, wrote Lloyd, 'would be an unspeakable blessing to society, and would be the means of conveying improvement, and suggesting information to teachers, and stirring them up and leading them to increase their efforts' (Select Committee on Education, 1834, p. 103). Indeed, the Newcastle Commission Report (1861d) concluded that nearly everyone considered the school inspection a 'wholesome stimulus to all concerned' (p. 16).

Collecting statistical data about the teacher

While inspectors, managers, and school visitors were urged to provide the teacher with advice on teaching, another explicit task of school inspections was the collection, tabulation and publication of data about the school and its teacher. As power depends on knowledge, collecting this educational information was central to the process of making the teacher as subject. Therefore, the general aim of inspection was to obtain the most thorough information possible about the school, the argument being that any person or institution that received government money should be open to supervision.

This constituted a new form of state steering from a distance with the inspectorate and other school visitors charged with the collection of detailed information about the teacher and the school. In such a way, the inspectorate, school managers (in the UK) and school trustees (in North America) became a vital link between the central government and local authorities, enabling the central administration to use local bodies, such as the voluntary societies, both as sources of intelligence and as a means for executing new policies and procedures.

In part, the inspector was to inquire into the school records, methods of instruction, which subjects were taught, the quality of the lessons, and the mode of control and discipline that the teacher depended upon. Inspectors' reports were detailed compilations of information about each school, its teacher and students. They were over ten pages in length and included 140 questions on the condition of the school and teachers, and were submitted at the end of each month (Committee of Council, 1841).[3]

Despite this format, these reports were much more than lists of quantitative data. Inspectors were expected to give their opinion of the teacher with respect to his attainments, character, and method of conducting the school. Many of the earlier reports tended to be narrative, observational accounts replete with descriptive analyses of the schools in their districts, and in some cases inspectors' personal reflections about the condition of the schools, teachers and their own responsibilities. This changed after the mid-century, however, as inspectors' reports shifted to more precise, standardised lists of quantitative data, a point taken up further in Chapter 8 (Ball, 1963; Committee on Council, 1857–58).

Some of this quantitative information was to be obtained by talking directly to the teacher or from an examination of the class logbooks, which teachers were obliged to maintain. These logbooks contained general information about the school and each pupil (attendance, dates of withdrawals, progress, etc.). Inspectors were obliged to look through the logbooks and to report whether or not they had been properly kept throughout the year (Committee of Council, 1861). After 1861, these logbooks took on added importance as the school grant was distributed on the basis of average attendance grants. Teachers were provided with clear instructions for logbook entries:

> The principal teacher must daily make in the logbook the briefest entry which will suffice to specify either ordinary progress, or whatever other facts concerning the school or its teachers, such as the date of withdrawals, commencement of duty, cautions, illness, &c. may required to be referred to at a future time, or may otherwise deserve to be recorded (Committee of Council, 1861, p. 375).

Further, the significance of the log book was underscored when teachers, in the case of a fire, were cautioned to first ensure that the school log book was safely secured *before* leading the children out of doors to their safety.

The collection, tabulation, and publication of detailed knowledge about the teacher were key elements in the process of making and shaping the good Victorian teacher. Monitoring what went on inside the schoolhouse through inspections and other official school visits was taken up outside of England too. In this next section, we take a look at these practices as they were played out in Ireland, continental Europe and North America.

External inspections: Comparative and international contexts

The English school inspectorate was influenced by inspection systems that were solidly in place in Europe and Ireland by the start of the Victorian period. The establishment of an educational inspectorate in Prussia and Holland had been shaped by the revolutionary efforts of the French empire. In Prussia, inspection became a key element of the highly centralised and closely regulated educational system. Managing committees comprised of clergymen, magistrates, and one or two elected householders were set up at the local commune or parish level; as well as at the district level. At the lower level, the local pastor or curate served as the inspector of the village school. At the district level, an inspector was appointed by clerical authorities and responsible for submitting reports on school inspections in their districts to the central authorities (Curtis, 1992).

In contrast to the formalised and tightly regulated Prussian system, the Dutch inspectorate allowed for much more flexibility. There was no large corps of inspectors general in Holland. In each district, a resident primary-school inspector visited each school at least twice a year. He was in charge of promoting teachers and chairing educational meetings. District inspectors were responsible for inquiring into school organisation and teaching. If improvements were necessary, inspectors were to advise teachers discreetly and to keep written notes of all visits. At the quarterly meetings of district boards of education, inspectors were expected to provide detailed reports in writing, outlining the number of schools visited, their general conditions, meetings with teachers, teacher examinations and other events concerning the conduct of education. This material formed the basis of an annual report that each inspector submitted to the district board meetings (Curtis, 1992).

The English model whereby the inspector was positioned as a friend and welcomed advisor to the teacher was largely drawn from the Dutch inspectorate. The Dutch model was viewed by Kay-Shuttleworth and other like-minded reformers as the best means to support and offer assistance to the local teacher. This was, as Curtis (1992) explains, because the Dutch system combined 'intense regulation and room for manoeuvre' (p. 31). Dutch inspectors were viewed locally as 'friends of education' and enjoyed independent powers to adapt central regulations without being viewed as visible objects of control and authority.

The English inspectorate was also influenced by similar developments in Ireland, which had an educational inspectorate in place by the early Victorian period (Ball, 1963). By the start of the Victorian period, building on the earlier work of the Kildare Place Society, Ireland had developed an elaborate inspection system. Each of the 25 districts had a superintendent who would visit local schools, receive monthly reports, and submit their standardised, quarterly reports to the Board of National Commissioners. Superintendents were expected to attend to the general order and condition of the school, to examine classes, attendance records, and school register and daily report book. As in Holland, inspectors were instructed not to give orders to teachers, but rather to be friendly, courteous, and to exhibit a 'courteous and conciliatory demeanour' (Quoted in Curtis, 1992, p. 44).

This model was also taken up in North America. Over the course of the Victorian period, most US states passed legislation creating inspectorates and boards of education (Green, 1990). An inspectorate came into being in Upper Canada with the 1843 Common School Act, which outlined the duties of the local and county superintendents, the term used to refer to school inspectors. These positions were collapsed into one with the 1846 School Act, which defined more clearly the responsibilities of the inspectors, or school district superintendents, as they were henceforth called. District superintendents were expected to visit all of the schools in their districts at least once a year and report on their progress and general condition to the Chief Superintendent of schools. They were responsible for examining and certifying candidates for one year teaching positions and for annulling certificates held by incompetent or unsuitable teachers (Curtis, 1992).

The 1846 School Act also defined the duties and powers of the locally elected trustees in Upper Canada, including the responsibilities for hiring, paying, and dismissing teachers. Teachers' employment was very much dependent upon the local trustee or manager. Contracts, drawn up between school teachers and their local trustees, stipulated the length of the contract, subjects to be taught, the teacher's duties, and the amount of pay according to the rules and regulations provided for by the School Act. Once hired, trustees provided teachers with the necessary portion of the school grant to which their school section was entitled. Trustees also had the power to dismiss or suspend teachers on account of any objection to their teaching, discipline, or conduct (Curtis, 1988).

The system of school visitors, taken from the Irish model, was also taken up in Canada and some of US states. For example, in Upper Canada, visitors, which included local clergy of all denominations, district wardens, township and town councillors, resident justices of the peace, as well as 'gentlemen of the neighbourhood' were allowed free admission to the school at any time, and 'full liberty' to observe the pupils, their books, lesson, apparatus, etc. (Curtis, 1992, p. 44). The Visitors' Book, which each teacher was obliged to keep in the class-room, was to be used for visitors' comments and advice for the teacher (Ryerson, 1850a). Teachers were urged to receive visitors courteously and welcome the advice and stimulation they provided (Public Schools, 1859). The Irish experience, upon which these and other inspection practices were based, was also taken up in many of the US states (Tyack, 1967) and England as we have seen above.

Making and shaping the teacher through inspections

Indeed, education reformers argued that schools and teachers could not be inspected too often or too much. Inspections would ensure that there was 'a vigilant eye everywhere' in the school (Committee of Council, 1843, p. 103). The combination of regular visits from inspectors, school managers, and official school visitors produced this situation and the school shifted from being a quasi-autonomous, flex-ible, and shifting site, grounded in close community relations to a disciplinary space where a myriad of inspection practices continually operated to make and shape the good teacher.

As he peered into the very depths of the school, nothing was to escape the inspector's notice. District superintendents in Upper Canada, for example, were urged to go beyond the character and methods of instruction, discipline, and school management in their reports to:

the interior regime of the Schools, – the aptitude, the zeal, the deport-ment of the Teachers – their relations with the Pupils, the Trustees and the neighbourhood, – the progress and attainments of the pupils, and in a word, the whole moral and social character and results of the instruction given, as far as can be ascertained (Ryerson, 1846a, p. 268).

This was not simply a matter of getting at the interior workings of the school, but investigating the interior regime of the teacher. This type of information could not be obtained from reports and statistical tables. School visits, observations, and personal conversations with teachers were required, so that the true efficiency of the school and character of the teacher could be determined and modified if necessary.

The teacher's mind, soul, and body were 'opened up' for inspection. The process, as Jeffrey and Woods (1998) explains in their discussion about the contemporary role of inspectors, resembles the unclothing of the teacher and the school. The inspector has the power to undress the teacher, gaze at and examine him in any way he sees fit. Once the inspector leaves, the teacher laid bare must re-dress, but their clothes (and their bodies) have changed through the process, reminding them of the continuous gaze that they can never escape.

In this way, the Victorian teacher was 'laid bare' for the inspector. S/he was expected to answer all of the inspector's questions, which covered not only their subjects, teaching methods and background instruction in the art of teaching, and general conditions and terms of their appointment to the school, length of teaching career, and status in the school (full-time teacher, or if occupied with other jobs), but also personal questions about their marital status, living conditions, and former occupation (Committee of Council, 1841). Nothing was left uncovered, and through this total visibility the teacher was made and shaped as a humble, obedient subject.

Despite rhetoric to the contrary, inspections were not simply visits to demonstrate support and share advice with the teacher. Inspection and school managers had the power to withhold pay (or augmentation of it) from teachers and dismiss them from their positions. The 1850 Annual Report of the Bath and Wells Diocesan Board sheds light on the direct effects of type of power on the school teacher:

> The master, mistresses, pupil teachers, and stipendiary monitors, *if* they would obtain the money which has been promised them, *must please the Government Inspector*, and must therefore use the text-books, employ the methods of teaching, and express the opinion which the Government Inspector fancies the best (National Society, 1850, pp. 90–1).

As this quotation reveals, there were very real effects associated with the operation of these powers. These are examples of sovereign power; power that was clearly recognisable and visible in the person of the inspector, trustee, manager and school visitor. The power to hire, certify, discipline and dismiss the teacher, for example, operated as potent tools to ensure that teachers who wished to maintain their positions conformed to official rules and regulations. These powers were direct and explicit and their effects played themselves out in the lives of Victorian teachers.

However, the Victorian school was also a disciplinary site where power in its dispersed form operated to control and regulate teachers. Inspectors, trustees, managers and official school visitors were to view their relationship with the teacher as a mutual one, based on cooperation and collaboration. This positioning of school visitors as kind, supportive advice-providing friends of the teacher illustrates the subtle, diffuse and seemingly innocuous ways that power can operate in disciplinary settings. In the US city of Portland, for example, teachers were told that they had to 'cheerfully cooperate' with the City Superintendent (Tyack, 1967, p. 488).

Contemporary accounts of inspection practices shed light on how teachers come to internalise expectations from inspectors, making it almost unnecessary for the inspector to be present in the school for the teacher to conform. Hence, while the physical presence of inspectors, school managers or other official visitors would likely spur the teacher to perform appropriately, their presence was not necessarily required for the efficient operation of disciplinary power. Teachers learned to reform their own behaviour and govern themselves appropriately, even when they were the only adults present in the classroom.

Clearly, the inspector, school manager and trustees had direct power over the teacher, given their authority to hire, pay, and fire teachers if they were deemed incapable or unable to fulfil their responsibilities. However, there were more subtle ways that power operated in the school, and these had a greater effect in the construction and governing of the teacher as a modern and moral subject. In this way, it is important to recognise that any discussion of direct power over teacher ought not to overshadow the more understated and unintended consequences of disciplinary technologies such as advice giving, supportive encouragement, and other seemingly innocuous practices.

Together, these disciplinary mechanisms hung over the teacher's head as a sword of Damocles. Inspections laid bare the teacher, opening him/her up for the external gaze of the various school visitors. Through this process, the teacher became visible and hence governable. As a moral subject, the teacher was expected to humbly welcome the advice and encouragement of his superiors. As a modern subject, as we will see next, he rose to the call to study and learn about the art and science of his noble profession.

Internal inspections: Self-inspection and the soul

The playground: A site of self introspection

In addition to being given pedagogical advice by inspectors and school managers, teachers were also called upon to engage in the study of their pupils and self-study of themselves. The dual practices of studying the child and the self were to take place in the school. The teacher was to observe children, how they conducted themselves and behaved when in school. Teachers were encouraged to learn to talk and associate with their pupils, cheerfully and with great pleasure. There were a number of strategies to help teachers better understand the nature of the child; the best being to take part in their occupations, activities, and games. Inspectors were urged to pay attention to whether teachers took advantage of such opportunities to become companions with their pupils through play and other friendly activities (Committee of Council, 1841; Symons, 1854; Salzmann, 1852).

The playground where the child's character, dispositions and feelings were most apparent provided the best setting for the teacher to understand thoroughly the true inner nature and future character of the developing child. One contemporary explained that:

> the teacher should not only see the child while under the restraint of school discipline, but should be able to observe the natural flow of his passions, as exhibited in his boyish gambols. And hence arises the necessity of the play-ground, as a concomitant of every school-establishment (Harris, 1848, p. 37).

Another schoolmaster reflected on the significance of the playground for his profession. 'The playground,' he wrote, 'without the teacher is...the engine without the engineer. If you have strength, join in your children's games, and teach them games; it is not beneath the teacher to play with the children...We ought not to be above doing it – nay, it is a branch of our calling, and a truly important one, never to be neglected' (Anon, 1848d, p. 194).

To this end, teacher training candidates were evaluated on their knowledge about the playground. At Stockwell College for School-mistresses, for instance, candidates were asked to explain the advantages of having a playground attached to the school on their final examination. The playground, the arena that Stow (1853) called the 'uncovered school,' provided the teacher not only with a setting for understanding the child, but the best opportunities for moral training. An 1840 Chartist pamphlet made this point clearly:

> While much moral instruction may be conveyed in the school-room, the play-ground will be found the best place for *moral training*; where all [the pupil's] faculties will be active, and when their dispositions and feelings will all be displayed in a different manner than when they are in the school-room, where silence, order and discipline should prevail. But when in the playground, the teacher should incite them to amusement and activity, in order to develop their characters (Lovett, 1840, p. 98).

Moral training, the making of the child as a self-governing moral individual, mirrored the work the teacher was to do on himself. This would involve deep and careful reflection on the meaning of human nature in the context of the lives of his pupils and of his own life. The teacher was reminded that there was much work to be done on the self:

> Keep and watch *your own* hearts, and then you will speedily become familiar with the hearts of others, without knowing which, you may lose some of the finest and the most delicate opportunities of accomplishing your great end, and may even break some of the fibres which you might otherwise have succeeded in winding round the truth and God (Viney, 1854, p. 223).

The inward search for self-knowledge was at the heart of the teaching process. 'Self-knowledge' wrote one author, 'requires that we should know ourselves in relation to the three states of our existence, – the past, the present, and the future' (Anon, 1854, p. 211). A part of this process necessitated that teachers recall and reflect upon the early years of their own childhood in order to better understand their young charges. In doing so, the teacher would likely realise that their pupils act and think the way they themselves had behaved and thought when they were younger (Harris, 1848; Salzmann, 1852).

Studying and governing the soul

Once the teacher had examined and reflected upon their own lives and lives of their pupils, they would be better equipped to look inside the inmost thoughts of their own souls and come to understand the human condition. True knowledge would come to mean understanding the soul of the child and one's own soul. The teacher needed to look deep within himself to understand his own strengths and weaknesses. Anyone who lacked strength, clarity of thought, tranquillity, and cheerfulness would realise through this reflective practice that the cause lay with the defective state of their soul (Anon, 1858; Salzmann, 1852).

The study of human intellectual and moral nature was ultimately bound up with this understanding of the human soul. Nineteenth century educationists interchanged the use of the words mind, body, soul and self. For instance, statements about defects in the body were sometimes made in relation to the state of the soul, and vice versa. In other examples, the soul was akin to the mind, and references were made to the need for knowledge to reside deep within the soul (Drew, 1856; Tate, 1857).

This suggests the breaking down of the traditional dualism between the mind and the body. The body and the mind were viewed as being captured within the soul. In effect, the soul was positioned as the self; constituted and regulated by the disciplinary technologies that acted on and shaped it. The soul then emerges as a new domain for observation, calculation and control. Challenging the mind/body dualism, the soul becomes 'the prison of the body', pointing to the ways that disciplinary technologies condition how we feel and act towards ourselves (Rose, 1989, p. 147).

The teacher's attention was to be directed towards the needs of the soul for knowledge, and then developing its faculties. Indeed, like the mind and body, once the soul was understood, it could be acted upon and regulated. Studying human nature would provide the teacher with the means by which first to understand and then regulate and control the soul. The ultimate aim was to constitute the self-regulating or self-governing soul in both the pupil and the self, which could best be achieved through self-understanding and then by developing an attachment between the soul of the teacher and the soul of the child (Drew, 1856; Salzmann, 1852; Tate, 1857).

Constituting the self as a moral subject

Indeed, teachers and their souls would come to be shaped and regulated through processes of self-reflection, study, and play. According to Foucault (2000c), such processes and practices 'permit individuals to effect by their own means, or with the help of others, a certain number of operations on their own bodies and souls, thoughts, conduct, and way of being, so as to transform themselves in order to attain a certain state of happiness, purity, wisdom, perfection, or immorality' (p. 255).

As a modern subject, the teacher internalised and acted upon the call to understand the philosophic and scientific basis of human nature, through close study of the child at play and intensive practices of self-reflection. In addition, as outlined in Chapter 5, teachers were to engage in the study and reflection of the principles and practices of his profession through formal training and participation in shorter summer or harvest school course work. Through careful, rational and objective study, both outside and within the school, the teacher would come to understand the relationship between human nature, pedagogic principles and his own daily practice.

However, these learning processes were not simply means by which the teacher could become a learned, cultivated, professional Modern Teacher. Many of these same practices operated to shape the moral conduct of the pupil and teacher. Moral training depended upon the study of the child and of the self, and then on the internalisation of techniques of self-governance. Together, the teacher and pupil would learn how to govern the moral self, guaranteeing the smooth and efficient operation of power in the classroom. Both would be constituted as subjects of moral conduct, not solely by what 'others' did to them (inspectors, managers or trustees), but through internalised, self-governing practices. Moreover, this illustrates the mirroring interplay between the teacher's work on his pupils to instruct them as subjects of moral conduct, and the work carried out on the self.

The making and shaping of the teacher as subject involved positioning the self as child. Hence, the teacher was incited to become child-like, by playing and interacting with the children's activities in the school, and to reflect upon his own childhood. By becoming a child once again, the teacher would be better positioned to understand fully human nature. The process went further however, as the teacher not only became like a child but also one with the child. Through study, play, and reflection, the teacher and pupil were to become one mind, one soul, one entity; fused together through technologies of moral conduct.

Self-reflection was central to this process. The Victorian teacher was called upon to 'Know Thyself' and to achieve this goal through a series of practices of the self including daily reading and reflecting. Experienced teachers were encouraged to reflect upon their teaching and subject matter, take the time to record daily thoughts, and engage in further self-improvement. 'However accomplished a schoolmaster may be,' wrote one English educationist, 'he will find upon testing his knowledge in practice, that there are points which have escaped his attention, and depths which he has failed to explore' (Anon, 1850c, p. 106).

Teachers were warned that the process of engaging in self-reflection would be difficult and necessitate a certain sense of humility and faithfulness:

> You must, with impartial rigour, casting aside all vanity and self-gratulation [sic], search into your course of instruction and its various parts; and throw aside, without a regret, all unsuitable matter, all bad method, although it may have become so familiarized by use as to be almost attractive. This task of self-scrutiny you will find a hard one...It will require...not only much right principle, but much moral courage (Anon, 1850c, p. 107).

However, there were rewards for teachers who were humble enough to reflect upon themselves. Study and daily reflection upon one's work would assist teachers to know and understand their subject matter, pupils, and the principles of teaching and learning. A teacher who did not engage in conscientious study and self-reflection would be incapable of providing his/her pupils with a good education.

These practices were not only technologies that constituted the self, but they were also techniques of control and regulation. Study, self-reflection, reading, and writing produced the self-governing teacher, who learned to internalise expectations of the meaning of the good teacher. Analysing these technologies of the self does not mean accepting at face value the knowledge that teachers were expected to have of themselves, their work, and their pupils. Rather, they are problematised as 'truth games' that enabled teachers to constitute themselves as moral subjects (Foucault, 2000b, p. 263).

Conclusion

This chapter has presented the making of the teacher as a modern and moral subject within the disciplinary space of the school. The school was transformed from a quasi-autonomous, flexible and shifting site negotiated between parents, the community and the teacher to a disciplinary space where a heterogeneous web of external and internal technologies worked themselves out on the mind, body and soul of the teacher.

This account has been concerned with understanding the conditions that make certain sets of practices seem normal and acceptable at particular places and times. By claiming that inspectors and other school visitors were teachers' friends and confidantes, a regime of inspection technologies, albeit subtle and diffuse, could be established that would come to be viewed as normal. As Foucault (1991) states, these practices, 'possess up to a point their own specific regularities, logic, strategy, self-evidence and "reason". It is a question of analysing a "regime of practices" – practices being understood...as places where what is said and what is done, rules imposed and reasons given, the planned and the taken for granted meet and interconnect' (p. 75).

Within the disciplinary regime of the school, there were two types of technologies. External technologies worked through inspectors, school managers and other official school visitors. These individuals sought to shape the teacher through power that was both sovereign and disciplinary. However, while the (sovereign) power to certify, hire, pay and dismiss teachers, appears to be a more vigorous tool to control teachers, there were other effective diffuse disciplinary mechanisms at work in the school. Giving advice and the collection of data about the teacher also subtly shaped the type of teacher considered most appropriate for educating Victorian children.

In this chapter, I also looked at internal technologies (or technologies of the self) to understand the ways in which teachers would have come to experience themselves as modern and moral subjects. Technologies of the self are constituted by the norms, values and expectations that individuals have of themselves. They include the intentional or voluntary means by which individuals seek to question, think about and understand themselves, and as a consequence shape and change their own thoughts, bodies, souls and general mode of being to fit a desired norm.

Together both external and internal technologies operated to make and govern the teacher as subject. For example, it was not only the inspector's annual visit that caused teachers to conform to official expectations, but anticipation of the visit that acted as a stimulus to conformity. As expectations, norms and values concerning what it meant to be a good teacher were internalised by teachers, many external technologies became technologies of the self.

Hence, while teachers may very well have carried on their everyday activities without interruption from outsiders, the anticipation of the arrival of the inspector, manager could act as a sufficient disciplinary control to ensure compliance to a set of norms, values and expectations. This is where external technologies of power and internal technologies of the self intertwine. Teachers became subject to a whole variety of new regulatory practices, including the gaze of the other, and their internalised values and expectations, in this new regime of truth.

This is power exercised through an impersonal, invisible and total gaze; a gaze not always physically present in the body of the school visitor, but always present in the mind of the teacher. For this type of disciplinary power to operate effectively, the subject must be seen. Hence, the teacher becomes known and visible through these practices. This relationship of visibility and invisibility is reciprocal. For the subject to be disciplined, s/he must be visible to the disciplinary gaze and know that this is so; while concomitantly, the gaze must be invisible so that it remains effective even when it is not directed towards him (Foucault, 1977). However, the gaze is not solely an external technology, but one that the teacher directs towards his own self or soul.

The second half of this chapter examined how teacher came to recognise themselves as moral subjects in conjunction with a set of technologies of the self. Through study of the child, especially in the playground, the teacher would be able to understand true human nature and come up with the most appropriate strategies for the development of the child as a moral and obedient individual. To do this, the teacher was incited to become a child again himself, play with his pupils, engage in their games and activities, and reflect upon what it was like to be young. These practices, in addition to formal study of the philosophic and pedagogic principles of their profession, would enable the teacher to know both the pupil-child and their own self-child. The Moral and Modern Teacher was therefore a self-regulating subject, as were the pupils in their schools. Both would become one unified self-governing soul, subjected to others (the pupil to the teacher; the teacher to the inspector, manager, trustee, etc.) and subject to oneself.

In shifting the analysis from the sovereign power located within the hands of certain individuals or institutions to the effects of disciplinary power, we can see the more subtle ways in which a particular type of teacher-subject was constituted. This is not a study of the *powerful* inspector, trustee/manager or school visitor, but of the *power-full* school room. Here in the school, where power circulated and was exercised, the teacher as a Modern and Moral subject was constituted and governed. These processes were also played out in another site, the training college, which is the topic of the next chapter.

Notes

1   There is evidence that slaves formed clandestine schools on plantations and slave masters allowed some oral education of slaves. However, up until 1830, slaves were completely excluded from formal educational institutions (Green, 1990).

2   The instructions to the first two appointed inspectors in England made this clear:

> You will therefore be careful, at visits of inspection to communicate with the parochial clergyman, or other minister of religion, connected with the school, and with the school committee, or…the chief promoter of the school, and will explain to them, that the one main object of your visit is to afford them your assistance in all efforts for improvement in which they may desire your aid; but that you are in no respect to interfere with the instruction, management or discipline of the school, or to press upon them any suggestions which they may be disinclined to receive (Committee of Council, 1841, p. 1).

3   Following basic identification questions about the teacher and school, the report contained 16 sections including: Tenure and Site of Building; Mechanical Arrangements; Religious and Moral Discipline; Means of Instruction; Organisation and Discipline; As Respects Rewards and Punishments; As Respects Method; Simultaneous or Mixed Method; Mutual Instruction and Mixed Method; Monitors and Pupil Teachers; Attendance, Registers, etc; Schoolmaster and Schoolmistress; Government of the School; Annual Income; and Annual Expenditure (Committee of Council, 1841, pp. 12–21).

7
Training Institutions as Sites of Disciplinary Control

From its first establishment this institution [has] been conducted on...a system eminently vigorous in its operation...The students are allowed no time to reflect on the difficulties of the path on which they are entering – they must *advance* in it...A state of constant mental activity...greatly aids in the maintenance of its discipline...To the right discipline of such an institution there is further required a regular and punctual adherence to whatever rules may have been prescribed for the government of it, the scrupulous observance of such as are conventional, the utmost consideration in all personal relations, and a just, impartial, and temperate use of the means of reproof and encouragement (Committee of Council, 1847, p. 408).

Every single aspect of students' lives was controlled and regulated within the Victorian teacher training colleges, such as St. John's at Battersea in London described in the quotation above. In these institutions, the student-teacher was governed and shaped as a good, moral teacher. This chapter and the next show how the Victorian teacher was constructed as an object and subject of power through a set of disciplinary technologies that operated within teacher training institutions. In this chapter, we will see how the teacher's character and body were shaped and regulated through admissions policies, timetabling, rules and regulations, and dress and drill policies and practices. Normalisation and disciplinary strategies in the colleges worked themselves out on the character and body of the teacher to construct teacher candidates as docile inmates. We begin with an overview of the teacher training institutions that were established during the Victorian period in England and abroad, and then take a look at the precise ways that teachers-in-training were shaped and governed through their experiences in these institutions. The focus again is on the Victorian teacher in England, but reference is made to similar practices and policies in normal schools in Europe and North America.

Overview of teacher training institutions: England and abroad

Formal teacher training had its roots in Europe in the early eighteenth century with the establishment of normal schools to prepare elementary school teachers. The term 'normal' stems from the Latin word 'norm' meaning 'rule', illustrating the role of these institution in instructing in the rules and principles of education. Its use was first adopted in Prussia, and then subsequently adopted in Switzerland and France. By the start of the Victorian period, there were 75 normal schools in France and over 100 in Prussia, and even elementary school teachers had training that lasted several years.

In contrast, prior to the 1830s there were very few formal, state-funded options for the training of teachers in the UK and North America. In both England and North America, there were some opportunities for aspiring teachers to learn the monitorial or Lancasterian method through short, intensive sessions in model schools or in centres attached to schools of experienced teachers. However, with the discrediting of the monitorial system and growing interest in progressive pedagogical principles and methods based on the Prussian model, reformers and educational promoters across the UK, Europe and North America began to push for the development of other formal teacher training institutions. Public inquiries, official reports and speeches, and newspaper articles claimed that the greatest problem facing prospects for the spread of compulsory education was the want of properly trained and certified teachers. In response to this clear need, educational reformers promoted the establishment of state-funded, formal teacher training (Herbst, 1989).

In 1839, the government in England disbursed a £10,000 grant for the erection of training institutions to the two voluntary religious societies who had been operating their own teacher training colleges. From that period onwards, under the stimulus of further grants, the number of training colleges multiplied. The National Society established three training institutions in London: St. John's (Battersea) in 1840; and a year later, St. Mark's and Whitelands Training Institutions at Chelsea, for schoolmasters and mistresses respectively. By 1845, the

National Society operated 22 training colleges, while the BFSS continued to run Borough Road in London.[1] The 1846 Committee of Council on Education Minutes established the principle of state assistance in the maintenance of the training colleges, and initiated a system of teacher certification following successful completion of standardised merit examinations and carrying with them state-funded salary augmentations (Committee of Council, 1847; Newcastle Commission, 1861b).

In the United States the first state normal school (not based on the monitorial method) was founded in Massachusetts in 1838. Over the next 20 years, other state-funded normal schools were founded in US states (e.g. Massachusetts, New York, Connecticut, Michigan, Rhode Island, New Jersey, Illinois, Pennsylvania and Minnesota) and in one city (St. Louis). By 1860, there were a dozen state and six privately run normal schools in the United States, and by 1865, this figure had risen to 22 (Binder, 1974; Herbst, 1989).

Normal schools were established with state funding for the training of elementary schoolmasters in Upper Canada, New Brunswick, and Nova Scotia in the 1840s–1850s. At the opening of the Normal School for Upper Canada in 1847, Ryerson explained that the 'word *Normal*, both in its etymology and common use, signifies "according to rule, or principle," and is employed to express the systematic teaching of the rudiments of learning' (Ryerson, 1846b, p. 97). Moreover, the Master of Method at the English training institutions was referred to as the Normal Master, representing 'the idea that there exists some norm or type in teaching, and the nearer the teacher comes to that norm the better will his teaching be' (Rich, 1933, p. 78). The word 'normal' indicates how training institutions operated to normalise the teacher through rules and regulations based on particular norms; norms that reflected the ideas about the good teacher reviewed in Chapter 5. The following discussion focuses on those training institution rules and regulations that operated to make and shape the Victorian teacher.

Selecting and shaping the teacher's character

Admissions procedures

To be accepted into a teacher training college, candidates had to be at least 18 years of age, in good physical health, of proper moral character, able to pay the annual fee, and successfully complete an entrance examination. The requisite qualities of the ideal candidate for training included '[g]ood moral character, amiability, truthfulness, and diligence...His temper and disposition; his abilities and attainments;

his tastes and habits; his age, size and physical strength, should all be known, as far as possible, beforehand' (Coleridge, 1841, p. 40).

What is significant about this quotation is both the list of desirable qualities of the training candidate and the fact that these characteristics should 'be known' and made visible before admission. Like school inspections, admissions procedures acted in such a way to lay bare the character, dispositions, and deportment of the training candidate in an attempt to know everything about the individual.

How was this to be done? First, in order to be admitted to the training institution, each applicant had to provide detailed information about his intellectual, physical, and moral state of being. While admissions procedures revealed interest in the healthy body (a point I take up below), much more attention was directed towards the moral character of the teacher-to-be. Moral character was evaluated through the submission of certificates and testimonials, describing the candidate's attainments, background, and moral character. Statements referred to the Christian background of the candidate, his or her modest, humble, deferential, and respectful character, and willingness to work in laborious, painstaking, and persevering ways (BFSS, 1859; Bradbury, 1975). Such practices were common in Prussian and North American normal schools where high moral and upright character was also a requirement for admission (Lemlech and Marks, 1976; Anon, 1849a).

Certificates and testimonials operated as technologies to select only candidates whose character mirrored the Christian moral-exemplar reformers aimed to fashion for the schools. Applicants were required to provide certificates and testimonials attesting to their religious background and moral character. Morality was synonymous with Christianity. Consequently, certificates of baptism in the Church of England were required for admission to National Society training institutions. However, baptismal certificates were not often considered sufficient to determine the true religious and moral character of the applicant. For this reason, St. Mark's students had to provide a declaration from their parents or guardians stating that they had attended Church of England services for at least one year prior to the date of the application. Borough Road applicants were also expected to provide statements confirming their membership in nonconformist Churches. These procedures ensured that only those who upheld in public the principles of the Christian faith would be accepted into the colleges (Coleridge, 1841; McGregor, 1978).

Church of England clergymen signed the letters of testimony for candidates to the National Society training colleges. At the Roman

Catholic St. Mary's Training College, the required certificate of conduct and character was to be signed by the local parish priest. Candidates to the Borough Road could submit letters signed by the local clergyman or minister of the religious persuasion with which they were connected. In most cases, these were non-Conformist ministers. However, letters from others in the local community such as trustees, inspectors, and superintendents were also accepted (Britton, 1964; Hughes, 1936).

Morality was also associated with the idea of calling and desire to act as God's representative on earth. Candidates often had to write their own letters of intent outlining the reasons why they wanted to become teachers, and demonstrating their aptitude for the task. Borough Road expected its candidates to be inspired by a genuine enthusiasm and desire for spreading the Christian religion. This letter, which accompanied an 1842 application for admission, reveals the candidate's understanding of this very point:

> I should be most happy to be fully occupied [as a teacher] as it would afford me increasing and widely extended opportunities of doing good, as it regards the diffusion of the great truths of our Christian Religion. All I desire is to live for the honour and glory of that God and Saviour who has done so much for me, in the advancement of his kingdom in the world (BFSS, 1841–1850).

Lastly, applicants were also required to sign declarations of intent confirming that they would devote themselves to the profession of school teaching. This practice was in response to the critique of itinerant and ephemeral teachers who did not take their calling to teach seriously. Students at Battersea and St. Mark's, for example, were all obliged to sign these forms, and to be thankful and grateful that they were accepted into the noble profession of teaching. This practice and the certificates of moral character as a condition of admission were also taken up at normal schools in Canada and in the United States (Lemlech and Marks, 1976; Anon, 1849a).

Such procedures illustrate the emphasis placed on the notion of calling, duty, and preparedness for a profession aimed at spreading the Christian faith. From the start, candidates were made well aware that the purpose of their future work was tightly connected to their roles as Christians amongst the children of the poor. Together these admissions procedures shaped the Christian character of the candidate reflecting the ideas and systems of reasoning about the Moral Teacher. Both the inner and outward dispositions of the candidate were assessed and if deemed appropriate, admitted into the training programme for further shaping and regulating. Those whose character and motivations did not conform to the norm were weeded out right from the start.

Monitoring and maximising time

Once admitted into the training institution, the daily lives of students were closely governed. From the probationary procedures throughout their program, the conduct and behaviour of students were shaped in such a way not only to normalise and control them, but also to make them humble, moral subjects. The minute regulation and breakdown of time characterised the teacher training institution schedule. All aspects of daily life were tightly ordered with one activity leading at a prearranged time into the next, and the whole sequence of activities imposed from above by a system of explicit formal rules. This precise breakdown of time and establishment of daily institutional rhythms allowed for the ceaseless and complete monitoring of students' actions, and shaping of an obedient and docile subject.

The close monitoring and use of time, practices well established in France and Prussian normal schools, were taken up in the English teacher training colleges where it was the norm for students to be woken by a bell as early as 5:30 a.m. After rising, washing, dressing, and making their beds, students had to engage in early morning household work, followed by morning prayers, scripture lessons, and other religious instruction. By 8:30 a.m. (almost a good three hours after rising) breakfast was served. Roll call for the first classes was taken at 9 a.m. and, as with all activities, students were expected to be punctual. Manville, a Battersea student in the mid-1850s, recalled the race to get to the morning lectures on time, noting that the principal, vice principal, and assistant master 'dominated one's thoughts; and one's actions, too, as regards speed, for two out of the three punctuality was indeed the soul of business' (Quoted in Roberts, 1946, p. 39).

Classes, generally an hour in length, continued all morning until dinner was served. Dinner was followed by further classes and practice teaching in the afternoon. After supper, there were more classes until evening prayers and bedtime, or what was called 'lock up' time at Chester College. Strict rules were posted in the dormitories concerning the time that books were to be put away and gaslights extinguished (Hutchinson, 1946). Such strict schedules, which were also taken up in the North American normal schools (Ryerson, 1853; Thornburg, 2004), allowed little time for idleness. Time continued to be precisely monitored during the weekends as well. On Sundays, students were expected to attend at least one Church service, where they continued to be closely observed. During a Church service, a Cheltenham College mistress, watched the female students with her 'eagle eye' to see that no one looked like fainting (More, 1992a, p. 144). In some cases, Sundays were spent attending religious lessons and engaging in choir practice.

When students were not engaged in timetabled activities on Sundays, they were to spend it in quiet solitude and a manner suitable to the Sabbath. Sunday was 'to be observed with great quietness and decorum, and all visiting discountenanced on that day' (Committee of Council, 1847–48, p. 403). To mirror a monastery like setting, the rule of silence was strictly enforced amongst the various English training colleges. At St. Mary's, for instance, meals were taken in silence while spiritual readings were read aloud. Inspector Marshall commented on this in his report:

> The great exactness of the rural and religious discipline and its visible effect upon the general character and deportment of the students, claims attention in the first place...Strict silence is observed everywhere throughout the day except in times of recreation (Committee of Council, 1852–53, p. 343).

During unstructured time, students were rarely, if ever, allowed any privacy at all. Each student was always within sight or earshot of someone else to ensure constant conformity to the norm. Kay-Shuttleworth (1862c) wrote that there was little leisure time at Battersea, for fear of 'associations formed among the students inconsistent with discipline' (p. 403).

Life at the female training institutions was no different. A student at St. Hilda's recalled that there was no common room to relax in during the day: 'such a luxury as a bed-sitting room was undreamed of...we took our spells of rest on the seats of the classrooms, sitting back to back for ease and comfort, or propping ourselves against a cushion supported by the partition dividing a long room into two' (Lawrence, 1958, p. 36).

Moreover, bedroom cubicles were out of bounds for St. Hilda's students until the evening. This was one of the many rules regarding the use of the dormitories in the English teacher training institutions. Battersea students were allowed, during their leisure hours (which were few and far between), access to their dormitories, for the purpose of private study only. However, this practice was the exception rather than the rule. For at all of the other training institutions, once students had left their dormitory in the morning, they were forbidden to re-enter it until they were to retire for bed. Special permission could be granted only if the student was ill or with another very good reason. One student at Culham Diocesan Training College recalled having to leave his chilly and comfortless cubicle at 6:30 a.m. and being prohibited from re-entering it until he went to bed at night. He wrote, 'No matter what was forgotten, what might be wanted from our scanty stores, no admittance was the rule, except by special permission' (Quoted in Horn, 1978, p. 94).[2]

Off-campus activities were similarly strictly regulated. Although students in most English training institutions were allowed to visit relatives on Sunday, it was common practice to make them write a statement describing the ways they had spent the day away from the college. In other cases, off-campus visits were simply forbidden in order to monitor student behaviour on the weekends. This was also the case at many North American normal schools where students boarded off-campus. At the Michigan State Normal School, for instance, students' time and behaviour both on and off-campus were monitored carefully. If students were caught outside of their boarding rooms during study hours, they would be reported to the principal and after two reports, expelled from the school (Thornburg, 2004).

What were the effects of these seemingly innocuous forms of control? The minute breakdown of time operated in such a way to shape students as docile subjects, who learned early in their training that conformity and obedience to the rules of the institution guaranteed success. There were very few opportunities for deviant behaviour, given that students were constantly engaged in activities and always under the watchful eye of the training institution headmaster, masters, and student monitors.

Time was not only strictly monitored, but also maximised. Time, students were told, was precious and not to be wasted:

> Redeem your time. Do not think it sufficient to attend regularly and diligently to appointed studies, but improve the intervals of time which will necessarily elapse between these stated employments. Secure the minutes, for minutes compose hours. Ten minutes, diligently improved every day, will amount to an hour in the course of a week; and an hour, thus snatched every day, will be equal in value to no small portion of a year (BFSS, 1838, Appendix IV).

Nothing in this disciplinary regime was to remain idle or useless. All time and energy was to be maximised to support the total transformation of the disciplined character and body. Another mechanism for achieving

these objectives was manual and domestic labour, a mandatory requirement in most teacher training programs.

Manual and practical labour

The focus on manual work at many of the training institutions in
England and abroad illuminated the coordinated linkage between the
precise and exhaustive use of time, the manipulation of the body, and
development of moral character. Self-sacrifice, prudence, simplicity of
life and frugality were emphasised during teacher training through
obligatory manual and domestic labour. Such ideas, advanced through
the work of Pestalozzi and De Fellenberg, were taken up in normal
schools in France, Prussia, Switzerland and Holland early in the nineteenth century, and provided the basis upon which St. John's at Battersea
was established. On a daily basis, Battersea teachers-in-training engaged
in many hours of steady and vigorous labour, including cleaning the
school premises, gardening, cooking, and other domestic duties. 'Satan'
wrote Armytage (1965), 'was never allowed to find a pair of idle hands at
Battersea' (p. 115).

While Battersea epitomised the idea of training the teacher to a life
of humility and self-denial, other training institutions adopted this
model, albeit to varying degrees. Borough Road candidates were kept
busy throughout the day with manual work as well as practical training. Dunn, Secretary to the BFSS, noted that the object of the institution was to keep students 'incessantly employed from five in the morning
until nine or ten at night' (Select Committee on Education, 1834,
p. 17).

Chester College was known for its particular focus on manual and
industrial labour. Students there engaged in building and decorating
the college including the chapel, and constructing their own school
furniture and apparatuses. Chester College students were obliged to go
out into the local community and beg for most of the construction
material. A great deal of their time was occupied in manual activities
such as carpentry, cabinet making, brass working, bookbinding, stone
cutting, painting and glass staining, lithography, filing and chipping,
practical chemistry, woodcarving, varnishing and map mounting.
Outdoor activities also included excavating and transporting earth to
prepare for their gardening work (Bradbury, 1975).

Attention to moral character development through industrial training
constituted an essential part of the programme at the female training
institutions as well. By the late 1850s, when manual labour was becoming
less common in the male training institutions, schoolmistresses in train-

ing were engaged each day in many hours of domestic work such as cooking, baking, laundry and cleaning. The National Society reported that Whitelands' students were 'carefully instructed in the subject of domestic economy, great attention being bestowed upon their industrial training; and they are also taught everything connected with plain cooking, and the preparation of food for the sick. Their services are also required in the laundry, where they both make themselves useful, and have every opportunity of acquiring a thorough knowledge of that department under the instruction of a competent laundress' (National Society, 1853, p. xiv).

As well as engaging in domestic activities, female teachers in training studied the art of domestic and industrial economy. These lessons were a part of what became known as the Common Things Movement, a utilitarian concept that gained wide popularity in the 1850s. Schoolmistresses studied 'common things' such as cooking and cleaning, and were instructed in the arts of plain needlework, knitting, sewing, marking, and darning. Their studies were replete with moral lessons for the teacher and the children of the labouring poor whom they would eventually be instructing. Lessons on weekly food expenditures and methods of cooking, for example, emphasised the need to use money economically, without haste or waste.

In 1855, Angela Burdett-Coutts, the principal of Whitelands, initiated an annual competition for a system of prizes for common things. Prizes were offered to students for their domestic work, including the best needlework, essays on the virtues of temperance and frugality, and on account of 'their general usefulness and practical skill in all household, domestic, and culinary matters' (Whitelands Training Institution, 1855, p. 2). In addition, as a part of their annual examination, students were required to submit a certificate on their work in these activities.

Practical pursuits and lessons on domestic economy were established at the female training institutions in order to enable schoolmistresses to empathise with the work and lives of the children they would teach. Schoolmistresses, it was argued, would be better prepared for their future work teaching the wives, sisters, and mothers of the poor and labouring classes. Manual activities at Battersea were similarly intended to provide male student-teachers 'for the discharge of serious duties in the humble sphere, and to nerve [sic] their minds for the trials and vicissitudes of life' (Kay-Shuttleworth, 1862a, p. 296). Moreover, engaging in practical and manual pursuits would create a bond of understanding between teaching candidates and their future pupils. Ryerson similarly justified the emphasis on practical education at the Normal

School in Upper Canada, by arguing that the object of education was to fit men 'for usefulness to that particular society of which they constitute an integral part – to form their principles and habits – to develop their talents and dispositions in such a way, and to the interests of the country in which they dwell' (Quoted in Fiorino, 1978, p. 67).

Preparing candidates for teaching the urban or rural working classes was the first of three purposes served by the integration of manual activities and industrial pursuits at the teacher training institutions. The second aim was to shape the moral character of the teacher in training. A humble and healthful character was to be produced through such regulated activities. Much of this work was intended to inculcate the values of humility and selflessness in the hearts and minds of students. One contemporary noted that domestic labour such as scrubbing and cleaning shoes at the female training colleges had 'a beneficial tendency in correcting faults of vanity, indolence, etc. and in giving a practical lesson in humility' (Quoted in Sturt, 1967, p. 148). Work was to be done for honour's sake, as the good teacher should prefer simple, practical, and manual work to empty intellectual pursuits that would render teachers conceited, assuming, and in contempt towards their social equals.

Finally, these activities operated along a dual axis to control students and enable them to regulate their own bodies and behaviour through the internalisation of a positive work ethic and respect for the careful use of time. Through these activities, teachers-in-training came to think of themselves as humble, obedient, moral subjects. Inspector Moseley commenting on the industrial pursuits at Chester College remarked that '[h]abits of indolence not having been allowed to grow upon them...inactivity being banished from the Institution, a thousand evils engendered of it are held in abeyance' (Committee of Council, 1845, p. 640).

Selecting and shaping the teacher's body

Admissions, timetabling, and exercises

Admissions procedures drew direct attention towards the physical body of the student. As noted above, male candidates had to be at least 18 and females 16 years of age, and in good medical health. To demonstrate whether they met the medical health requirements, candidates had to submit a certificate attesting to their good medical health. Applicants to English training institutions were required to submit certificates, on forms provided by the college, from a qualified doctor attesting to the state of their medical health (Coleridge, 1841;

British and Foreign School Society, 1859; Committee of Council, 1847).

Questions on these forms were detailed, indicating the interest paid to the body and physical health of both male and female teachers. Evidence concerning both their past and present medical health was required and whether vaccinations were up-to-date. In some cases, medical practitioners were asked directly whether they considered the candidate fit to become a teacher.[3] These concerns with the body of the student were made in relation to the critique of the teacher as an aged 'cripple' and reflects the normalisation strategies operating across the training institution. Normal 'healthy' bodies were good and acceptable bodies that could be further trained, manipulated, and controlled. Unhealthy bodies were deemed beyond repair and signs of weak and immoral characters (British and Foreign School Society, 1859).

Once admitted to the training institution, the body became a site for the construction of expectations, norms, and values about the good teacher. A set of procedures was developed to order (and control) the space of the training institution through the uniform ordering of bodies. Upon arrival, students were blocked together into divisions (upper and lower; first and second; senior and junior) and timetabled accordingly.

In the co-educational colleges, very strict regulations were developed to separate male and female training candidates. There was no direct communication between the men's and women's sides of the building at the Borough Road. The only exception was by a private door, which was opened once a day to permit the young women to take their seats in the back of the theatre, for the daily lecture that the principal gave on the art of teaching and governing a school. Moreover, there were many strict rules regarding social intercourse with members of the opposite sex. Male students at Culham College in England were prohibited from speaking to girls or visiting nearby small towns. The 1879 punishment book revealed that one student was suspended 'for being in Abingdon, talking to a woman, on Saturday evening' (Horn, 1978, p. 94).

This strict division between male and female students and regulation of behaviour between the sexes occurred at other co-educational training colleges outside of England. The main building for the Normal School of Upper Canada was designed with separate entrances for males and females and separate model schools for boys and girls, to maintain the complete separation between men and women. At co-educational normal schools in Canada and the United States, male and female students were expressly forbidden from talking with or meeting with one another, both on the college campus and outside of classes. Lodgings were segregated by sex, given that female teachers-in-training were viewed as individuals requiring protection and care. Boarding houses were inspected regularly to ensure that they adhered to these rules and if not, their license was revoked (Hodgins, 1911; Sangster, 1871; Thornburg, 2004).

However, there was another purpose to the separation of students based on gender and the blocking of students into divisions through-out their training. Separating and blocking groups of students allowed for college authorities to control closely the behaviour and conduct of all teacher candidates. Foucault (1977), in his account of the prison, shows how this blocking together of people and strict regimented time-table ensured that all activities could be controlled, and rhythms and cycles of repetition regulated.

The training institution, like other institutions that operate on these principles, could function more efficiently under these circumstances. Goffman, in his study of the asylum, explains how a variety of human needs can be most effectively handled in the institutional setting by blocking groups of people. The implications are that the inmates can be supervised by personnel whose chief activity is not guidance or peri-odic inspection, but surveillance. Under these conditions, 'one person's infraction is likely to stand out in relief against the visible, constantly examined compliance of the others' (Goffman, 1961, p. 18).

The key to surveillance is the large blocking and ordering of man-ageable bodies. In the training institutions, bodies were not only dis-tributed along the timetable grid, but they were also shaped and normalised through a variety of drills, physical exercises, rules, and regulations. Training college students were obliged to participate in exercise and military drills, and in so doing, care for their own physical health. In the women's colleges the primary outdoor recreation was the compulsory daily walk in 'crocodile' formation, as unsupervised walking was strictly forbidden. Female students at Stockwell College, for example, were expected to 'take exercise, in company with some fellow Student, at the hour fixed for that purpose' (BFSS, n.d.). At Batter-sea, following the example set at the normal schools in Switzerland, the principal led students in long, organised walking excursions in the country on weekends.

Compulsory gymnastic exercises were also introduced at Battersea, St. Mark's, Borough Road and at several other male and female training institutions. Gymnastics, along with marching drill exercises, which consisted of marching and Indian club swinging were all considered an important element of the discipline and moral tone of the training colleges (Rich, 1933). These practices were also taken up in North America. Upper Canadian teachers-in-training participated in military drill exercises at the normal school. Military drill (marching and formations) had been introduced into Canadian schools during American Civil War, as much in response to concerns about Canada's military preparedness, as a means by which to promote patriotism and citizenship (Houston and Prentice, 1988).

In addition, some English male training colleges had volunteer companies. Later in the century, a number of male students at St. Mark's and Battersea joined the South Middlesex regiment. Canon Cromwell, a St. Mark's student, reviewed the advantages of such a military association:

> The effect of this association with the outer world was to make [the students] more manly. At the same time, they were learning to realize more and more intensely the vast importance of good discipline everywhere (Quoted in Warwick, 1966, p. 161).

Marching, counter-marching, rifle-drill, inspection, and manoeuvres later replaced the club-drill, which had been popular at St. Mark's and Battersea. Marching, drill and other compulsory exercises were considered especially conducive to promoting the good health and habits of the student teacher. Through these disciplinary practices, students were made to take responsibility for their own physical well-being. However, these exercises and posture development were not simply carried out for the sake of developing good habits and health, order, and propriety in the training college students, but to influence the formation of these habits in their future pupils. Such exercises, according to Kay-Shuttleworth (1862a) would 'enable the master to detect at a glance the cause of any disorder in inconvenient postures and ill-timed and inappropriate motions, which is a part of the duty of an experienced master to control *by a sign*' (p. 318). Compulsory exercises, drills, and the strict ordering of bodies in the training institution can therefore be considered precise technologies to shape and govern the individual and social body of teachers and their future pupils.

Through these types of mandatory physical exercises, the individual body became an articulated and precisely defined object of regulation. These types of exercises represent the general way that all time, actions, and movements were controlled at the training institution. This is the regulation of behaviour and conduct though the precise use of time and space. Nothing remained idle or useless. Everything including the use of time, space and the body, was called upon to form correct behaviours. A new set of restraints was brought into play through the tight monitoring and breakdown of each gesture and each movement, producing another means of adjusting the body to temporal imperatives. 'Time', as Foucault (1977) writes, 'penetrates the body and with it all the meticulous controls of power' (p. 152).

The normalisation of the body: Uniforms and dress codes

Clothing also constituted part of the web of technologies that normalised and governed the body and the character of the teacher in training. Rules and regulations concerning students' clothing and the enforced use of uniforms were intended to produce humble, selfless, and modest students. Upon entry to the male training colleges, students were stripped of their own possessions and clothing, and provided with uniforms belonging to the institution. For instance, upon entering Chester College, male students were given a plain cap and gown to wear, similar to the plain clothing worn by students in normal schools in Switzerland and other continental European countries. Such procedures are reminiscent of the asylums that Goffman (1961) studied where numbered inmates were shaped and coded into objects to be processed through the institution.

Students in some other colleges were provided with uniforms, further stripping away their individual identities to inculcate the group mentality through this levelling process. During the early years of Battersea, younger pupils were expected to wear the 'Green Birds' uniform, which consisted of jacket suits of dark rifle-green and black leather-peaked caps. Students at St. Marks had two sets of clothing: one Sunday suit and another working suit. The Sunday and Chapel going suit was comprised of a black, single-vested frock coat, waistcoat, trousers, gaiters, a black silk hat, and a white cravat. In contrast, the daily work suit consisted of a round, short velveteen jacket and waistcoat, with a pair of fustian trousers, heavy shoes, a brown holland blouse and a straw hat. In addition, beards and moustaches, which were considered signs of manhood, were also strictly forbidden.

Rules of propriety, dress, and decorum, especially for women training candidates, reflected the idea of the humble and modest teacher. While there were no specific uniforms for females in training, very clear dress codes specified that clothing be neat, well-kept, plain, modest and simple. Flower, ornaments, bright colours, jewels, ribbons, trimming and bows were to be avoided. Female students at Whitelands were reminded daily of the institution's dress code. A sign entitled 'Regulations Respecting Dress: The utmost simplicity of dress and modesty of demeanour are to be observed, and strict attention must be paid to the rules of this Institution' was posted in the dormitory. Moreover, lessons contained moral tales of the importance of avoiding showy dress. Students were reminded how dress reveals much about one's temper, manners, and character. Outward finery could never conceal a bad disposition. Rather, students were instructed to adorn themselves with 'the ornament of a meek and quiet spirit' (Whitelands Training Institution, 1855, pp. 11–12).

The common uniform and dress codes were intended to shape and regulate both the inward and outward dispositions of the teacher in training. The body of the teacher was offered up to new forms of power and knowledge through the operation of these technologies. Subjectivation, according to Foucault (1980a), occurs through the practices that shape our body and behaviour. The regulation of social life becomes the regulation of the body: 'Now the phenomenon of the social body is the effect not of a consensus but of the materiality of power operating on the very bodies of the individuals' (Foucault, 1980a, p. 55).

Uniforms and dress codes inscribed humility, modesty, and docility on the character and body of the teacher. In this respect, the body, through these rules and regulations, was dominated by the system of ideas concerning the Moral Teacher. The moral effects of the uniforms was not lost on Coleridge, the principal of St. Mark's, who remarked that while 'a uniform dress prevents many inconveniences, it has in several ways an excellent moral effect' (Coleridge, 1842a, p. 23).

Rules banning moustaches and beards, and uniforms with shorts trousers and jackets for men shaped the child-like body of the schoolmaster. Not surprisingly, one student at St. Mark's felt that the Sunday outfit made teacher candidates look like 'very young and needy Curates', while the workday clothes, especially the short jackets which were the same type that railway porters wore, embarrassed and shamed them. He wrote that although, 'not brought up as a young "dandy", I felt somewhat ashamed of myself when we all marched out, as we often did, in a string, two and two, through the streets or along the roads for a long walk together' (Quoted in Hutchinson, 1946, p. 21).

This illustrates the productive effects of uniforms and dress codes in shaping how the Victorian teacher in training came think of himself as a child-like, humble individual. Uniforms, as part of a regime of truth about the good teacher, normalised the collective body of students. Visibility, through the uniform, was central to this process. A common uniform and dress code constituted one body that could be seen and therefore more easily regulated. Coleridge (1842a) explained that a common uniform reminded students that they are all on the same footing. The uniform, he wrote 'belongs to them as members of a body, not as individuals – an important distinction, which must not be lost sight of in estimating the effect of collegiate establishments' (p. 23).

However as Dussel (2001) has explained in her account of the role of school uniforms in the history of the regulation of bodies in modern educational systems, the uniform as a form of corporeal regulation not only ordered and controlled school space, but also established a classification device to individualise school children. In this way, uniforms produced both conformity and individuality in schools and in larger society. As a classificatory device, uniforms and dress codes promoted a disciplined relationship to oneself, distinguishing teachers from the rest of society, and ensuring that they conform to the norms associated with the discourse of the good teacher.

Complete and complex systems of authority

Thus far, we have seen how the myriad of rules and regulations governed the daily lives of students at the training institutions. How was the micro-management of the details of the students' lives to be achieved? Complete and complex systems of authority were established to ensure that every aspect of students' lives were micro-monitored in precise and total ways, beginning from the ground-up with the work of the student monitors.

Student monitors and deviation registers

Battersea was the first college in England to rely upon a student-monitor system. The prefect, as he was called there, watched 'with an ever-vigilant eye the moral and intellectual progress of every individual' (Kay-Shuttleworth, 1862a, p. 332). Monitors were appointed from amongst the eldest and most responsible students. At St. Mark's the first ten students enrolled were considered the school monitors. After 1850, monitors and monitresses in England were generally chosen from amongst those on the Queen's Scholarship list.

The role of the monitor was to watch over the other students in order to ensure that order, decorum, and discipline were maintained. Through this system, which had been adopted from normal schools in continental Europe, monitors would become accustomed to using 'a mild vigilance, to fidelity, impartiality, and firmness' with their peers, who would in turn 'learn subordination to those who, on account of these qualifications, exercise a limited degree of control over them' (Kay-Shuttleworth, 1862a, p. 333).

Monitors also played a role in North American boarding houses for teachers in training. In Upper Canada, student monitors, or 'behavioural supervisors' were appointed to each boarding house to monitor the behaviour and conduct of teachers-in-training. While normal schoolmasters inspected student lodgings on a bi-weekly basis, it was left up to the monitors to ensure that propriety and good conduct were maintained on a daily basis within the boarding houses (Curtis, 1988; Prentice, 1990).

In England, there were a variety of areas of responsibility for the monitors and sometimes separate individuals were appointed for specific jobs. First, monitors were responsible for keeping good order in the dormitories. During bath times, monitors lined along hallway to keep order and see that everyone served in turn. Monitors were also charged with arranging and monitoring prayers in the dormitories, and for lighting, regulating, and extinguishing gaslights throughout the college.

Student monitors kept order in the dining hall, lecture room, and during private study periods. At Chester College, they directed the manner in which work was done, and at Homerton College took attendance and prepared the lecture room for class duties. In many respects, monitors were regarded as sacrosanct. Their position carried with it certain privileges such as being allowed to go outside the college walls when alone. Monitors, in some colleges, acted as mail carriers and town messengers, taking articles from students to the local tailor or shoemaker (Digby and Searby, 1981; Horn, 1978; Hutchinson, 1946).

There were a number of sanctions or penalties that the student monitors could impose to ensure correct behaviour. To do this, they were required to maintain a record of conduct or regulation book recording misdemeanours, and to report all violations of order and good conduct directly to the principal or normal schoolmasters. Conduct or deviation registers were detailed records that ordered and accounted for student conduct and behaviour. The register system at Battersea is fascinating to consider. Three deviation registers, which were maintained by the monitors, were intended to record any errors that interfered with the formation of moral habits. In the Time Deviation Register, any aberrations to punctuality were noted by recording the precise number of minutes a student arrived late to class. The other two registers recorded information about household and outdoor work.

Each register contained five categories: punctuality, subordination, industry, cleanliness and other. For each of these headings, the monitor would assign a number (from one to four) indicating the extent of deviation from the norm. The sum of the numbers recorded in the books denoted the extent of the errors in each student's habits and manners. The final mark was combined into a 'moral coefficient' that determined which degree of certificate (first, second or third) would be granted to each student.

Each morning after prayers, the deviation registers were presented to the principal Kay-Shuttleworth and read in front of the entire school. He explained how this simple procedure operated to discipline students:

> At this period the relation which the entire discipline holds to the future pursuits of the pupils is from time to time made familiar to them by simple expositions of the principles by which it is regulated. The tendency towards any error in the general conduct is indicated by the registers, and is at this period, if necessary, made the subject of mild expostulation. Such expostulations have been needed in relation to such *precision* in the orderly management of the detail of *work* and *household service* as can perhaps only be attained by greater experience than the pupils have yet enjoyed (Kay-Shuttleworth, 1862a, p. 332).

In this way, conduct or deviation registers operated as efficient technologies to secure complete discipline and obedience. On the success of this technology to ensure conformity to institutional rules at Battersea, Etherington (1969) writes that the 'damaging effect of being known to have erred was sufficient to make other punishments unnecessary, and breaches of discipline were rare' (p. 150).

The paradox is the ostensible freedom that this disciplinary system allowed for. There was no need for the principal or masters to watch over every minute detail of the institution's daily operations. The student monitor and deviation register system were efficient microtechnologies to ensure the ordered and regulated operation of training college life. Correct behaviour was guaranteed through normalisation strategies that worked in an ascending direction, in diffuse and detailed ways.

The principal, masters, and the panopticon

While power circulated in fluid and web-like ways, it was also present in its sovereign, top-down form. The principal and training college masters played a role in guaranteeing the smooth operation of power in the training institutions. College masters were responsible for watching closely over their students. A probationary trial for upwards of three months after having been admitted to the training institution was established to allow the college staff to develop an adequate opinion of the candidate's personal habits, disposition, and style.

Infractions of college rules were to be reported directly to the principal. Dunn explained the role of the Borough Road principal in ensuring the constant vigilance of each student's character:

> It is extremely difficult for them to deceive us after the very rigid investigations entered into at their admission. During the three months' probation they live in the house of the institution, and the eye of the superintendent is continually over them, we therefore feel it almost impossible that they can deceive us as to their real character (Select Committee on Education, 1834, p. 18).

Nothing was to escape the continuous attention of the principal. The principal, it was said, should be *'wise as a serpent,'* someone who was attentive to every minute detail of the life of the institution (Kay-Shuttleworth, 1862c, p. 405). This was one of the reasons why the principal lived on the college ground with his office located immediately at the entrance to the main building.

In the US female training colleges, a female preceptress was appointed to attend to the special needs of the female students. She shared her administrative power and responsibilities with the male principal. Preceptress was a title associated with female seminaries (in Europe) and other earlier forms of women's schooling. As the monastic connotation of her title suggests, she was to be was responsible for the deportment and character development of the female teachers-in-training, acting as a 'model of upright Christian character...[undertaking] the tutoring of the neophyte' (Quoted in Thornburg, 2004, pp. 89–90).

In the English male teacher training colleges, the principal was to be like a kind father or overseer of his pupils. Like school inspectors, he was also positioned as a respectful friend of the other college masters, supporting not challenging their authority. In summing up his relationship with the other college staff, Kay-Shuttleworth wrote that it was not his desire to 'assume a tone of authority, but to make [himself] acquainted with the views of each master' either separately or in his office, seldom thinking it desirable to enter the master's classroom during a lesson, except when his presence was a compliment to the master's teaching (Quoted in Smith, 1974, p. 110).

The principal need not be physically present himself, but merely present in the minds and bodies of the other masters and students. Students had only to think that the eye of the principal was upon them for their conduct and behaviour to be secured. This prepared teacher candidates for future self-regulation of their behaviour in between the school inspector's visits. The assumed presence of the principal, the role of the monitors, and learned self-government combined to form a complete and complex system of authority to control and shape the training candidate. According to one student, the secret of maintaining a high standard of discipline at Battersea remained not only in the hands of the principal, but with the entire 'organisation of the College, the accommodation of the routine to the needs of mind and body, the forcible and practical character of teaching, and the energy, thoroughness, and consistency of [the principal's] administration' (Adkins, 1906, pp. 138–9).

The teacher candidate played a role in ensuring his/her own good conduct as well. Each student learned and internalised the importance of obedience to the norm. Self-government was an essential part of the training of the teacher. Hence, Borough Road candidates received the following instructions upon admittance to the institution:

> In presenting you with a list of certain regulations to which you will be expected scrupulously to conform while an inmate of this establishment, the committee are desirous to calling your attention to a few hints...Let your mind frequently and seriously revert to the objects which are to be attained by your residence in the Society's house. You have at once to acquire and to communicate, to learn and to teach, to govern and to submit to government (BFSS, 1838, pp. 154–6).

Learning how to govern and how to submit to self-government both guided the training of the teacher. The training institution provided a model that the teacher was expected to replicate in his own classroom. Such external and self-governing practices in the teacher training institutions were also taken up in Europe (e.g. Prussia, Switzerland, France) and in North America. Indeed, most of the disciplinary processes and practice outlined in this chapter were also in place in normal schools and teacher training colleges outside of England, attesting to the global dimension of these forms of regulatory control over the lives of teachers in training (Harp, 1998; Herbst, 1989; Houston & Prentice, 1988; Smaller, 1997; Thornburg, 2004).

Conclusion

Admissions procedures, timetabling, and the rules and regulations characteristic of the nineteenth century teacher training institution suggest that they were examples of what Goffman (1961) has termed the total institution. Goffman's analysis of total institutions such as mental asylums, prisons, and military establishments provides one way to understand the operation of power in the teacher training institution. In breaking down the barriers that normally separate sleeping, playing and working in regular life, Goffman explains that all aspects of life in the total institution are conducted in the same place and under the same single authority. Each phase of the member's daily activity is carried on in the immediate company of a large number of others. All phases of the day's activities are tightly scheduled, with a system of explicit formal rules and body of officials set up to regulate the whole sequence of activities. Finally, various enforced activities are brought together into a single rational plan purportedly designed to fulfil the official aims of the institution.

However, the teacher training institutions presented here are representative not only of the total institution, but also of institutions characteristic of disciplinary societies. With the birth of the modern world, Foucault argues that we have moved from extreme and external forms of punishment to a disciplinary society whereby internalised discipline or surveillance ensures the efficient functioning of power. His account of the modern prison in *Discipline and Punish* bears resemblance to Goffman's description of the central characteristics of total institutions, although the emphasis with Foucault is not so much on the determinism of social structures, but on the productive capacity of disciplinary power.

Foucault (1977) described two techniques by which the new invisible disciplinary power is implemented. The first is the system of hierarchical observation in which the apparatus of observation as a whole produces power and distributes individuals within its continuous and permanent gaze. Foucault extends Bentham's idea that the perfection of surveillance makes the actual exercise of power unnecessary. In this notion of panoptic surveillance, visible and unverifiable power makes the individual self-controlling as s/he is conscious of being observed, assessed, and classified. Individuals learn to judge themselves as if some external eye was constantly monitoring their performance, encouraging the internalisation of the evaluative criteria of those in power, and thereby providing a new basis for regulation.

The second technique is what Foucault (1977) calls normalising judgement. Like hierarchical observation, this also develops initially on a small scale. He discusses the role of micro-penalties in a variety of settings, not previously scrutinised by the state:

> The workshop, the school, the army were subject to a whole micro-penalty of time (lateness, absences, interruptions of tasks), of activity (inattention, negligence, lack of zeal), of behaviour (impoliteness, disobedience) of speech (idle chatter, insolence), of the body ('incorrect' attitudes, irregular gestures, lack of cleanliness), of sexuality (impurity, indecency) (p. 178).

The basis for such judgements was the norm, taking us back to the origins of the word 'normal'. 'Normal' or 'good' behaviour was rewarded while 'bad' behaviour was punished, demonstrating that the ultimate aim of disciplinary power was normalisation, not repression.

Both techniques, hierarchical observation and normalising judgements, operated in the nineteenth century teacher training institution to construct and govern the teacher-in-training. From the start, the teacher's inner (character) and outer (corporeal) dispositions became targets of investigation and control. Admissions processes operated to ensure that only candidates who possessed the correct or 'normal' character and bodily traits were chosen for training.

Once having been admitted, students were surveilled carefully and constantly to ensure that their assumptions, aspirations, actions, and capacities aligned with the institution's goals to train teachers for the moral reformation of the population. These included mandatory manual labour and practical work, physical exercises and drills to instil in training candidates a sense of humility and obedience and prepare them for their future roles as moral exemplars for the children of the poor and labouring populations. Uniforms and dress codes constituted another element of the web of moral technologies to construct docile, obedient, and moral subjects. Such technologies normalised the teacher, locating a space bounded by the set of ideas that comprised the discourse of the Moral Teacher.

Together, these technologies shaped and regulated tightly and continuously the inner and outer disposition of the teacher. Male and female bodies were not only distributed along the timetable grid, but they were also shaped and normalised through a variety of physical exercises, rules, and regulations. Moreover, the teacher learned to think of himself as a moral, obedient, humble, and child-like subject through the operation of these practices, rules and regulations.

Practices such as admissions procedures, the strict regulation of time and space through timetables, rules, and regulations have been analysed in this chapter as disciplinary technologies. The regime of constant, regimented, and ordered activities enabled the smooth and disciplined operation of each institution. Order was maintained not because the principal was all-powerful, but through more subtle mechanisms. Disciplinary power was exercised within the training institutions through the dual processes of hierarchical observation and normalising judgements. The establishment of systems such as student monitors and more importantly, instilling in students the habit of self-government, ensured the effective and efficient functioning of power. Indeed, it is possible to think of the training institution as a perfect panopticon where a 'state of conscious and permanent visibility' ensured the automatic and constant functioning of disciplinary power (Foucault, 1977, p. 210).

In this chapter, we have seen how the teacher's character and body were shaped and regulated through admissions policies, timetabling, the course of study, rules and regulations, and dress and drill policies and practices in the teacher training institutions. The next chapter continues this analysis through a discussion of the productive effects of the examination, training institution syllabi and documentation procedures to make and shape the good Victorian teacher.

Notes

1 From 1839 onwards, Church of England dioceses across the country established their own training colleges, a system which dominated teacher training in England for the rest of the century. These included the Dioceses of Canterbury, Chester, Bath and Wells, York, Durham, Exeter, Gloucester, Carmarthen, Warrington, Winchester, Salisbury, Lichfield, Chichester, Bristol and Oxford. The Newcastle Commission Report revealed that by 1858, there were 33 colleges under government inspection catering to over 2000 students in England. Of these, 15 were all-male training colleges, 13 for women, and five for both genders. Out of the total, almost 80 per cent were run by the National Society, two were operated by the BFSS, and the rest of the smaller colleges operated by the

Roman Catholic Church, the Wesleyans and the Congregationalists (Newcastle Commission, 1861b, pp. 643–5).

2   The student, Benjamin Bailey, continued his description of the morning routine:

> Oh! the miseries of those dreadfully cold mornings, when with chilblains on our hands, for want of a few pounds spent in heating the College we had to wash and dress in the bitter weather, with no possible change of warmth, before going in to study for the dreary hour before Chapel, previous to which the student whose turn it was, swept the Class Room and lit the fire; coal, etc. being fetched by another student on similar duty (Horn, 1978, p. 94).

3   For example, the Borough Road medical certificate for male candidates, which was to be completed and signed by a 'duly qualified Practitioner' included the following questions:

> How long have you known him? Have you attended him, and for what illness?
>
> Has he any constitutional predisposition to disease, such as a tendency to consumption?
>
> Has he been vaccinated, or had the smallpox? Has he any physical infirmity? Are the organs of vision and hearing perfect?
>
> Is the candidate: 1) Strong and in good health?
>
> 2) Not strong, but free from any positive illness, and likely to continue to act as a Teacher?
>
> 3) In bad health?   a) Likely to recover and become fit to act as a Teacher?
>
> b) Not likely to become fit to act as a Teacher?

(British and Foreign School Society, 1859).

8
Examining and Documenting the Teacher

Foucault (1977) traces the rise and development of a number of different institutions over the course of the nineteenth century, which signalled the beginnings of the disciplinary world. Within such institutions, a number of technologies were developed to discipline individuals through the two techniques described in the previous chapter: normalising judgements and hierarchical observation. The examination, a seemingly innocuous technique of knowledge, was one of these new 'means of correct training' (Foucault, 1977, p. 84). Another, the collection of statistical information about population groups, was made possible by the quantitative data left behind by the examination.

The modern school, like the prison that spread throughout the nineteenth century western world, was the most obvious of institutions that deployed disciplinary technologies. Schools became an apparatus of continuous examination and collection of data where pupils were transformed through this new field of power and knowledge. However, as this chapter will show, it was not only the pupil who was transformed and disciplined by the examination, but also the teacher.

This chapter extends the arguments made in the last chapter about the disciplinary strategies deployed in the teacher training institutions. I argue that the examination and grading, in combination with the wider Victorian occupation with the documentation and publication of data about groups of people, marked the shift to the disciplinary world. Specifically, the combination of two dual technologies: the examining/grading of the teacher's knowledge and the documenting/publishing of systems of knowledge and reasoning about the teacher, operated to construct and discipline the teacher as a subject and object of power.

First I review the examinations that took place in the school and training institution, some for the purposes of certification, others as a constant means to assess and regulate the teaching candidate. We will see how they became a constant and continuous part of teacher training and certification. Over the course of the Victorian period, examinations were also transformed into ritualised public events, and simultaneously shifted from being primarily oral to standardised written forms of evaluation. This shift towards standardised examinations allowed for the specific marking of each examination, a process through which the teacher could be more precisely graded, classified, and certified.

This last feature of the Victorian educational examination connects to the second broad theme of this chapter: the collection and publication of detailed data about the teacher. Some of the information that was collected and made publicly available included teacher examination and certification results. However, as the drive to gather, tabulate, and publish data about the teacher gained momentum throughout the century, more and more detailed information about teachers began to comprise the general data bank about the teaching population. These processes and their effects are discussed in the second half of the chapter.

Examining the teacher

The constant and continuous examining of the teacher

Over the course of the nineteenth century, mirroring wider changes in the educational world, the examination became a permanent feature of teachers' training and professional lives, in England and abroad. In 1846, a new examination system for English pupil teachers, students in training colleges, and uncertified practicing teachers was established. These examinations and others that the pupil-teacher, teacher-in-training and classroom teacher confronted will be surveyed here to show the extent to which the Victorian teacher became a continually examined subject.

By mid-century, teacher training candidates were subject to a whole variety of examinations throughout their course of studies. Besides entrance examinations, there were practice teaching examinations, criticism lesson examinations, and regular examination practices for the final certification examinations. During the 1840s, in an attempt to address the problem of low attainments amongst applicants, training colleges across England instituted entrance examinations (Kay-Shuttleworth, 1862a). During these early days of formal teacher training, entrance examinations varied depending upon each institution's needs and requirements. However, most generally covered spelling, reading, writing, the basic rules of arithmetic, geography, and history, scriptural history and the Church Catechism (Etherington, 1969; McGregor, 1978).

By the early 1850s, a standardised entrance examination was established across most training colleges in response to the arrival of the first cohort of pupil teachers. Pupil teachers were senior school pupils who were already accustomed to the concept of regular assessment, having been examined on an annual basis during their five-year apprenticeship in a local school. Once the pupil teacher had successfully completed his apprenticeship, he was encouraged to attend one of the training colleges. Queen's Scholarships were awarded to pupil teachers upon successful completion of an annual examination, which carried with them annual maintenance grants. Some training colleges also instituted (or continued) general entrance examinations for candidates who had not previously been pupil-teachers to weed out students whose knowledge and skills were weak (Committee of Council, 1854–55).

Once admitted to the training institution, candidates embarked upon their course of study, which included a regular stream of examinations throughout the training year. Training candidates were examined in a variety of ways on their practical teaching skills. Criticism lessons, the practice known today as mock lessons or micro-teaching, were held and formally assessed anywhere from once per month to three times per week (Committee of Council, 1851, 1859).

Practice teaching examinations provided another mechanism through which teaching skills and methods could be assessed. Generally, students observed and taught classes in either the local practising or model school. Training candidates were supervised by the model/practice school teacher(s) who worked under the superintendence of the training institution principal or headmaster. Training candidates were divided into smaller groups or divisions, usually based on the year or session of training, and spent time each week in the model/practising school observing and then teaching classes.[1]

Practice teaching was evaluated on an ongoing basis by the model schoolmaster and culminated with the formal inspection examination. Results of daily practice teaching lessons were forwarded from the model schoolmaster to the training college principal. The local practising schoolmaster sent the St. Mark's principal weekly reports on the progress of each student under the headings: attendance, temper, and teaching (Coleridge, 1842b).

The culminating practice teaching examination took place over the course of a few days, either preceding or following the written part of the annual certification examination. Battersea students spent three days teaching lessons in the practising school in the presence of the local inspector. One inspector explained that during the examination he watched the teacher and the method of his lesson, along with 'his skill in keeping the class attentive, his readiness, tact, manner, power of illustration, and language' (Quoted in More, 1992a, p. 99).

Written examinations provided authorities with another mode of assessing training candidates' knowledge of teaching methods and skills. Regular written examinations, covering teaching skills and methods as well as content area knowledge, as a form of preparation for the final certification examination, became another feature of the training college. Weekly examinations were held at Battersea in the early 1840s to check students' progress. An hour was spent each day preparing for written examinations whereby students silently answered questions written on the board in the presence of a tutor. Examination papers were corrected and at the end of each week and month, averages were calculated and entered in the examination book, which was used to award certificates (Kay-Shuttleworth, 1862c).

By the 1860s, the entire training college course of study was organised around the examination. In 1873, 27 days per year were taken up in examinations and inspections at St. Mark's. The annual examinations and inspections included the Science and Arts Department examination in May, the June college inspection, followed by the religious teaching inspection in July. Written examinations on religious teaching and music inspections were held in October, drawing examinations in November, and the Certificate of Merit Examination in December. Warwick (1966) aptly calls this phase in English teacher training the 'the age of examinations and inspections' (p. 144).

The certification examination was arguably the most important of all the examinations that teachers in training faced. Examinations, upwards of a week in length, were held at the colleges in December for training candidates and district examinations took place at Easter for acting teachers. The latter were implemented for classroom teachers who were given the option of being examined for certification without having to attend sessions at one of the colleges. Most of the certificate examinations were comprised of ten to 16 different subjects, held over the course of an entire week. The 1850 examination consisted of 11 papers that ranged from three to four hours, for a total examination that was 37 hours in length (Committee on Council, 1851).

From the time they began their initial apprenticeship, throughout the course of their formal training, and professional careers, teachers were confronted with a continuous stream of examinations. Within the training institutions there were entrance examinations, criticism lessons, practice teaching examinations, and regular written examinations. Teacher training culminated with final examinations, at which point candidates received a certificate to teach. Otherwise, uncertified acting teachers sat the training college examinations to gain and maintain their certification to teach. Finally, examinations in the form of school inspections, which need to be viewed as a part of this complex of examinations, continued throughout the teacher's professional life.

Examining the teacher: Comparative and international contexts

Over the course of the nineteenth century, teaching became a profession associated not solely with the examination of others (pupils), but of the teacher's own knowledge and skills. In this regard, the examination did not signify the end of an individual's apprenticeship or training. Rather, it became a permanent and continuous feature of the teacher's professional life. These practices were common in continental Europe by the mid-nineteenth century, and were taken up in North America as well by that point. In both France and Prussia, teachers were considered civil servants, which meant that they were carefully monitored by the state. From the early nineteenth century, there were rigorous state examinations for Prussian and French teachers to become licensed. In Prussia, teacher candidates were certified after an examination before both lay and religious parties. Standardised examinations were a common feature in the training colleges as well. In France, a national system of examinations regulated entry into different levels of state service and into institutions of higher learning, including the normal schools. Inspectors examined teachers for promotion and salary augmentation and, as in England, encouraged teachers to engage in learning through their associations and institutes (Curtis, 1992; Green, 1990).

Examinations were a common feature of the North American educational landscape by mid-century as well. In Upper Canada, for example, the normal school students sat entrance examinations, practice teaching examinations, criticism lesson examinations, and semi-annual examinations. Written examinations were held once every six weeks, and based on material covered in class lectures. As in England, they were long and rigorous. The 1850 certification examination consisted of ten different papers, each ranging from three to four hours. In addition, students spent eight hours in public examinations, for a total combined examination time of thirty hours (Ryerson, 1851). In contrast to England (and Europe), up until 1870, uncertified Upper Canadian teachers were not able to sit normal school certification examinations. Rather, certification examinations for acting teachers were first held by district superintendents and then after 1850, by County Boards of Public Instruction (Althouse, 1967; Curtis, 1988; Prentice, 1990). County superintendents also administered certification examinations to local teachers in the US, covering a wide range of subject and pedagogical matters (Gezi and Myers, 1968).

The examination as public theatre: Constructing the visible teacher

Becoming and being a teacher under constant examination entailed learning and internalising the correct methods for performing while being assessed. The concept of the examination as a performance was enhanced by the development of strategies that made the examined teacher a visible object of knowledge and target of power. The criticism lesson, a form of examination that became a core feature of teacher training in England and North America by the 1860s, is analysed here as a germane example of this particular disciplinary process. In particular, the criticism lesson at Borough Road is described in detail to illustrate the precise ways that the teacher's body became a target to be reshaped.

During the criticism lesson all Borough Road training candidates, the college principal, and the model schoolmaster would congregate in one of the gallery classrooms, where one candidate, the 'victim', (Rich, 1933, p. 101) would give a collective lesson to one hundred boys. They would then move to the lecture theatre where the student who had been giving the lesson would face a critical oral 'examination' from the staff and the other training candidates on the lesson (Committee of Council, 1860, pp. 309–11).

The criticism lesson was an innovation that had come to England and Upper Canada from the Glasgow Normal Seminary via McLeod (who became the methods instructor at Battersea) and others trained by Stow. Stow's work in training teachers emphasised initiating the training candidate into the correct use of methods through practice teaching coupled with the criticism lesson. His 1853 book *The Training System*, published numerous times throughout the nineteenth century in Britain and North America, systemically outlined the significance of the teacher's physical body in the teaching process. In this regard, Stow appears as a key transitional figure associated with this particular shift to disciplinarity in teacher training.

Stow showed how both the criticism lesson and practice teaching examinations provided an opportunity for demonstrating not only the teacher's knowledge and skill, but for showcasing and shaping the physical body. In particular, attention was directed towards the voice in the shaping of the teaching body. Stow (1853) wrote: 'The voice and the eye constitute, unquestionably, fully one-half of the power of a trainer of young. Thus a trainer's manner may be said to be "half his fortune"' (pp. 320–1).

Students evaluating the criticism lesson were cautioned to provide clear, definitive, and constructive criticisms. To assist them in this task, they were provided with criticism forms, which were intended to direct their attention to the salient points in the lesson and 'to prevent criticism from becoming pointless and diffuse' (Gladman, 1876, p. 157). Students were also urged to direct their attention to the teacher candidate's 'eye and ear' and 'position and posture.' In particular, attention was to be drawn towards whether the candidate's use of language was grammatical, 'free from provincialisms' and the correct tone (Gladman, 1876, p. 157).[2]

This concern with grammar, pronunciation, and tone was taken up in inspectors' reports and in educational journals. In their reports, English inspectors referred to careless and inappropriate use and articulation of words, grammar, pronunciation, and speed of speaking. Comments on the unfortunate use and prevalence of provincial dialects and 'brogue or coarse accents' were recorded as well (Britton, 1964). Students at the training colleges were reminded that correct emphases and intonation were especially important and a sure guarantee to maintaining classroom order (Viney, 1854).[3] Such concerns were expressed by normal school instructors and school inspectors in North America and Europe as well (Harp, 1998; Anon, 1871).

Training manuals, books, and educational articles contained detailed prescriptive advice for teachers regarding appropriate use of their voice and body. Stow (1853) expressly instructed teachers that:

> The voice ought to be full, clear, and *varied*, according to the subject under consideration, at the same time mild and easy in expressing unimportant matters. In drawing the lesson it ought to be low, slow, and affectionate; firm, yet mild, in checking error, and in giving reproof; and always distinct in articulation....No defect in the manner, tone of voice, or grammar is overlooked. Every mispronunciation,

error, or defect in stating the successive points of the subject of the lesson...is plainly expressed (pp. 50–1).

These texts and the practices (such as practice teaching examinations and criticism lessons) associated with them demonstrate the ways whereby the teacher's body was to be constructed. The body was constructed in terms of what the teacher did or was supposed to do. Hence, the unambiguous advice to teachers concerning the correct body positions they were to maintain, the tone, volume, and speed of speaking, and proper use of pronunciation and grammar.

Vick (1997), in an article entitled the 'Body of the Teacher' points out that nineteenth century texts, such as Stow's *The Training System*, focus on the abstract category term 'the teacher' rather than 'teachers' or 'teaching'. The use of this language, writes Vick, 'invites us to think in terms of their defining attributes rather than their materiality embodied particularities. In doing so, they effectively disembody them' (p. 4). The texts describe what a teacher should be according to the actions ascribed to the body and the voice. Such performative strategies shape and define the body of the good teacher.

However, actions were not only inscribed on the body, but also key middle-class Victorian values, such as respectability, morality, decency and propriety. This explains the attention directed towards the teacher's accent and tone of voice as marks of middle-class respectability. Foucault, following upon Nietzsche's concept of genealogy, describes how history is written on the body. The role of the genealogist is to expose 'the body totally imprinted by history and the process of history's destruction of the body' (Foucault, 2000a, p. 376). The paradox is that while the cultural values of history become a part of the body, they must simultaneously destroy and reshape the body. In order for Victorian middle-class values to be written on the teaching body, the body had to be transfigured as a *tabula rasa*, a process described in Chapter 7 through training college admission procedures, mandatory physical exercises, and rules and regulations concerning uniforms and dress codes.

Embodied activities provided the proof of appropriate delivery of performance. Through his own actions, whether it be concealing a provincial dialect or shifting his body position on the lecture theatre stage, the teaching body was reshaped. These practices operated to construct the teacher as a docile and willing target of critique. As Stow (1853) reminded the teaching candidate, during the criticism lesson, 'submit *silently* to the criticism of all' (p. 350). The teacher learned to perform correctly and without complaint before the examining audience, whose very gaze operated to control and regulate each minute behaviour and action.

Whilst the humble, obedient teacher was expected to submit to the watchful gaze of the inspector, training college masters, and his peers, during these examinations, he stood above them, as performer perched on a stage. Stow's recommendation that teachers stand on a raised gallery to deliver their lesson is suggestive of the notion of the teacher as performer. The 'staging' of the teacher, or teaching candidate as performer, made possible the efficient examination of the teacher. In other words, the heightened visibility of the teacher (elevated above the audience on stage) did not so much indicate his superior position to the examiners, but made the examination both possible and performative.

Visibility makes possible not only the examination, but also the effective governing of the teacher. Foucault (1977) explains the working of this type of disciplinary power that:

> is exercised through its invisibility; at the same time it imposes on those whom it subjects a principle of compulsory visibility. In discipline, the subjects have to be seen. Their visibility assures the hold of power that is exercised over them. It is the fact of being constantly seen that maintains the disciplined individual in his subjection (p. 187).

A drawing from St. Mark's (circa 1846) illustrates this idea (see Figure 8.1). In the drawing, the student teacher stands up on the gallery in the lecture theatre, dressed in a fine suit, book in one hand, other hand pointing towards the children to whom the lesson is directed. He stands in the middle of the stage lit up under a large ceiling lamp with two full-size upright boards behind him as teaching props. The audience sits attentively in crowded rows around the room watching the lesson unfold. At the back, a group of college staff and inspectors are presumably discussing the progress of the lesson. The training candidate is a visible performer, captured by the bright lights and eyes targeted on his body, disciplined within the space of visibility.

While the teaching candidate may appear centre stage and in control of the lesson, the question that needs to be asked is who actually controls this examination space? Power circulates through these transparent fields of normalising judgement, capturing and controlling the examined subject's every movement. These technologies of visibility

Figure 8.1   Examination of the Students of St. Mark's College, Thursday, June 7th, c. 1846

EXAMINATION OF THE STUDENTS OF ST. MARK'S COLLEGE, THURSDAY, JUNE 7.   c. 1846

Source: *College of St. Mark's and St. Johns Archives* (Plymouth)

make divergence from the norm virtually impossible, as the teacher becomes fixed by the gaze of the other. In effect, there is no one person that controls the examination space. The way the space has been physically arranged facilitates the efficient circulation of power through the audience and teacher.

To return to the drawing for a moment, it is possible to detect a fresco of ancient world scenes. The high walls are also lined with book-shelves and paintings. This points to the nature of the physical spaces where the teaching examination was played out. Both the criticism lesson and the model schools where practice teaching were evaluated occurred in buildings resembling theatres or religious chapels. The practice school at St. Mark's was built alongside the college Chapel in the form of an Italian baptistery (Dent, 1977). In a similar spirit, the Normal School for Upper Canada purchased the neighbouring Lyceum Theatre to function as a model school for training candidates to practice their teaching techniques (*DHE VII* 1847 in Hodgins, 1894).

In addition, the room where the criticism lesson took place was called the lecture *theatre*, which points to the performative nature of the examination space. Alexander (1977), in his history of the English teacher training colleges, writes that the criticism lecture theatre became a part of the 'mystique of college life...[and]...established as the focal point of the practical training and the normal master's work' (p. 312). The lecture theatre, which remained popular throughout the century, provided a rehearsal stage for future public examinations that the teaching candidate faced both at the end of his training and later throughout his career. Here in these examination theatres, the teaching candidate performed being a teacher before the audience of spectators.

With the audience as spectator and the teacher as performer, it is not difficult to view the examination as a theatrical spectacle. What became increasingly central to the examination of the teacher was the visibility of it all. As an open, 'staged' process, the teacher became an object of attention and subject of control. Ball (2001), in analysing contemporary modes of regulation in the public sector, describes the '*flow* of performativities both continuous and eventful – that is *spectacular*' (p. 211). This is what we see in the lives of Victorian teachers: a constant 'flow' of public examination performances that were visible and spectacular events.

The rituals and rules of the examination: Constructing the obedient teacher

However, it was not only the spectacle of the examination that produced governable subjects, but the concomitant development of a regime of rules and regulations associated with the public examination. One of the most significant features of the nineteenth century examination was its formalised public nature. Much of this was related to the novelty of the examination to the Victorians, who were curious to participate as audience members in examinations of pupils and their teachers.

School examinations were popular, public events in England and abroad. Many responded to offers advertised in local newspapers to obtain tickets in order to attend examinations of school children and pupil teachers. School examinations were often full day events replete with great formality and pomp. Some examinations began with prayers, others with a speech from an important local dignitary. Often there was a break mid-way through the examination, after which the proceedings resumed. At the end, more speeches were made and prizes distributed for the best results.[4] During one public examination of pupil teachers, a local newspaper reported the excitement of the audience members in hearing the answers to the questions. At 4 p.m., the audience was 'regaled' with tea and cake, and two and a half hours later, the examination resumed. On its conclusion, the local Reverend distributed prizes and testimonials to students who had provided the best answers, and noted his satisfaction with the progress of the scholars and passed his 'high compliment [to] the school master, for his talent and indefatigable zeal' (Anon, 1848c, p. 328).

Acknowledging the teacher's role in preparing his pupils for the examination illustrates how these events were not solely about assessing schoolchildren's knowledge and skills, but actually about examining the work of the teacher. As the *Educational Record* claimed, it was the teachers who were examined, not their pupils, during these public events (Danylewycz and Prentice, 1986). This was certainly the case after 1861 in England, following the passage of the Revised Code, when school grants (and hence the teacher's salary) were tied to student performance on examinations.

The semi-annual examinations of training college students were also public events. At least one full day of the weeklong final examinations was usually devoted to public examinations, which like school examinations were advertised in local newspapers. These practices became common in North America as well. The 1849 spring examination at the Normal School for Upper Canada, for example, took place over the course of five days, two of which were public. After publicly demonstrating Hullah's system of vocal music on the final day of the examination, the Governor General's Prizes were distributed. This was followed by a number of speeches by the Head Master, the Chief Superintendent of Education, and the Honourable Chief Justice on behalf of the Governor General. The latter explained 'how much pleasure and profit he had experienced in attending the public Examination...and in witnessing the very able manner in which it had been conducted, the practical and thorough system of instruction pursued, and the great progress which the Students had made' (Anon, 1849b, p. 56). The Chief Superintendent followed again with a statistical overview of the normal school, after which the Lord Bishop of Toronto concluded the exercises by pronouncing the Benediction.

Training college examinations were steeped in the rituals reminiscent of Church services. Prayers at the start and completion of the public examination set the appropriate tone. They were intended to strike in the hearts and minds of the students the seriousness of the proceedings. Inspector Watkins recalled the ritual of the first English training college certification examination that he presided over. Beginning and concluding the eight-hour examination day with prayers was not, according to Watkins, 'without its effects on the hearts of those who were assembled for so important a purpose' (Ball, 1983, p. 89).

While such practices were intended to create the correct attitude, one of seriousness and solemnity, they also operated to instil fear and nervousness into the hearts and minds of the examinees. One Battersea student recalled the experience of the practice teaching part of the final examination:

> We spent three days in giving lessons at the practising school... Then many a heart, which in the quiet routine of home duties would have possessed itself in confidence, quailed under the possessor's consciousness of being the special subject of remark by Her Majesty's Inspectors of Schools. A kindly word of approval or congratulations from these gentlemen assured not a few, whom the pomp and circumstance of their judicial supervision had thrown into a state of utter trepidation (Adkins, 1906, p. 122).

The 'pomp and circumstance', along with the strict monitoring of time and expectation of punctuality contributed to the orderly and ritualistic proceedings of the examination. Students internalised the significance of the examination, arriving on time, beginning their examination promptly, and writing in a serious, 'steady and business-like' fashion (Committee of Council, 1850, p. 322). Inspector Watkins was impressed with the strict punctuality of the candidates and scrupulous attentiveness to the directions given to them, leading him gladly to 'testify to the excellence of their conduct and their right feelings, their brotherly spirit towards each other, and their ready obedience to myself' (Committee of Council, 1847–48, p. 89).

In order to guarantee absolute obedience, a regime of rules and regulations was established around the examination. In particular, strategies were developed to prevent cheating, an offence that authorities took very seriously, from taking place. Questions and instructions on examinations were changed frequently and sometimes varied from paper to paper (Curtis, 1988; Committee of Council, 1856). Inspectors in England were advised to send the Education Department lists of candidates in their order of sitting to be used in deciding on cases of copying. To dissuade students from cheating, the inspector also had to warn students that, 'as all the papers on the same subject are read over together, there is little or no chance that delinquency of this kind will escape detection' (Hurt, 1971, p. 130).

Penalties for cheating during examinations were severe. Prior to their 1871 General Examination, Borough Road students were warned that any candidate who was detected bringing into the examination room any book or writing from which they could copy answers, or assisting other students or 'conniving of any misconduct of this kind' would be dismissed from the examination, forgo receiving a certificate and be suspended for three years from all examinations. The warning concluded firmly, stating that 'No exception to this penalty has ever been allowed. The plea of accident, or forgetfulness, will not be received' (British and Foreign School Society, 1871).

Such rules attest to the seriousness and significance attributed to the teacher examination. While they aimed to generate obedience, they simultaneously instilled a sense of fear and anxiety in the minds of the examinees. In this regard, the examination can also be viewed as a form of punishment for the teacher. Authorities were well aware of the negative emotional effects of the examination on the teacher. A letter to Whitelands graduates from the college head mistress about the upcoming certification examination acknowledged that it was natural to regard the examination with 'a certain feeling of repugnance and to shrink from it in consequence' (National Society, 184749, p. 3).

Many acting teachers were overwhelmed with the stress of taking the certification examination. Watkins remarked that a number of the schoolmistresses in his district were so nervous they could not do themselves justice on the examination. Two of them, he noted, 'were so unwell that they were absent during the greater part of the hours allotted to one or two subjects' (Committee of Council, 1850, p. 776).

Training college students were as likely to view the certification examination with trepidation and fear. One mid-century male training candidate recalled the six-day examination:

> Each recorded what he knew, and what he did not know, of Biblical knowledge, Church history, algebra, trigonometry, calculus, geometry, mechanics, English history, English Language and literature, grammar, etymology, geography, method, the Catechism, etc. Each read a portion of Milton's immortal work and relied on some questions relative to his own personal history and pursuits. Here terminated the

examination, with the issue of which so many hopes and misgivings are associated (Adkins, 1906, p. 122).

Given this student's description of the event, it is no surprise that the 1847 Supplementary Account at Battersea included a charge for 2 *l.* 10 s. for wine and brandy for students who were low and nervous at examination time (St. Mark's College, 1845–54, p. 12).

Such compensatory practices were rare however, especially as the century progressed and the examination became less of an anomaly and increasingly a regular feature of teacher training. With these changes, teachers learned how to learn (and perform) under the regime of the examination. Rules, regulations, and codes of conduct associated with the examination became the norm and through these technologies, the teacher was shaped as an obedient subject.

The written, standardised and graded examination

This regime of rules and rituals was related to the novelty of the public examination to the Victorians, and desire amongst educational reformers to see that teachers, their training and certification were given the serious respect they deserved. The concept of the written and graded examination was also new to the Victorians. Up until 1800, most education examinations in England had been oral. The first written examinations were developed at Oxford and Cambridge from the mid-eighteenth to the early nineteenth century. Up until that point, university examinations had been primarily oral and consequently evaluated on a qualitative rather than quantitative basis (Hoskin, 1979).

During the nineteenth century, written examinations were also adopted by numerous societies in England to control entry to their professions (e.g. Law, Veterinary Surgeons, and Pharmaceutical). The introduction of these examinations was as part of the wider, middle-class Victorian reform movement, which heightened public support for the implementation of standardised and written examinations (Simon, 1960; Spence, 1972). Teachers were no exception to this general trend. By the early 1870s, only 25 years after the beginnings of formal teacher training, certification examinations were standardised, primarily fact-based and entirely written.

Standardisation and simplification of content accompanied this shift from the oral to the written examination. Prior to 1850, there was little conformity and uniformity in the content of training college curriculum or examinations. By 1850, the curriculum and examinations began to be standardised. A new syllabus, linked to the common examination, was introduced into the training colleges for the December 1854 examinations. By the late 1850s, a uniform and primarily written system of training college examinations had been achieved (Committee of Council, 1852).[5]

The content of the English training college examinations mirrored the course of study, and in this way training candidates learned to learn under an examination-based system. The (lower) first year examination was comprised of Scripture, Catechism and Liturgy and Church History, as well as arithmetic, mechanics, English Grammar, geography, history, Euclid, algebra, drawing and vocal music. The (higher) second year examination covered history, geography, arithmetic, physical science (natural philosophy), higher mathematics, and algebra. In addition, students in the second year were examined in drawing and vocal music, as well as Scripture, Catechism and Church History (Committee of Council, 1854).

A look at the three-hour history section of the 1850 training college examination provides some insight into the breadth and type of knowledge expected of students. The history paper covered ancient, British and colonial history, while scriptural history was covered in a separate paper. Sample questions from three of the five different sections of the examination shed light on the knowledge required:

- In what ways is the history of the great Constantine associated with that of Britain?
- Who were the Sovereigns between Edward III and Henry VIII, and what were their respective claims to the succession?
- When, and under what circumstances, were the colonies of New England and Virginia first settled? How long was this after the discovery of America? (Committee of Council, 1851)

Scripts from the Borough Road 1860 Midsummer Examination provides some insight into the depth and detail of knowledge expected from students. Geography examination papers contained in depth answers, hand-drawn maps which were finely detailed and to scale, and charts of information contained precise information on each country's physical geography. Corrections to the maps indicate that the examiners paid very particular attention to detail. The history examination scripts contained lengthy, detailed answers as well, some upwards of 23 pages of writing (Hurt, 1971; BFSS, 1860).

The content on examinations was similarly broad in the North American normal schools (*DHE XIV* 1858–60 in Hodgins, 1894;

Ryerson, 1850a; Thornburg, 2004). Many of the questions on the written examinations in English and other training institutions stressed the factual and required specific responses that facilitated grading. However, specialist knowledge was valued within the context of a broader, humanistic education. That explains the combination of factual, short answer questions alongside questions that demanded deeper, philosophical thinking.

The latter, however, slowly disappeared over the course of the century with the shift towards questions that relied on specific, correct answers that could be easily marked. With the passage of the 1861 Revised Code, training colleges in England could only gain their full grant entitlement for a student when s/he passed the final examination and satisfactorily completed his probationary period in a government inspected school (Committee of Council, 1862). This led to the elimination of the more ambitious, broad, open-ended questions from the training college examination to the inclusion of more narrow, factual, objective questions.

To assist students in memorising large amounts of information in preparation for these written examinations, mechanical modes of learning were gradually taken up at the training colleges. Dry, detail-driven lectures and dictated notes 'tended to limit the scope of the most imaginative lecturer, and literary appreciation was smothered under the onslaught of paraphrases, analysis, parse, allusion, and explanation of difficult words, all necessary if the student was to pass the "literature" papers' (Warwick, 1966, p. 144).

Mass quantitative grading only became possible as examination questions shifted from being oral and qualitative to written and fact-based. This was, to quote from an English Board of Education report: 'an age which believed in the virtue of facts...and had little, if any, faith in knowledge which could not be tested by examination, or in results which could not be calculated in figures' (Spence, 1972, p. 84). To this end, complex marking schemes were simplified over the course of the century with the drive towards written, uniform, fact-recall examinations.

Different class teaching certificates were similarly based on these precise and detailed marking schemes. According to the 1857 marking scheme for the male training institutions, 35 to 500 marks was equivalent to a third class certificate and 650 to a first class certificate (Committee of Council, 1857, pp. 15–17). Such precise and uniform marking schemes would not have been possible earlier in the century when examinations tended to have been oral, qualitative, and not standardised across programmes and professions. Hoskin has written about the shift from the oral to the written, graded examination, emphasising the profound significance of the nineteenth century shift to writing, constant rigorous examinations, and the numerical grading of examination results. According to Hoskin (1993), for the first time in history, students 'learned under constant examination and for grades, knowing that they were to be examined and graded on what and how they wrote' (p. 273). What Hoskin (1993) calls these 'three little practices': writing, examining, and grading, created in the examined subject a new positive power of knowledge. Students and their teachers learned to learn under these new conditions, and through this, new knowledge systems and new knowledge selves were constituted. This shift is another marker of the beginnings of the disciplinary world.

The collection and publication of data about the teacher

The transformation to disciplinarity was signalled not only by the development of these three little practices, but also by the establishment of new procedures for the collection and compilation of statistical data about teachers. If the examination concerned itself with assessing an individual's knowledge, the process of collecting statistical data related to the desire to know more about that individual. This second part of this chapter builds upon the first in showing how the processes of collecting, tabulating, and publishing data about the teacher – alongside the processes of examining and grading – operated to construct the teacher as an object of knowledge and subject of power.

First, an overview and recapitulation of the various mechanisms that were used to compile and organise data about the teaching population is provided. These processes cannot be understood without reference to the wider context of Victorian statistical data collection within which the educational world was situated. This broader context is surveyed in the second section and then I analyse the effects of examining/grading the teacher and collecting/publishing data about the teacher. Collecting statistical data, whether of the general population or of the teaching population, was premised on the notion that governing a population depends on precise, written, recorded knowledge about that population. Additionally, these mechanisms operate not only to control populations, but also to make them. In this way, through these dual processes, the teacher, as an element of the teaching population, was constructed as a visible, calculable and comparable modern subject.

Examination/certification data about the teacher

In Victorian England, increasingly complex and detailed teacher certification categories were created to identify and differentiate between teachers' capacities. Following the results of certificate examinations, teachers would be issued certificates that would qualify them to teach and receive salary augmentations. Teachers were informed of their examination results in a Committee of Council circular containing a certification and augmentation broadsheet. The broadsheet outlined in considerable detail the 18 different augmentations that the Committee were prepared to pay, according to gender and to the Class and Group numbers appearing on the Certificate. Consequently, there were nine different rates of salary augmentation to match each Certificate of Merit: Upper, Middle and Lower Class, each subdivided into first, second and third divisions (Committee of Council, 1849).

In North America, teachers were awarded county or district certificates following the results of district examinations. This system existed alongside the normal school certification system, which also consisted of a differentiated series of certificates. As in England, salary augmentations were based on class certification (*DHE XXV* 1871–74 in Hodgins, 1894).

What became obvious to reformers and educationists was that this type of precise information about teacher certification should be made more widely available. As such, more and more information about teacher examinations and certification entered the public domain. In England, lists of teachers who had been awarded Certificates, the results of training college certification examinations, as well as students in training college by year, division, gender, counties/region of origin were published in the journals of the two religious societies and the Committee of Council Minutes (Committee of Council, 1847). In Upper Canada, the 1850 School Act developed new rules for classifying teachers. An increase in the drive to collect, tabulate and publish information about teachers followed from this change. Henceforth, the annual reports of the Chief Superintendent contained detailed, tabulated information on the status of acting teachers, including their certification, training, rank, gender, and religious persuasion. Results of the normal school certification examinations were also published in the *Journal of Education for Upper Canada* and the Chief Superintendent's annual reports.

Training college data about the teacher

This drive to collect and carefully organise information about the teaching population was taken up in the training institutions as well.

From the moment that the candidate entered the training institution, detailed information was collected about him. The General Register, used at National Society training institutions, contained information on the name, age, previous education, state of acquirements on admission (from entrance examination results), and health of each teaching candidate. Information on the station of life and residence of his parents, recommendations, and premium payments were also recorded in the register. The register also contained columns for final examination results, class, standing, certification (if awarded) as well as details concerning the teacher's character and qualifications when 'sent out', his posting (if he secured one), and salary. The 'additional memoranda' section was used most often to record the date of death. Hence, the Register comprised a total data bank about teachers, throughout their training and teaching years, right up until they died.

The General Register was one of the many standardised registers and reports that were used to record detailed information about training candidates. At St. Mark's, for example, besides the General Register, college authorities relied upon information from the Book of Application for Masters, The Industrial Master's Weekly Report of Labour and Discipline, the Industrial Report, Court-Yard Report, Drawing Report, School Report, Report of Lessons and Report of Exercises to keep close tabs on the academic progress and conduct of their students (Coleridge, 1842b).

Many of these reports recorded information about teaching candidates' conduct, attention, and progress while in training. The Deviation Register was amongst the mechanisms developed to systematically record information about the behaviour and moral conduct of the teacher in training. The key to the Deviation Register, which was used to record instances of incorrect conduct, lay in its precise use of numbers. The admissions and deviation registers are two examples of the collection of data on the teacher's moral conduct and behaviour. Most of the data collected in the training colleges, however, concerned the academic progress of the teacher in training.

Collecting data about the teacher: The role of the inspector

Statistical data about the teaching population was also compiled in inspectors' reports. The production and circulation of instructions and printed books of forms from the central authorities specified the structure and content of these reports. The Inspectorate in England submitted their annual reports to the Committee of Council office, and in some cases to the National Society or local diocese.

Up until the middle of the century, inspectors' reports were replete with detailed, qualitative descriptions of each of the schools in their district. As noted in Chapter 6, there was little uniformity from one inspector to the next, and reports tended to be long, opinionated narratives. However, it was not long before the rules and regulations concerning inspectors and their reports fell in line with wider trends towards standardisation and quantification. As such, reports became shorter, more factual, and uniform. In a circular from the Committee of Council, inspectors were reminded that their duty was to collect educational data 'rather than that of speculation and inference' (Committee of Council, 1857, p. 249). This shift to the standardisation and simplification of inspectors' reports occurred in North America as well.

Standardised forms provided the authorities with a quantitative and uniform measure of the state of the education system and in particular, the teaching force. They constructed truths about schools and their teachers. Official knowledge was constructed in particular ways, as the forms utilised framed information in line with the current view of what needed to be done and known (Curtis, 1992).[6]

The compilation of information about schools and their teachers enabled central authorities to develop more effective policies and practices for the governance of the teaching populations. The inspectorate existed within a web of new agencies and institutions, such as prisons, lunatic asylums, registry offices, and other governmental bodies that all depended upon the careful collection of statistical information to facilitate the implementation of official policy. It is to this broader context of statistical reforms that spread throughout many western societies over the course of the nineteenth century that the next section turns.

The collection of statistics: Comparative and international contexts

Nineteenth century transformations in the nature of the nation-state provided the impetus for the collection of national statistics of the population. From the 1830s onwards, national statistics were perceived as a vital characteristic of the nation-state under construction such as the British North American colonies, or in those states seeking to assert their legitimacy, such as Prussia, the United States and England. New authorities were established to classify, enumerate and tabulate subjects for the purposes of taxation, military recruitment and in some cases, political representation. The most significant of these new technologies were the statistical bureaus created by a wide range of western nation-states, each unique in its own way, although paralleling each other across North America, Europe and Britain (Desrosieres, 1998, 1999).

The term 'statistics' comes from the seventeenth century German idea of the scientific and systematic study of the state. This meaning of statistics points to the relationship between the official collection of statistics and nation-state building. Hence, we witness the use of official statistics not only to build, but also to unify and administer the German nation-state (Hacking, 1990). The collection of statistical information was similarly central to the process of unifying the nation-state and building a democracy in post-revolutionary France. Following Concordet's proposal, the Bureau de Statistique was established in 1800 to assemble and classify information on the population ranging from births and deaths to their moral qualities and behaviour, as well as data on the economy and territory. Collecting this data was also connected to the process of creating equivalences (through the metric system, unification of weights and measures, generalising the French language, dividing French territory into same size departments, etc). In this way, statistics became the mirror of the nation (Desrosieries, 1998).

Behind the collection of statistical data about the people, commerce and production of the nation lay the hope of democracy. These dreams of democratic potential through numbers dates to the French Revolution with the Enlightenment aim to free people from the darkness and ignorance of despotism through the authority of their own reason. Social quantification and scientific reasoning would allow the rational man to become an active political citizen (Rose, 1999).

The collection of social statistics was also essential to the development of the English democratic, liberal state as well. The nineteenth century framework which determined the development of official English statistics was based on the principles of free enterprise, the importance of local powers and the development of workhouses as relief for the poor. A complex of offices and bureaus for the collection of statistics developed over the course of the century. Administrative and moral statisticians remained distinct, as indicated by the establishment of two separate statistical bureaus, the Board of Trade, which collected economic statistics and the General Register Office (GRO) for the collection of social statistics. The GRO, driven in large part by the work of social reformers, was concerned about the relationship of poverty, disease and death due to the dual processes of industrialisation and urbanisation (Hacking, 1990; Desrosieres, 1998).

The concept of the census was central to the process of statistical collection and governing of the state. The first census in England was carried out in 1810 and every ten years after that. Likewise, having been mandated by the Constitution, a decennial census was carried out in the United States to determine tax and representation based on population. Debates to extend the census in the mid-nineteenth century were framed within the relationship between knowledge and governance. Senator Hunter in 1849 explained that 'the American statesman [must] obtain a full and accurate view of all parts of that vast society whose machinery he directs' and later in 1880, Representative Cox argued that 'a country without a census cannot be well-governed' (Quoted in Rose, 1999, p. xx).

By 1852, following statistical developments in Britain and the United States, a decennial census was established in the province of Canada (Curtis, 2001). Canadians had been urged to adopt the census developed by the London Statistical Society, an organisation founded on the assumption that facts and interpretation could and should be kept separate. The 1837 manifesto of the LSS stated this point clearly:

> The Statistical Society will consider it to be the first and essential rule of its conduct to exclude carefully all Opinions from its transactions and publications – to confine its attention rigorously to facts – and, as far as may be found possible, to facts which can be stated numerically and arranged in tables (Quoted in Desrosieres, 1998, p. xx).

Hence, the earlier German meaning of the word 'statistics' concerning the relationship between the official collection of general information and nation-state building, had narrowed to mean the collection of detailed numerical data about populations.

Through the invention of new quantitative categories into which people could be placed and counted, the qualitative world was transformed into manageable categories. This collection of data influenced not only the ways in which people thought of themselves, their possibilities and potentialities, but also how they conceived of society. They enabled order to be found in a capricious, chaotic world. Chance, according to Hacking (1990), was tamed and brought under the influence of a new kind of natural statistical law.

Taming chance implies the taming of the population. The problem facing governments, from the nineteenth century onward, has been on how to govern their populations from a distance. The collection and compilation of data about the population through procedures such as the census produced the knowledge necessary to govern the nation-state. The census allowed for a wide range of objects to be grasped and compared at a single glance. The population became something to be known, analysed, and controlled. In this way, statistics acted as a process of objectification, providing solid data on which the social world could be managed (Hacking, 1990).

Numbers and data connect those who exercised power with the persons, processes, and problems they seek to govern. However, these are not strategies confined to totalitarian states. On the contrary, political life in the modern democratic state has come to be linked to these new numbering strategies. Quantification, Rose (1999) argues, has a central and characteristic role in democratic governments; they are interrelated and constitute one another. He explains, 'Democratic power is calculated power, and numbers are intrinsic to the forms of justification that give legitimacy to political power in democracies' (p. xx).

Eighteenth century theorists of the police constructed this link between a democratic politics of calculated administration of the population and information. They argued that there could be no well-ordered and functioning government apparatus without specific knowledge of the population, including births, deaths, and activities. Nineteenth century social statisticians in England, Europe and North America retained the link between government and information, but as Rose points out, in a more enlightened form. Wise government and judicious legislation were dependent upon statistical knowledge of the population to be governed if society's social, economic, and political problems were to be alleviated (Rose, 1999).

Unsurprisingly, English statistical developments, early in the 19th century, were largely related to the desire to manage deviant populations. Official statistical reports from the first three decades confined themselves largely with collecting information about crime and the poor (Cullen, 1975). Foucault (1977), in his history of the prison, has shown how disciplining the prisoner involved the development of new taxonomies for identifying criminal behaviour. An archive of record keeping was developed to verify offences, judgements, descriptions of individual behaviours, identification of rank, and locations of confinement. These new modes of classification of criminal behaviour made possible the development of new civil laws and forms of punishment.

The key is that power depends on knowledge to operate efficiently. Nineteenth century social statisticians based their work on this link between the governing of the population and specific knowledge about that population. Good government and judicious legislation were dependent upon statistical knowledge of the population to be governed. The hope of democracy and freedom lay within these practices, without which the chaos that Hacking (1990) refers to would reign.

While most nineteenth century statistical developments were driven by the desire to govern populations, there were other effects stemming from these initiatives. The collection and compilation of information about the population, not only led to the governing of the population, but the very construction of it. Statistical data, compiled through strategies such as the census, allowed for the population to be constructed through the invention of new categories into which individuals could be placed and counted.

As Curtis (2001), and others following Foucault, have argued, statistical procedures such as the census 'make up' populations. The concept of population cannot exist outside of the collection and organisation of observations about social life. The census allows for the investment of social groupings and relations into forms that can be governed and administered. In doing so, individuals could come to think of themselves as particular population groups. In effect, they are constituted through the reasoning principles that inhere in the statistical data about them (Desrosieres, 1998; Rose, 1999; Popkewitz, 2001).

Statistical data and constructing the teacher

The various processes associated with the collection of data about teachers mirrored the wider nineteenth century passion for numbers and statistical precision in measurement. First (and this relates to examination/grading trends as well), more uniform practices were developed to collect information about teachers. Inspectors' reports, school and training college registers, training college examinations, and other forms used across the training institutions were all standardised and simplified over the course of the century. This change reflected wider transformations within state departments and agencies to compile documentary material and standardise reporting practices.

Second, data collection (and interpretation) procedures came to rely on the use of increasingly precise categories. There was no longer *a* population to be governed, but particular populations that could be administered in ways that were as precise as the categories within which they were placed. Hence, the development of new mechanisms to carefully categorise the teacher into detailed categories. The classification of teachers, through certification charts, training college and inspectors' charts and tables outlining examination results, details about the teaching force (gender, age, rank, years of teaching experience, education, certification status), and training college registers enabled the scrupulous categorisation of the teaching population. In this way, statistical data that could be easily and precisely calibrated and classified came to comprise the new cumulative archive of the teacher.

After mid-century, there was no such thing as 'the teacher' any longer, but a series of labels that divided and differentiated the teaching population. For example, in Victorian England there was the pupil-teacher, the student teacher, the schoolmaster and schoolmistress, the registered teacher, and the headmaster. The invention of categories into which teachers could be slotted and ordered influenced and shaped the ways that they could think about themselves, their limits, potentials, and chances in life. As Hacking (1990) explains:

> [E]numeration requires categorization, and that defining new classes of people for the purposes of statistics has consequences for the ways in which we conceive of others and think of our own possibilities and potentialities (p. 6).

Such consequences of categorising populations depend upon the degree to which the categorised can be induced or coerced to conduct themselves appropriately. This points to how statistical categories provide the conditions for the governing (and self-governing) of population groups. The forms of knowledge that would allow for the most efficient operation of power were those that were precise, detailed, and numerical. Through the systematic collection of this type of information, classification (and therefore governance) of the teaching population could and did occur.

Moreover, what these practices did was create a situation whereby teachers could be ranked on a scale and compared with others in the same population grouping. The collection and publication of data about teachers allowed for the comparison of individual bodies. Teachers were examined, graded, recorded, and ranked into certification classes based on underlying criteria. The dual set of technologies, examining/grading and collecting/publishing data, operated to make the teacher judgeable and comparable. This is one of the marks of the Modern Teacher. The development of precise charts and tables that allow for comparisons to take place has become essential for the critical scrutiny of authority in contemporary society (Rose, 1999).

Although counting and classification technologies individualise the general teaching population, they also impose homogeneity on the group. This is the paradox: while these mechanisms are concerned with teachers as a group – as the average, the 'normal' – they simultaneously act to distinguish, divide and discipline them. The contradiction is that there exists both a focus on difference between individuals, while at the same time insistence on uniformity and conformity (Foucault, 1977).

Moreover, examining, grading, collecting and codifying statistical data about teachers made possible the normalisation of the teacher. Through these processes, norms concerning the appropriate knowledge, skills, dispositions and character of the teaching population were articulated. For instance, only teachers who proclaimed their adherence to the Christian faith could gain entry to English training institutions. Once admitted, certification was at least partly dependent upon the teaching candidate's Biblical history and scriptural knowledge. These practices qualified the teacher who was religious (i.e. Christian) and disqualified the non-religious individual from teaching. In other words, such statistical practices and policies functioned to capture the teacher within a regime of norms that reflected Victorian Christian values.

The knowledge that underpinned how the Victorian teacher was normalised, in combination with the diffuse operation of power, made possible a particular type of governance specific to the modern, disciplinary world. As the teacher offered up herself, her knowledge, and skills for examination; and as data about the teacher's capacities was collected and organised into precise categories, the teacher was constructed as a governable subject. As explained above, the uniform, fact-based examination, numerical forms of grading and collection of quantitative statistical data, are all characteristic features of governance in modern, democratic societies (Rose, 1999).

What is obvious is that during the Victorian period a myriad of new disciplinary practices related to the elementary school teacher were established or refined and made more precise. These new practices, ranging from the examining, grading, and certifying to the collection of data about teachers, created new spaces of governance. In this new disciplinary world, there was nothing that could not be counted, classified, and controlled.

Conclusion

Victorian education reformers, educationists and inspectors in England and abroad argued that teachers would only be viewed as professionals and paid accordingly with the establishment of formal teacher training institutions, and a centralised and therefore standardised system of examination and certification. They viewed the establishment of systems to train, examine, certify, collect, tabulate and publish information about the teacher as new routes to progress and professionalism. These technologies, comprised of disciplinary power and knowledge, created the conditions for both the making and shaping of the teaching population in all its depths and grainy details.

These processes, policies, and procedures illustrate the way in which power and truth are connected in modern society. They yield 'truths' about the teachers, 'truths' that place teachers in hierarchies, organised around the idea of the norm. Both the written examination and numerical statistical practices, which became continuous and constant rituals in the lives of Victorian teachers, were central in providing knowledge about the teacher's skills, knowledge, disposition and capacities.

Initially, they were public phenomena, and characterised by a set of specific rules and regulations that were repeated endlessly across schools, training colleges, and other educational sites. Over time, together, they made the wide and standardised collection of numerical data possible.

The effects of the dual set of disciplinary practices, the examining/ grading of the teacher and the collecting/publishing of statistical data about the teacher, cannot be understood in separation from one another. Examinations, or more precisely, the quantitative grading of standardised examinations, produced a mark, a trace of the teacher that could be accumulated on a chart or table. The teacher became that examination mark, the certification grade, and the total number on the Deviation Register. These new inscriptions, which were collected and organised in various official reports, allowed for the categorisation and comparison of the teaching population.

In this way, the teacher could be divided and differentiated from others in that same population. What could be judged, compared, and governed was not some essentialised concept of the teacher, but each individual's recorded capacities and dispositions. Examinations, certifications, registers, and reports were all tools that made these processes possible. They created new governing and calculating spaces in the lives of Victorian teachers, as they did abroad in Europe and North America. They, in combination with other technologies deployed in the training colleges and schools, 'made up' the teacher as an object of knowledge and subject of modern disciplinary power. Taken together then, the written, graded examination and systematic collection of statistical data about teachers constituted a powerful set of disciplinary technologies to govern and shape the nature of teachers and teaching.

Notes

1 The amount of time spent on practical teaching varied. In 1855, the number of hours devoted to practise teaching for schoolmistresses ranged from 70 to 340, with the average being almost 200. Of all the English training colleges, Borough Road placed the most emphasis on practical training. Students there engaged in four and a half to five hours of practice teaching in the model school **each day**. In contrast, by 1860, first year students at Battersea had been attending the practising village school for four weeks in total over the course of the year (Rich, 1933; Committee of Council, 1860).

2 Notes were also to be recorded on the neatness, completeness, and character of writing of the lesson, as well as the actual matter, method, recapitulation, and questioning that took place. Attention was also drawn to the teacher's use of classroom equipment and his ability to manage the class. Finally, students were to assess the results of the lesson in terms of the intellectual and moral training that had been imparted. Gladman (1876) who lectured at Borough Road on school methods instructed students in the correct use of the criticism form:

> In criticizing others, avoid indefiniteness; try to bear in mind some instance of the merit or demerit that you are noticing, and be prepared to illustrate your point by referring to it. Let your criticism be straightforward, avoid carping and fault-finding, but at the same time remember that the purpose of the exercise is to expose faults and to notice merits, and do your duty with decision and firmness (p. 157).

3 In his address at Homerton College, Reverend Viney (1854) reminded students that:

> in connexion with appropriate language, cultivate the habit of pleasing intonation. Words are the projectiles – the voice is the power which projects. If possible, let this instrument be perfect, and understand its capabilities. Of all the instruments ever made by man, none have ever approached this in power, volume, sweetness. Monotony, drawling, twang, how do they often spoil even a good and useful lesson. What a marvellous influence tones possess! Have we not all been often melted by mere intonation, and are not children most susceptible to its influence? (p. 224).

4 The author of an article 'Educational Quacks; or, the Puffing System in Education' (1838) described with a great deal of sarcasm, the solemnity and display associated with these public examination events:

> The auspicious morning came, a large public building had been engaged – the bills announced that a gentleman of high literary celebrity was expected to take the chair. Tickets were enclosed to every family within a convenient distance, and their company on the occasion respectfully solicited. Such measures skilfully executed brought a large audience, and at the appointed hour was seen Mr. Filbertgibbet on the stage of his theatre, with three divisions of

his 'young gentlemen;' all duly prepared with white cotton gloves and beautiful white frills. At a given signal all rose up and made an unmentionable obeisance to the company; and then began the examination – elocutionary exercises....The examination lasted four hours, during which time the schoolmaster, a somewhat pursey [sic] man, 'larded the lean earth' by constant dripping. Everybody except a few sly old foxes who knew the process, were electrified and abundance of fame grew round the brows of the pedagogue and his assistants (Anon, 1838, p. 337).

5   The new course of study became known as 'Moseley's syllabus' given that Inspector Moseley had advocated for a common examination for the colleges. In proposing the standardisation of the training syllabus, Moseley's thinking was guided by three principles: first 'to not add or to take from the existing subjects of the examination', second 'to give the greatest weight to those subjects which are the subjects of elementary education', and lastly to 'inculcate the principle of "not attempting more than can be done well"' (Committee of Council, 1854–55, p. 15).

6   Curtis contends that it is irrelevant whether or not the inspectors erred in their reports, neglecting to complete them in full or deliberately making mistakes, which were later returned to the local superintendents for correction and revision. Educational facts, writes Curtis (1992):

> were the opinions, guesses, judgments, and evaluations of a group of respectable men, interpreted again in the interests of educational improvement by the central authority...the estimates, guesses and perceptions of inspectors formed a corpus of hegemonic knowledge. The reports were 'read' in ways that educational administrators deemed appropriate or useful in given circumstances. Oppositional voices did not make it into the official record (pp. 191–2).

9
Conclusion: Paradoxes and the Present

This book has shown how the Victorian teacher was governed and constructed as a modern and moral subject through a set of disciplinary technologies. These technologies produced a teacher who was at once both a humble, docile and obedient moral exemplar, and a cultivated, studious, and educated philosopher. Studying the making and shaping of the teacher has entailed researching a set of historical practices, which made up and shaped the good teacher. This has not been an investigation of the origins of the teacher as subject, nor has it been research to determine what the lives of teachers were really like in Victorian England. Rather, it has been a study of how particular truths about the teacher have come into being and the workings out of a set of strategies (associated with those 'truths') to know and govern the teacher.

Two sites where the teacher came to be constituted as subject were described in this book: the school and the training institution. These were panoptic spaces constituted by a heterogeneous complex of ideas and disciplinary practices where what was said, done, and expected, the rules and regulations imposed, and the consequences for breaking those rules interconnected and operated to control, regulate, and normalise the teacher. The good teacher was shaped as a modern and moral subject through what I have called external and internal technologies. External technologies operated via the inspector, school managers and trustees, training institution masters and principals, and in some cases, other community members. Internal technologies were those practices of the self, through which the teacher internalised a set of norms, values, rules, and expectations about what it meant to be a modern and moral subject. Technologies of the self, such as daily reflections, readings, study, and prayers in the training institutions, enabled teachers to regulate their own behaviour, conduct and thoughts in order to become and think of themselves as good teachers.

Through the combined effects of these external and internal technologies, the teacher became not only a target of discourse (its object and invention), but also its vehicle (its subject and agent). Specifically, the body, mind, character, and soul of the teacher were the target of these disciplinary technologies. Within the training institution, the body became an object and target of power through admissions procedures, mandatory drill and physical exercises, uniforms and dress codes. Through these technologies, the body was made docile, something that could be subjected, transformed and controlled.

The character of the teacher was also a target of technological control, both within the school and the training institution. Teachers learned the art of obedience, humility, modesty, patience, and propriety through self-study and reflection, mandatory participation in manual labour and practical work, conformity to institutional rules and regulations, including obedience to the strict use of time and space. Through such practices, the teacher as a Moral Subject was constituted and governed.

Finally, the teacher's mind was targeted within the training institutions as well through the broad range of courses, lectures, and examinations related to pedagogy, didactics, humanistic, and scientific subject matter courses. Outside of the training institution, the teacher was urged to develop his/her own intellectual capacities through self-study, enrolment in harvest school courses and teachers' institutes, attendance at local lectures and daily reflections. Through such technologies of the self, the teacher would become a cultivated, rational intellectual philosopher. This was the making of the teacher as a Modern Subject.

Above all, the teacher (and the pupil's) soul became an object of knowledge and control. To truly understand human nature, the teacher was to study the child in all her depths and details. Concomitantly, to know and understand the self, the teacher was compelled to contemplate and care for his own soul. The playground, a site where the teacher could once again become a child, presented the best forum for this work to be done. Through such self-cultivating internal work, the teacher would be enabled to govern the child and their own self.

Power in both its sovereign and diffuse web-like forms was central to the operation of these internal and external technologies. Power, as I have shown, only exists when it is put into action. In its sovereign form, power was exercised by the inspector or the training college master, who was able to control and dominate the teacher through a variety of strategies such as school inspections, the enforcement of training institution rules and regulations, and the administration of examinations.

However, in this book, I have emphasised the dispersed, diffuse, and fragmented ways in which power operated to control and regulate the teacher. The analysis of the playing out of these diffuse power relations showed how the school and teacher training institution were transformed into disciplinary sites based on the twin notions of hierarchical observation and normalisation strategies. Moreover, the final chapter demonstrated how the examination and collection of statistical data operated as technologies to make the teacher a visible, calculable, and governable subject.

Tensions and paradoxes

In many ways, the assumptions, norms, and values associated with the Modern Teacher were incongruous with the systems of reasoning concerning the Moral Teacher. The Modern Teacher was an educated philosopher and a cultivated pedagogic expert as reflected by the drawing of the schoolmaster on the back cover of this book. The Moral Teacher, as shown in the front cover picture of the schoolmistress, was a pious and humble Christian, innately patient, kind, and nurturing. The Modern Teacher's classroom was characterised by order, discipline, reason, and rationality. Joyful playing and love pervaded the classroom of the Moral Teacher. As models of an ideal, these teachers and their classrooms would appear to be incompatible and contradictory.

Constructing the teacher who was expected to reflect the Enlightenment commitment to science, reason and progress, as well as moral Christian sentiments of humility and self-sacrifice reflected the wider tensions in Victorian society. English Victorian society contained its own internal struggles (and shifts in balance of power) to reconcile faith in the principles of the Established Church and values associated with traditional society with the forces of modernity. The middle of the century witnessed an uproar over the results of the 1851 Census which indicated that the majority of the working classes were not attending Church, while at the same time Darwin's *On the Origin of Species* (1859) was published, and the wheels of industrialism and urbanisation reflected the Enlightenment commitment to progress through science, reason, and rationality. Such were the contradictory and complex times in which the teacher as subject emerged in England.

There are educational examples of the tensions, struggles and debates that characterised Victorian society. While most Victorians were in agreement over their support for education, they debated the costs in terms of taxes, secularisation, and potential problems associated with educating the poor. Educational reformers' pedagogical ideas were also plagued with contradictions. Drawing upon models from Prussia, many reformers supported both the idea of a humanistic, Pestalozzian, child-centred curriculum, as well as schools to prepare students to be loyal, obedient citizens committed to the nationalism of the state.

Moreover, as reformers and statisticians pushed for the development and spread of standardised methods to collect information about populations through the census and examinations, others were less optimistic about the spread of these new practices. National examination systems, for example, worried some Victorians, including the educational reformer/inspector Matthew Arnold (1910), who argued that if knowledge became nothing more than a collection of un-related facts that could be tabulated and codified, then its liberating and democratic potential would be lost.

This study of the making and shaping of the teacher reflects these wider tensions and contradictions associated with Victorian society. The result of this struggle between conceptions associated with Modern Teacher and Moral Teacher was a fragmented and unstable subject. Herein lies the paradox of the discourse of the good Victorian teacher. The Modern Teacher was to be elevated above the working classes, and educated to be an expert in philosophical, pedagogic and didactical knowledge. Here was the noble philosopher whose work was informed by the Enlightenment potential for reason and rationality. Yet the Moral Teacher was expected to remain humble, modest, and self-denying. She was trained to a life of self-sacrifice, prudence, and simplicity. The gentle, kind, and loving teacher played with the child to find the key to her pupil's hearts and her own soul. Love and affection, not reason and rationality, motivated the Moral Teacher.

Moreover, the emphasis in the historical record on the especial moral (patient, kind, and nurturing) qualities of the schoolmistress, against the modern (educated, rational, and cultivated) schoolmaster illuminates the gendered nature of the discourse of the good teacher. The male Modern Teacher was scientifically and philosophically engaged with the most contemporary pedagogic principles and practices. He was thoroughly knowledgeable not only of the elementary school subjects but a wide range of classical and literary studies. The female Moral Teacher, infused with the Christian principle, was a moral exemplar for her pupils. However, the key is that each individual teacher, whether male and female, was expected to be all of these things. In this way, this new cultural history of the Victorian teacher has been a story characterised by paradox, tension, and contradiction.

In many respects, these tensions worked themselves out with the feminisation of the teaching profession. As the nineteenth century progressed, with the increasing need for an inexpensive and steady supply of teachers for growing public school systems, more and more women were hired to teach in elementary schools. In a corresponding move, men were more likely to take up positions as educational administrators and secondary school teachers.

This increase in female teachers at the primary level of schooling was made possible (and reinforced) by popular conceptions about women's innate mothering capacities. The very qualities associated with the Moral Teacher were considered particularly appropriate for the teaching of younger children. Conversely, the characteristics associated with the Modern Teacher, in particular the focus on knowledge and subject matter, were viewed as being more important for teaching at the secondary level. Not only was the sexual division of the educational occupational ladder made possible by the systems of reasoning associated with the discourse of the good teacher, but in effect operated to resolve some of the tensions inherent in the discourse. This points to another area for future research for historians interested in understanding the longer-term effects of the discourse of the good Victorian teacher in terms of the more clearly differentiated educational models that developed later in the century.

New cultural history and comparative studies

Together, this comparative history of the making of the teacher as an object of attention and subject of control has been researched and written using the new cultural history strategies of archaeology and genealogy with discourse providing the conceptual and organising framework. Archaeology has provided the methodological means to interrogate systems of reasoning about Victorian society, education, and the teacher; genealogy to problematise disciplinary practices targeted at governing the teacher.

In describing how the Victorian teacher came to be constructed and governed, I have emphasised the productive nature of discourse. Discourse, from a Foucauldian perspective, was used to draw out the interconnected relationship between disciplinary knowledge about the teacher and technologies to control and regulate the teacher. Ideas and practices, far from existing within separate domains, are inextricably linked. For the disciplinary practices analysed in Part III of the book could not have come into existence without the related system of ideas and reasoning about the good teacher that were described in Chapter 5.

Similarly, ideas (about the good teacher) mean nothing without their corresponding practices. Hence, for example, the idea of the teacher as a humble servant of God cannot be understood apart from the practices taken up in the teaching institutions, such as attendance at mandatory religious services and humbling manual garden work. Similarly, the idea of the teacher as a cultivated, well read, intellectual cannot be understood apart from certification examination questions that required a wide range of pedagogic and didactical knowledge, as well as the advice inspectors gave teachers to study the art and science of teaching.

Moreover, discourse cannot be understood solely as a medium of expression. Rather, the object of this research needs to be viewed not as teachers or teaching, but discourse as an objective phenomenon in and of itself. Indeed, discursive space has become the *tertium comparationis* (basis of comparison) rather than individuals, institutions, countries or even regions. This additional shift concerns the emergence of the subject across geographical boundaries, to show how social spaces or regions have been discursively constructed in modern societies. Analysing the effects of disciplinary technologies located in discursive spaces is a way to understand and make problematic the ways whereby individuals are constructed and governed.

This also points to the rationale for incorporating a comparative and international dimension into this study of the Victorian teacher. While the focus has been on the teacher in England, it is clear from this study that the systems of reasoning and practices associated with the making and shaping of the English Victorian teacher were also taken up within Europe and North America. Other comparative research on this topic would help to better understand the spread and effects of the discourse of the good teacher across a wider range of settings, including countries in Africa, for example, where education systems were constructed after the Victorian period. Integrating comparative and international contexts into the text of this book has also allowed the reader to see how a similar set of processes associated with the making of the good teacher (including the development of formal teacher training, inspections and certification) were taken up across a range of settings. During the Victorian period, some of these settings were industrialised and urbanised, others rural and pioneer, some comprised primarily of homogeneous populations and others of indigenous and immigrant populations, some fully formed nation-states and others undergoing the process of nation-state building. Despite these differences, the good teacher in all of these settings was constructed as a Modern and Moral subject.

Addressing criticisms of new cultural history

One of the criticisms of new cultural history and the broader field of post-modernism within which it is situated concerns its disdain for notions of reality and truth, and corresponding focus on the idea of social construction. Some historians have critiqued new cultural history for its rejection of the search for truth. As Elton (1997) explains, 'it is the search for truth that must guide our labours, which is why that attack on the very possibility of discovering the truth of history is so very devastating' (p. 179). With so much attention devoted to social construction, critics ask if there is anything real left at all. Hacking in his book *The Social Construction of What?* describes the debate about whether reality exists independently of the human mind or is merely a construction of it. In attempting to strike a middle ground, Hacking (1999) calls for researchers to freshen up the concept of social-construction, and recall its literal meaning, that of building or assembling from parts. He writes:

> Anything worth calling a construction was or is constructed in quite definite stages, where the later stages are built upon, or out of, the product of earlier stages. Anything worth calling a construction has a history. But not just any history. It has to be a history of building (p. 50).

Indeed, this has been a history of the building or making of the teacher. But what about the criticism that social-construction research avoids questions about the nature of reality?

I am not arguing that the socially constructed teacher as a modern and moral subject was not real. Rather, I am calling into question the ways in which that reality about teachers came to be thought of as true. Discourse has been used as a theoretical concept to trace the creation of new truths about what it means to be a good teacher. This is not a rejection of reason or reality altogether, but rather an examination of the ways in which certain discourses were established to construct, control, and regulate the teacher. In other words, the ontological basis of teachers' lives has not been my focus of attention, but *how* it is that we have come to know and think about the teacher in particular ways. This is not simply an issue of offering up multiple truths, but questioning how is it that we come to research the world and accept something as being true.

In their rejection of the search for truth, some new cultural historians have been accused of ignoring some of the basic methodological guidelines of scholarly historical research. New cultural historians, according to this argument, are more concerned with creatively imagining and inventing the past, rather than carefully and painstakingly documenting the past. Himmelfarb (1997) decries the lack of regard for the 'canon of evidence' amongst new cultural (or post-modern) historians who have even influenced some older traditional historians 'who now feel sufficiently liberated to dispense with such impediments to creativity as footnotes' (p. 171).

Others have noted the practice amongst new cultural historians to juxtapose seemingly unrelated events, ignoring issues of historical specificity unless they can fit easily into their own discursive analysis. Specifically, Foucault has been criticised for problems with his archival research methods, mishandling evidence and careless referencing of sources. Windshuttle (1998) concludes that Foucault's histories are 'inadequate in terms of both their methodological approaches and in the way they deploy evidence and research findings, or to be more precise, in his cavalier attitude to the need for evidence to be accurate or for research to be at all comprehensive' (p. 35).

However, others such as Hoskin (1990) claim that 'despite the egregious errors in [Foucault's] history, he had that ability, or knack, or nose even, for sensing the significant' (p. 48). Perhaps this ability to draw significant theoretical conclusions from the study of the past can compensate for substandard scholarship. I do not agree though. For this book, I carried out detailed archival and secondary research on education, teachers and teaching, and then turned to new cultural history to help me make sense of my data. This process allowed me to understand better a past history of teachers and teaching, and provoke me to think more deeply about the present.

Connecting the past to the present

A few years ago, I began pondering the problematic of new forms of regulation and control over teachers. This led me to think further about the types of teachers that we want for our schools today. This study began in the present with my own experiences as a teacher in

England, Canada and the United States. Over my ten years of teaching I noticed a shift to reforms based on notions such as accountability, performance, standards and standardisation, choice and competition. Strangely (to me), this language seemed more indicative of business-based models to improve the effectiveness and efficiency of the private sector, rather than models to reform education. However, they have been widely taken up as taken-for-granted solutions to improving the quality of education, teachers and teaching. Among these include the development of professional and ethical standards and establishing more rigorous procedures for teacher certification and licensing. We have also seen the establishment of a range of mechanisms for evaluating and monitoring teachers such as inspections, threshold assessments, teacher testing, performance-based appraisals and capability procedures. Reforms based on accountability, audit and quality assurance models have also been taken up in pre-service (initial) and in-service (continuing) teacher education programs.

In some ways, there are links between the Victorian discourse of the good teacher and contemporary notions of the good teacher. The Victorians established or enhanced the key practices associated with the making of the good teacher, including teacher training institutions, and formal processes for certifying, inspecting and examining teachers. These are still with us today. However, while teachers are still targets of regulatory control through these practices, the basic notions of what it means to be a good teacher have changed considerably. In place of the good Victorian teacher who was a philosophic, intellectual and pious, moral exemplar, today's good teacher is an accountable, efficient, technologically-savvy professional. Indeed, we hear little about love and literary pursuits in today's discourse of the good teacher.

It was my reservations about contemporary notions about the good teacher and related forms of disciplinary control that took me out of the secondary school classroom and into the archives of the past. There was little assumption throughout my study that the past would in some way hold the key to fixing or correcting the problems of the present by providing a prescription for change. Nor did I think that the past would provide a continuous link to the present day playing out of power relations in schools, teacher education institutions, and other educational settings.

However, I believe that the type of theorising that I have engaged in is valuable in deepening our understanding not only of the past, but also of our present. In describing a set of discourses related to education and the teacher, discourses that differ from those that are played out today, it is possible to see how systems of ideas and practices can and do change. The ways that we have come to reason about teachers today (as being accountable, efficient and effective) are different from the ways that Victorians thought, spoke, and wrote about teachers. In questioning how certain historical discourses shaped and created systems of reasoning that were thought of as truth, it becomes possible to see how contemporary discourses also produce regimes of truth that come to be viewed as normal.

In this way, new cultural history challenges fatalistic determinism and helps to shake up our taken-for-granted assumptions about contemporary educational discourses. As Rose (1999) writes, the task of inquiry is to disturb 'that which forms the groundwork of the present, to make once more strange and to cause us to wonder how it came to appear so natural' (p. 58). In this way, I have engaged in a history of the present.

New alternative options and possibilities for change arise by underscoring the historical specificity and contesting the normalising discourses of what it means to be a teacher, and how we go about recruiting, educating, hiring and retaining teachers for our schools today. For those engaged in contemporary educational reform, it is beneficial to recall that conceptions of the good teacher, the good school, and more broadly the good education system, can and do change. This is not a new insight. Almost 40 years ago, the educational historian Simon (1966) reminded us that 'there can be no more liberating influence than the knowledge that things have not always been so and need not remain as they are' (p. 91).

Similarly, following this same line of argument, writing, researching, and reflecting about this book highlights for me the possibilities for alternative research methods and strategies. Making visible the assumptions, practices, processes and rules that structure our research enables the opening up of new possibilities for historical and comparative education research. In this way, new cultural history plays multiple roles in deconstructing certainties about the past, problematising the ways that truth has been constructed, and presenting alternative methodological and theoretical strategies.

This book is an attempt to open up new paradigmatic possibilities for educational research, by questioning some of the self-evident assumptions, certainties and expectations about what is considered appropriate, valid and objective research. Modernist assumptions are behind the practical, policy-oriented focus of much educational research. The expectation to include a final paragraph on the practical implications of theorising stems from these assumptions and the critique that new cultural history privileges theory over action. Research that neglects to carry out such emancipatory aims is viewed as being somewhat less legitimate and valid.

However, while this conclusion does not offer a clear-cut agenda for change or blueprint for good teaching, it does provide a way for thinking differently and outside of old limits, rather than legitimating what is already known. The task of the new cultural historian is to show how the words and things that we have come to accept as self-evident do not have to be accepted as such. Criticism is essential for social change, for as soon as it is possible to think, see, and write about things differently from other places and times, transformation becomes both immediately necessary and completely possible (Foucault, 1988). It is within this space that we can begin to think differently, more openly and attentively, about the kind of teachers we want for our schools today.

Bibliography

Adkins, T. (1906) *The Story of St. John's College, Battersea: The Story of a Notable Experiment*. London, National Society.

Albisetti, J. C. (1993) 'The feminization of teaching in the nineteenth century: A comparative perspective'. *History of Education*, 22(3), 253–62.

Aldrich, R. (1995) *School and Society in Victorian Britain*. London, Garland.

Alexander, J. L. (1977) *Collegiate Teacher Training in England and Wales: A Study in the Historical Determinants of Educational Provision and Practice in the Mid-Nineteenth Century*. Unpublished PhD thesis, London, University of London.

Althouse, J. G. (1967) *The Ontario Teacher: A Historical Account of Progress, 1800–1910*. Toronto, Ontario Teachers' Federation.

Anon (1838) 'Educational quacks; or, the puffing system in education'. *Educational Magazine: New Series*, I (October), 337.

Anon (1839) 'Papers on Education [on the establishment of Privy Council Committee]'. *Parliamentary Papers*, XLI, 255–9.

Anon (1840) 'Aphorisms'. *Educational Magazine (New Series)*, II (August), 113.

Anon (1847) 'Royal Commission to inquire into the state of education in the counties of Carmarthen, Glamorgan, and Pembroke'. *Parliamentary Papers*, XXVII, 1, 3–500.

Anon (1848a) 'Religion the basis and end of education'. *Quarterly Educational Magazine and Record of the Home and Colonial School Society*, I, 105.

Anon (1848b) 'The importance of selecting good teachers'. *Journal of Education for Upper Canada*, 1 (March), 87.

Anon (1848c) 'Questions proposed at the annual inspection of the training college, Battersea', 1848. *English Journal of Education*, II, 292.

Anon (1848d) 'How to make teaching agreeable'. *Quarterly Educational Magazine and Record of the Home and Colonial School Society*, I, 318–23.

Anon (1849a) 'Terms of admission into the normal school for Upper Canada'. *Public Archives of Ontario*, Series RG 2-12.

Anon (1849b) 'Rules for teachers'. *Journal of Education for Upper Canada*, II (April), 50.

Anon (1849c) 'Love to see them happy'. *Journal of Education for Upper Canada*, II (October), 158.

Anon (1850a) 'The art of teaching'. *Journal of Education for Upper Canada*, III (April), 52–4.

Anon (1850b) 'Teacher's self-heed essential to his success'. *Journal of Education for Upper Canada*, III (June), 83.

Anon (1850c) 'Method, and the principles of teaching'. *English Journal of Education, New Series*, IV, 105–10.

Anon (1851) 'On methods of teaching'. *English Journal of Education, New Series*, V, 415–20.

Anon (1852) 'On teaching power'. *English Journal of Education, New Series*, VI, 409–14.

Anon (1857) 'Fondness for teaching'. *Journal of Education for Upper Canada*, X (Feb), 24.

Anon (1858) 'Know your pupils'. *English Journal of Education – New Series*, XII (December), 461–2.

Anon (1861) 'Middle class and primary education in England'. *Cornhill Magazine*, 51–7.

Anon (1863) 'Value of female teachers in common schools'. *Journal of Education for Upper Canada*, XVI (April), 104.

Anon (1867) 'Principles of education'. *Educational Record*, VII, 85.

Anon (1871) 'First principles of education'. *Journal of Education for Upper Canada*, XIV (April), 26.

Archibald, A. (1845) *England in 1815 and 1845: or, a Sufficient and Contracted Currency*. Edinburgh, W. Blackwood and Sons.

Armytage, W. A. G. (1965) *Four Hundred Years of English Education*. London, Cambridge University Press.

Arnold, M. (1910) *Reports on Elementary Schools 1852–1882*. London, Eyre and Spottiswoode.

Baber, R. H. (1850) *A Letter Addressed to the Members of the Council of Whitelands Training Institution for Schoolmistresses*. London, Levey, Robson and Franklyn.

Bailyn, B. (1960) *Education in the Forming of American Society*. Williamsburg, VA, Institute of Early American History and Culture.

Bain, A. (1896) *Education as a Science*. London, Kegan Paul.

Ball, N. (1963) *Her Majesty's Inspectorate*. Edinburgh, Oliver and Boyd.

Ball, N. (1983) *Educating the People: A Documentary History of Elementary Schooling in England 1840–1870*. London, Maurice Temple Smith.

Ball, S. J. (1990) *Politics and Policy Making in Education: Explorations in Policy Sociology*. London, Routledge.

Ball, S. J. (2003) 'The teacher's soul and the terrors of performativity'. *Journal of Education Policy*, 18(2), 215–28.

Ball, S. (2001) 'Performativities and fabrications in the education economy: Towards the performative society', in D. Glesson and C. Husbands (eds) *The Performing School: Managing Teaching and Learning in a Performance Culture*, pp. 210–26. London, Routledge/Falmer.

Barnard, H. (ed.) (1859) *Pestalozzi and Pestalozzianism*. New York, F. C. Brownell.

Bartley, G. C. T. (1871) *The Schools for the People*. London, Bell & Daldy.

Barnard, H. C. (1947) *A History of English Education from 1760*. London, University of London Press.

Beard, C. A. (1983) 'Written History as an Act of Faith'. Annual address of the president of the American Historical Association, delivered at Urbana. December 28, 1933. *American Historical Review*, 39(2), 219–31.

Becker, C. (1983) 'Everyman His Own Historian'. Annual address of the president of the American Historical Association, delivered at Minneapolis. December 29, 1931. *American Historical Review*, 37(2), 221–36.

Bergen, B. H. (1988) 'Only a schoolmaster: Gender, class and the effort to professionalize elementary teaching in England 1870–1910', in J. Ozga (ed.) *Schoolwork: Approaches to the Labour Process of Teaching*, pp. 39–60. Milton Keynes, Open University Press.

Biber, E. (1831) *Henry Pestalozzi and His Plan of Education*. London, John Souter.

Binder, F. M. (1974) *The Age of the Common School, 1830–1865*. New York, John Wiley and Sons.

Birch, D. (2008) *Our Victorian Education*. Oxford, Blackwell.

Bledstein, B. J. (1976) *The Culture of Professionalism: The Middle Class and the Development of Higher Education in America*. New York, Norton.

Bloomfield, B. C. (1960–1961) 'Sir James Phillips Kay-Shuttleworth (1804–1877): A trial bibliography'. *British Journal of Educational Studies*, 9, 155–77.

Bowles, S. and Gintis, H. (1976) *Schooling in Capitalist America: Educational Reform and the Contradictions of Economic Life*. New York, Basic Books.

Bradbury, J. L. (1975) *Chester College and the Training of Teachers, 1839–1975*. Chester, Chester College.

Briggs, A. (1984) *A Social History of England*. London, Book Club Associates.

Briggs, W. (1896) 'Schools and teachers', in D. Boyle (ed.) *The Township of Scarboro 1796–1896*, pp. 177–96. Toronto, William Briggs.

British and Foreign School Society (n.d.) *Training College, Stockwell – General Regulations to be Observed by Students During Their Residence*. British and Foreign School Society Archive Centre, Middlesex, Brunel University.

British and Foreign School Society (1838) *Annual Report*. British and Foreign School Society Archive Centre, Middlesex, Brunel University.

British and Foreign School Society (1841–1850) *Student Testimonials*. British and Foreign School Society Archive Centre, Middlesex, Brunel University.

British and Foreign School Society (1859) *Admission Form, Borough Road Training College*. British and Foreign School Society Archive Centre, Middlesex, Brunel University.

British and Foreign School Society (1860) *Borough Road Training Institution 1860 Midsummer Examination Scripts*. British and Foreign School Society Archive Centre, Middlesex, Brunel University.

British and Foreign School Society (1871) *General Examination 1871 Notice*. British and Foreign School Society Archive Centre, Middlesex, Brunel University.

Britton, J. A. (1964) *The Origin and Subsequent Development of St. Mary's College (Hammersmith) 1847–1899*. Unpublished M.A. Thesis, Education, London, University of London.

Brougham, H. (1828) 'Speech in the House of Commons, 29 January 1828'. *Education Miscellanies*, I, 1825–31.

Brown, T. (1822) *Lectures on the Philosophy of the Human Mind (Vols 1–3)*. Andover, Mark Newman.

Bryant, M. (1979) *The Unexpected Revolution: A Study in the History of the Education of Women and Girls in the Nineteenth Century*. London, University of London Institute of Education.

Burke, P. (2008) *What is Cultural History? (2nd edn)*. Cambridge, Polity Press.

Burnet, J. (1972) *Ethnic Groups in Upper Canada (Vol. 1)*. Toronto, Ontario Historical Society.

Burroughs, P. (1969) *The Colonial Reformers in Canada: 1830–1849*. Toronto, Maclelland and Stewart.

Burstyn, J. N. (1977) 'Women's education in England during the nineteenth century: A review of the literature, 1970–1976'. *History of Education*, 6(1), 11–19.

Butcher, W. W. (1886) *Canadian Newspaper Directory*. Toronto, Canadian Newspaper Advertising Agency.

Butler, J. (1990) *Gender Trouble: Feminism and the Subversion of Identity*. London, Routledge.

Button, H. W. and Provenzo, E. (1983) *History of Education and Culture in America*. New Jersey, Prentice Hall.

Canuck, A. (1905) *Early Pioneer Life in Upper Canada*. Toronto, William Briggs.

Careless, J. M. S. (1967) *The Union of the Canadas: The Growth of Canadian Institutions 1841–1857*. Toronto, McClelland and Stewart.

Carr, E. H. (1977) *What is History?* London, Penguin Books.

Charlton, R. J. M. (1856) 'Christian education in relation to the development of a pure and enlightened Christianity'. *The Educator; or, Home, the School, and the Teacher. The Quarterly Journal of the Congregational Board of Education (New Series)*, II, 1–9.

Chitty, C. (2004) *Education Policy in Britain*. Basingstoke, Palgrave Macmillan.

Cohen, S. (1999) *Challenging Orthodoxies: Toward a New Cultural History of Education*. New York: Peter Lang.

Coleridge, D. (1841) 'Papers relating to the Society's Training-College for Schoolmasters at Stanley Grove, Chelsea'. *Tract on Education*, XI (1852), 39–43.

Coleridge, D. (1842a)' A letter on the National Society's training-college for schoolmasters, Stanley Grove, Chelsea: Addressed to the Rev. John Sinclair, Secretary of the Society'. *Tracts on Education*, 11, 1–43.

Coleridge, D. (1842b) *A Second Letter on the National Society's Training Institution for Schoolmasters, St. Mark's College, Chelsea*. Plymouth, College of St. Mark and St. John Archives.

Coleridge, D. (1862) *The Teachers of the People*. London, Gilbert and Rivington.

Committee of Council on Education (1840) 'Minutes, 1840'. *Parliamentary Papers*, XL.

—— (1841) 'Minutes, 1840–1'. *Parliamentary Papers*, XX.

—— (1842) 'Minutes, 1841–2'. *Parliamentary Papers*, XXXIII.

—— (1843) 'Minutes, 1842–3'. *Parliamentary Papers*, XL.

—— (1845) 'Minutes, 1843–4'. *Parliamentary Papers*, XXXV.

—— (1846) 'Minutes, 1845'. *Parliamentary Papers*, XXXII.

—— (1847) 'Minutes, 1846'. *Parliamentary Papers*, XLV.

—— (1847–48) 'Minutes, 1847'. *Parliamentary Papers*, L.

—— (1849) 'Minutes, 1848–9'. *Parliamentary Papers*, XLII.

—— (1850) 'Minutes, 1850'. *Parliamentary Papers*, XLIII.

—— (1851) 'Minutes, 1850–1'. *Parliamentary Papers*, XLIV.

—— (1852) 'Minutes, 1851–2'. *Parliamentary Papers*, XL.

—— (1852–53) 'Minutes, 1852–3'. *Parliamentary Papers*, LXXXIX.

—— (1854) 'Minutes, 1854'. *Parliamentary Papers*, LI.

—— (1854–55) 'Copies of all Minutes of Privy Council on Education (June 1839– March 1855)'. *Parliamentary Papers*, XLI, 191–296.

—— (1856) 'Minutes, 1855'. *Parliamentary Papers*, XLVII.

—— (1857) 'Minutes, 1856'. *Parliamentary Papers*, XXXIII.

—— (1857–58) 'Minutes, 1857'. *Parliamentary Papers*, XLVI.

—— (1859) 'Report, 1858–9'. *Parliamentary Papers*, XXI, 1.

—— (1860) 'Minutes and Regulations of the Committee of the Privy Council on Education, reduced into the form of a Code'. *Parliamentary Papers*, LIII, 275–315.

—— (1861) 'Revised code of minutes and regulations of the Committee of the Privy Council on Education'. *Parliamentary Papers*, XLVIII, 369–84.

—— (1862) 'Minute confirming the alterations of the Revised Code of Regulations'. *Parliamentary Papers*, XLI, 115–89.

Cook, R. and Mitchinson, W. (eds) (1976) *The Proper Sphere: Woman's Place in Canadian Society*. Toronto, Oxford University Press.

Cook, T. G. (ed.) (1974) *The History of Education in Europe*. London, Metheun.

Copleman, D. M. (1996) *London's Women Teachers: Gender, Class and Feminism 1870–1930*. London, Routledge.

Coppa, F. (1995) 'From liberalism to fascism: The church-state conflict over Italy's schools'. *The History Teacher*, 28(2), 135–48.

Cubberley, E. P. (1947) *Public Education in the United States: A Study and Interpretation of American Educational History*. Cambridge, MA, Houghton Mifflin Co.

Cullen, M. J. (1975) *The Statistical Movement in Early Victorian Britain*. New York, Harvester Press.

Curtis, B. (1981) *Preconditions of the Canadian State: Educational Reform and the Construction of a Public in Upper Canada: 1837–1846*. Toronto, University of Toronto.

Curtis, B. (1988) *Building the Educational State: Canada West, 1836–1871*. London, Ontario.

Curtis, B. (1992) *True Government by Choice Men? Inspection, Education, and State Formation in Canada West*. Toronto, University of Toronto Press.

Curtis, B. (2001) *The Politics of Population: State Formation, Statistics, and the Census of Canada, 1840–1875*. Toronto, University of Toronto Press.

Curtis, S. J. (1967) *History of Education in Great Britain*. London, University Tutorial Press.

Curtis, S. J. and Boultwood, M. E. A. (1961) *A Short History of Educational Ideas*. London, University Tutorial Press.

Dahlmann-Hanse, J. (1961) 'The transformation of schools in Denmark'. *Phi Delta Kappan*, 43(2), 54–9.

Danylewycz, M. and Prentice, A. (1986) 'Teachers' work: Changing patterns and perceptions in the emerging school systems of nineteenth-and early twentieth century Central Canada'. *Labour/Le Travail*, 17 (Spring), 59–80.

Darwin, C. (1859) *On the Origin of Species*. London, John Murray.

Dent, H. C. (1971) 'An historical perspective', in S. Hewett (ed.) *The Training of Teachers: A Factual Survey*, pp. 12–26. London, University of London Press.

Dent, H. C. (1977) *The Training of Teachers in England and Wales 1800–1975*. London, Hodder and Stoughton.

Derycke, H. (2007) 'Catholic schooling in France: Understanding "La guerre scholaire"', in G. Grace and J. O'Keefe (eds) *International Handbook of Catholic Education: Challenges for School Systems*, pp. 329–46. Dordrecht, the Netherlands: Springer.

Desrosieres, A. (1998) *The Politics of Large Numbers*. Cambridge, Harvard University Press.

Desrosieres, A. (1999) 'The history of statistics as a genre: Styles of writing and social uses'. Conference Paper Presentation: *Statistical Internationalism, State Practices, and National Traditions: Progress Report and Prospects in the History of Statistics*. Montreal, University of Quebec.

Digby, A. and Searby, P. (1981) *Children, School and Society in Nineteenth-Century England*. London, Macmillan Press.

Donaldson, J. (1876) 'The science of education', in H. Barnard (ed.) *Education, the School, and the Teacher, in English Literature*, pp. 481–96. Hartford, Brown & Gross.

Drew, G. C. (1856) 'The educators' instruments – Hints on method'. *The Educator; or, Home, the School, and the Teacher (The Quarterly Journal of the Congregational Board of Education) – New Series*, II, 3–12.

Duncombe, C. (1836) 'Report on education and proposed Common School Bill', in J. G. Hodgins (ed.) *Documentary History of Education in Upper Canada, III*, p. 101. Toronto, Warwick Bros. & Rutter.

Dunn, H. (1837) *Principles of Teaching; or the Normal School Manual: Containing Practical Suggestions on the Government and Instruction of Children*. London, Sunday School Union.

Dunning, R. (1854a) 'Training colleges and the training of teachers: First letter to the Lord President of the Council'. *The Educational Expositor*, 1(15), 166–73.

Dunning, R. (1854b) 'Training colleges and the training of teachers: Second letter to the Lord President of the Council'. *The Educational Expositer*, II(19), 334–8.

Durham, Lord (1839) *The Report and Despatches of The Earl of Durham, Her Majesty's High Commissioner and Governor General of British North America*. London, Ridgways.

Dussel, I. (2001) 'School uniforms and the disciplining of appearances', in T. S. Popkewitz, B. M. Franklin and M. A. Pereyra (eds) *Cultural History and Education: Critical Essays on Knowledge and Schooling*, pp. 207–41. New York, Routledge/Falmer.

Eggleston, E. (1871) *The Hoosier School-Master*. London, George Routledge and Sons.

Elton, G. (1997) 'Return to essentials', in K. Jenkins (ed.) *The Postmodern History Reader*, pp. 175–9. London, Routledge.

Errington, J. (1994) 'Ladies and school mistresses: Educating women in early nineteenth-century Upper Canada'. *Historical Studies in Education/Revue D'Histoire De L'Education*, 6(1), 71–96.

Etherington, W. (1969) *A History of St. John's College, York 1841–1914*. Unpublished M.Ed. Thesis, Education, Leicester, University of Leicester.

Fiorello, J. R. (1969) *General Education in the Preparation of Teachers at Westfield State College, 1839–1960*. Unpublished PhD Thesis, University of Connecticut.

Fiorino, A. (1978) 'The moral education of Egerton Ryerson's idea of education', in N. McDonald and A. Chaiton (eds) *Egerton Ryerson and His Times*, pp. 59–80. Toronto, Macmillan Company of Canada.

Fletcher, L. (1970) 'The development of periodicals addressed to teachers in Britain before 1870'. *Journal of Educational Administration and History*, II(2), 9–19.

Foucault, M. (1967) *Madness and Civilization: A History of Insanity in the Age of Reason*. London, Tavistock Publications.

Foucault, M. (1972) *The Archaeology of Knowledge and Discourse on Language*. New York, Pantheon Books.

Foucault, M. (1977) *Discipline and Punish: The Birth of the Prison* (Trans. Alan Sheridan). New York, Vintage.

Foucault, M. (1980a) 'Body/Power', in C. Gordon (ed.) *Michel Foucault: Power/Knowledge: Selected Interviews and Other Writings 1972–1977*, pp. 55–62. New York, Pantheon.

Foucault, M. (1980b) 'Truth and power', in C. Gordon (ed.) *Power/Knowledge: Selected Interviews and Other Writings 1972–1977 by Michel Foucault*, pp. 109–33. New York, Pantheon.

Foucault, M. (1980c) 'Two lectures: 7 & 14 January 1976', in C. Gordon (ed.) *Power/Knowledge: Selected Interviews and Other Writings 1972–1977 by Michel Foucault*, pp. 78–108. New York, Pantheon.

Foucault, M. (1988) '"On Power" interview with Pierre Boncenne', in L. D. Kritzman (ed.) *Michel Foucault: Politics Philosophy Culture: Interviews and Other Writings 1977–1984*, pp. 96–109. New York, Routledge.

Foucault, M. (1991) 'Questions of method', in G. Burchell, C. Gordon and P. Miller (eds) *The Foucault Effect: Studies in Governmentality*, pp. 73–86. Chicago, The University of Chicago Press.

Foucault, M. (2000a) 'Nietzsche, genealogy, history', in J. D. Faubion (ed.) *Aesthetics, Method and Epistemology: Essential Works of Foucault: 1954–1984, II*, pp. 369–92. London, Penguin.

Foucault, M. (2000b) 'On the genealogy of ethics: An overview of work in progress', in P. Rabinow (ed.) *Ethics, Subjectivity and Truth: Essential Works of Foucault: 1954–1984, I*, pp. 255–80. London, Penguin.

Foucault, M. (2000c) 'Technologies of the self', in J. D. Faubion (ed.) *Ethics, Subjectivity and Truth: Essential Works of Foucault 1954–1984, I*, pp. 223–51. London, Penguin.

Fraser, Rev. J. (1866) 'Schools inquiry commissions report on the common school system of the United States and of the provinces of upper and lower Canada'. *Parliamentary Papers*, XXVI, 216–20.

Gardner, P. W. (1984) *The Lost Elementary Schools of Victorian England*. Kent, Croom Helm.

General Correspondence Incoming, Department of Education (1844–65) *Series RG 2-12 Public Archives of Ontario*. Toronto.

Gezi, K. I. and Myers, J. E. (1968) *Teaching in American Culture*. New York, Holt, Rinehart and Winston.

Gidney, R. D. (1975) 'Elementary education in Upper Canada: A reassessment', in M. B. Katz and P. H. Mattingly (eds) *Education and Social Change: Themes from Ontario's Past*, pp. 3–27. New York, New York University Press.

Gidney, R. D. (1980) 'Making nineteenth-century school systems: The Upper Canadian experience and its relevance to English historiography'. *History of Education*, 9(2), 101–16.

Gidney, R. D. and Millar, W. P. J. (1994) *Professional Gentlemen: The Professions in Nineteenth Century Ontario*. Toronto, University of Toronto Press.

Gillis, A. R. (1994) 'Literacy and the civilization of violence in 19th-century France'. *Sociological Forum*, 9(3), 371–401.

Gladman, F. J. (1876) *School Method: Notes and Hints (from Lectures Delivered at the Borough Road Training College)*. London, Jarrold & Sons.

Goffman, E. (1961) *Asylums: Essays on the Social Situation of Mental Patients and Other Inmates*. Harmondsworth, Middlesex, Penguin.

Goldstein, J. (1995) 'Foucault and the post-revolutionary self: The uses of Cousinan pedagogy in nineteenth-century France', in J. Goldstein (ed.), *Foucault and the Writing of History*, pp. 99–115. Oxford, Blackwell.

Goldstrom, J. M. (1977) 'The content of education and the socialization of the working-class child 1830–1860', in P. McCann (ed.) *Popular Education and Socialization in the Nineteenth Century*, pp. 91–109. London, Methuen & Co.

Gomersall, M. (1997) *Working-class Girls in Nineteenth-Century England: Life, Work and Schooling*. London, Macmillan Press.

Good, H. and Teller, J. (1973) *A History of American Education*. New York, Macmillan.

Gordon, P. and Szreter, R. (1989) 'Introduction', P. Gordon and R. Szreter (ed.) *History of Education: The Making of a Discipline*, pp. 1–18. Exeter, Woburn Press.

Gosden, P. H. J. H. (1969) *How They Were Taught: An Anthology of Contemporary Accounts of Learning and Teaching in England, 1800–1950*. Oxford, Basil Blackwell.

Graham, E. (1974) 'Schoolmarms and early teaching', in J. Acton, P. Goldsmith and B. Shepard (eds) *Women at Work, Ontario 1850–1930*, pp. 165–210. Toronto, Canadian Women's Educational Press.

Green, A. (1990) *Education and State Formation: The Rise of Education Systems in England, France and the USA*. New York, St. Martin's Press.

Hacking, I. (1990) *The Taming of Chance*. Cambridge, Cambridge University Press.

Hacking, I. (1999) *The Social Construction of What?* Cambridge, Cambridge University Press.

Hamilton, E. (1838) 'The philosophy of education: No. 1 "On the cultivation of the faculties, perception and attention"'. *Educational Magazine (New Series)*, I (March), 99.

Harkness, A. (1896) *Iroquois High School 1845–1895: A Story of Fifty Years*. Toronto, William Briggs.

Hargreaves, A. and Evans, E. (1997) *Beyond Educational Reform: Bringing Teachers Back In*. Buckingham, Open University Press.

Harp, S. L. (1998) *Learning to be Loyal: Primary Schooling as Nation Building in Alsace and Lorraine, 1850–1940*. Dekalb, IL, Northern Illinois University Press.

Harrigan, P. (1992) 'The development of a corps of public school teachers in Canada, 1870–1980'. *History of Education Quarterly*, 32(4), 483–521.

Harris, T. (1848) 'Moral training: From an essay read before the British Teachers' Association on Sat. November 4th, 1848'. *Educational Record*, I, 37.

Heap, R. and Prentice, A. L. (eds) (1991) *Gender and Education in Ontario: An Historical Reader*. Toronto, Canadian Scholars' Press.

Helsby, G. and McCulloch, G. (eds) (1997) *Teachers and the National Curriculum*. London, Cassell.

Herbst, J. (1989) *And Sadly Teach: Teacher Education and Professionalization in American Culture*. Madison, University of Wisconsin Press.

Hewlett, E. L. (1932) *The Work of the British and Foreign School Society in the Training of Teachers*. Unpublished M.Ed. Thesis, The Training College, University of Manchester, Swansea.

Higginson, J. H. (1939) *The Dame Schools of Great Britain*. Unpublished M.A. Thesis, Education, Leeds, University of Leeds.

Himmelfarb, G. (1997) 'Telling it as you like it: Postmodernist history and the flight from fact', in K. Jenkins (ed.) *The Postmodern History Reader*, pp. 158–74. London: Routledge.

Hodgins, J. G. (ed.) (1894) *Documentary History of Education in Upper Canada from the Passing of the Constitutional Act of 1791 to the Close of Rev. Ryerson's Administration of the Education Department in 1876 (28 vols.)*. Henceforth, *DHE*. Toronto, Warwick Bros. & Rutter.

Hodgins, J. G. (ed.) (1911) *Historical Educational Papers and Documents Illustrative of the Educational System of Ontario*. Toronto, L. K. Cameron.

Hodgson, J. S. (1839) *Consideration of Phrenology in Connexion with an Intellectual, Moral, and Religious Education*. London, No publisher.

Horn, P. (1978) *Education in Rural England 1800–1914*. London, Gill & Macmillan.

Hoskin, K. W. (1979) 'The examination, disciplinary power and rational schooling'. *History of Education*, 8(2), 135–46.

Hoskin, K. W. (1990) 'Foucault under examination: The crypto-educationalist unmasked', S. Ball (ed.) *Foucault and Education: Disciplines and Knowledge*, pp. 29–56. London, Routledge.

Hoskin, K. W. (1993) 'Education and the genesis of disciplinarity: The unexpected reversal', in E. Messer-Davidow, D. Shumway and D. J. Sylvan (eds) *Knowledges: Historical and Critical Studies in Disciplinarity*, pp. 271–304. Charlottesville, University Press of Virginia.

House of Commons (1847) 'Plan of education'. *Hansard's Parliamentary Debates*, XCI, 947–1032.

Houston, S. E. (1975) 'Politics, schools, and social change in upper Canada', in M. B. Katz and P. H. Mattingly (eds) *Education and Social Change: Themes from Ontario's Past*, pp. 28–56. New York, New York University Press.

Houston, S. E. and Prentice, A. (1988) *Schooling and Scholars in Nineteenth Century Ontario*. Toronto, University of Toronto Press.

Hubbell, G. (1910) *The Life of Horace Mann, Educator, Patriot and Reformer*. Philadelphia, Kessinger Publishing.

Hughes, G. W. (1936) *The Social and Economic Status of the Elementary School Teacher in England 1833–1870*. Unpublished M.Ed. Thesis, Education. Manchester, University of Manchester.

Hunt, L. (ed.) (1989) *The New Cultural History*. Berkeley, University of California Press.

Hunter, I. (1994) *Rethinking the School: Subjectivity, Bureaucracy, Criticism*. New York, St. Martin's Press.

Hurt, J. (1971) *Education in Evolution: Church, State, Society and Popular Education 1800–1870*. London, Rupert Hart-Davis.

Hutchinson, J. (1946) 'Early days at St. Mark's', in M. Roberts (ed.) *Notes on College History: 1840–1865*, pp. 12–21. London, George White for The College of St. Mark and St. John.

J. S. G. (1854) 'Is teaching the grave of the intellect', *English Journal of Education – New Series*, XIV, 200–3.

Jarman, T. L. (1951) *Landmarks in the History of Education: English Education as Part of the European Tradition*. London, Murray.

Jeffrey, B. and Woods, P. (1998) *Testing Teachers: The Effects of School Inspections on Primary Teachers*. London, Falmer.

Jenkins, K. (1995) *On 'What is History?' From Carr and Elton to Rorty and White*. London, Routledge.

Jenkins, K. (1998) 'Introduction: On being open about our closures', in K. Jenkins (ed.) *The Postmodern History Reader*, pp. 1–35. London, Routledge.

Johnson, C. (1904) *Old Time Schools and Schoolbooks*. New York, The Macmillan Company.

Johnson, R. (1970) 'Educational policy and social control in early Victorian England'. *Past and Present*, 49, 96–119.

Johnson, R. (1977) 'Educating the educators: "Experts" and the state 1833–9', in A. P. Donajgrodski (ed.) *Social Control in Nineteenth Century Britain*, pp. 77–107. Totowa, New Jersey, Croom Helm.

Jones, A. (1963) *Changing Concepts of Teacher Education from 1800 to the Present Day: A Study of the English System*. Unpublished M.Ed. Thesis, Education, Leicester.

Jones, D. (1990) 'The genealogy of the urban schoolteacher', in S. J. Ball (ed.) *Foucault and Education: Disciplines and Knowledge*, pp. 57–77. London, Routledge.

Jones, L. G. E. (1924) *The Training of Teachers in England and Wales: A Critical Survey*. London, Oxford University Press.

Jones, M. (1860) *A Brief Account of the Home and Colonial Institution: And of the Pestalozzian System as Taught and Practiced in its Schools*. London, Groombridge and sons.

Jones, K. and Williamson, K. (1979) 'The birth of the schoolroom'. *Ideology and Consciousness*, Autumn, 59–110.

Judges, A. V. (1951) 'James Kay-Shuttleworth, pioneer of national education', in A. V. Judges (ed.) *Pioneers of English Education: A Course of Lectures Given at King's College, London*, pp. 104–27. London, Faber and Faber.

Kaestle, C. (1983) *Pillars of the Republic: Common Schools and American Society, 1780–1860*. New York, Hill and Wang.

Kaestle, C. and Vinovskis, M. (1980) *Education and Social Change in Nineteenth Century Massachusetts*. New York, Cambridge University Press.

Kamm, J. (1965) *Hope Deferred: Girls' Education in English History*. London, Routledge.

Katz, M. B. (1968) *The Irony of Early School Reform: Educational Innovation in Mid-Nineteenth Century Massachusetts*. Cambridge, MA, Harvard University Press.

Katz, M. B. (1975) *Class, Bureaucracy, and Schools: The Illusion of Educational Change in America*. New York, Praeger.

Katz, M. (1976) 'The origins of public education: A reassessment'. *History of Education Quarterly*, 16(4), 381–409.

Kay, D. J. (1862) 'The moral and physical condition of the working classes of Manchester in 1832', in S. J. Kay-Shuttleworth (ed.) *Four Periods of Public Education as Reviewed in 1832, 1839, 1846, 1862*, pp. 1–84. London, Spottiswoode and Co.

Kay-Shuttleworth, S. J. (ed.) (1841) *Four Periods of Public Education as Reviewed in 1832, 1839, 1846, 1862*. London, Spottiswoode and Co.

Kay-Shuttleworth, S. J. (1853) *Public Education as Affected by the Minutes of the Committee of Privy Council from 1846 to 1852 with Suggestions as to Future Policy*. London, Longman, Brown, Green, and Longmans.

Kay-Shuttleworth, S. J. (1862a) 'First report on the origin and organisation of the Training College at Battersea, 1841', in S. J. Kay-Shuttleworth (ed.) *Four Periods of Public Education as Reviewed in 1832, 1839, 1846, 1862*, pp. 294–386. London, Spottiswoode and Co.

Kay-Shuttleworth, S. J. (1862b) 'Recent measures for the promotion of education in England, 1839', in S. J. Kay-Shuttleworth (ed.) *Four Periods of Public Education as Reviewed in 1832, 1839, 1846, 1862*, pp. 187–286. Brighton, Harvester Press.

Kay-Shuttleworth, S. J. (1862c) 'Second report on the schools for the training of parochial schoolmasters at Battersea, 1843', in S. J. Kay-Shuttleworth (ed.) *Four Periods of Public Education as Reviewed in 1832, 1839, 1846, 1862*, pp. 387–431. London, Spottiswoode and Co.

Kay-Shuttleworth, S. J. (1862d) 'Sketch of the progress of Manchester in thirty years, from 1832 to 1862', in S. J. Kay-Shuttleworth (ed.) *Four Periods of Public Education as Reviewed in 1832, 1839, 1846, 1862*, pp. 87–170. London, Spottiswoode and Co.

Knight, E. W. (ed.) (1930) *Reports on European Education*. New York, McGraw-Hill.

Landon, J. (1894) *The Principles and Practice of Teaching and Class Management*. London, Alfred M. Holden.

Laquer, T. W. (1976) *Religion and Respectability: Sunday Schools and Working-Class Culture, 1780–1850*. New Haven, Yale University Press.

Larsen, M. (2010) 'Troubling the discourse of teacher centrality: A comparative perspective'. *Journal of Education Policy*, 26(2), 207–31.

Larson, M. S. (1977) *The Rise of Professionalism: A Sociological Analysis*. Berkeley, University of California Press.

Laurie, S. (1902) *The Training of Teachers, Methods of Instruction: Selected Papers*. Cambridge, Cambridge University Press.

Lawrence, A. (1958) *St. Hilda's College 1858–1958*. Darlington, William Dresser and Sons.

Lawson, J. and Silver, H. (1973) *A Social History of Education in England*. London, Methuen & Co.

Leinster-Mackay, D. P. (1978) 'A question of ephemerality: Indices for longevity of 19th century private schools'. *Journal of Educational Administration and History*, 10(2), 1–7.

Leinster-Mackay, D. P. (1983) 'Private or public schools: The education debate in laissez-faire England'. *Journal of Educational Administration and History*, 15(2), 1–6.

Lemlech, J. and Marks, M. B. (1976) *The American Teacher, 1776–1976*. Bloomington, Phi Delta Kappa Educational Foundation.

Le Vaux, G. V. (1875) *The Science and Art of Teaching, or, the Principles and Practice of Education*. Toronto, Copp Clark.

Lizars, R. and Lizars, K. M. (1896) *In the Days of the Canada Company: The Story of the Settlement of the Huron Tract and a View of the Social Life of the Period 1825–1850*. Toronto, William Briggs.

Locke, J. (1690) *An Essay Concerning Human Understanding*. London, Three Bibles in St. Pauls.

Love, J. (1978) 'The professionalization of teachers in the mid-nineteenth century upper Canada', in N. McDonald and A. Chaiton (eds) *Egerton Ryerson and His Times*, pp. 109–27. Toronto, Macmillan Company of Canada.

Love, J. (1984) 'Anti-American ideology and education reform in 19th century Upper Canada', in J. D. Wilson (ed.) *An Imperfect Past: Education and Society in Canadian History*, pp. 170–80. Vancouver, Centre for the Study of Curriculum and Instruction.

Lovett, W. (1840) *Chartism, a New Organisation for the People: Embracing a Plan for the Education and Improvement of the People, Politically and Socially*. London, J. Watson.

Lowe, R. (1996) 'Postmodernity and historians of education: A view from Britain'. *Paedagogica Historica*, 32(2), 307–23.

Lyotard, J. F. (1984) *The Postmodern Condition: A Report on Knowledge*. Minneapolis, University of Minnesota Press.

Mahony, P. and Hextall, I. (2000) *Reconstructing Teaching: Standards, Performance and Accountability*. London, Routledge/Falmer.

Manchester Statistical Society (1835) 'Report of a committee of the Manchester Statistical Society on the State of Education in the Borough of Manchester'. *Education Pamphlets, 4*. London, James Ridgway and Son.

Manchester Statistical Society (1836) 'Report of a committee of the Manchester Statistical Society on the State of Education in the Borough of Salford'. *Education Pamphlets, 5*. London, James Ridgway and Son.

Mann, H. (1841) 'Fifth Annual Report (The effect of education upon the worldly fortunes of Men)', in M. Mann (ed.) *Life and Works of Horace Mann*, p. 1868. Boston, Walker, Fuller and Co.

Mann, H. (1843) 'Seventh Annual Report (Variation and description of European schools)', in M. Mann (ed.) *Life and Works of Horace Mann*, p. 1868. Boston, Walker, Fuller and Co.

Mann, H. (1845) 'Eighth Annual Report (Duties of the future)', in M. Mann (ed.) *Life and Works of Horace Mann*, p. 1868. Boston, Walker, Fuller and Co.

Mann, H. (1846) 'Tenth Annual Report (The common school system of Massachusetts)', in M. Mann (ed.) *Life and Works of Horace Mann*, p. 1868. Boston, Walker, Fuller and Co.

Mann, H. (1848) 'Twelfth Annual Report (The capacity of the common school system to improve the pecuniary condition)', in M. Mann (ed.) *Life and Works of Horace Mann*, p. 1868. Boston, Walker, Fuller and Co.

Maynes, M. J. (1985) *Schooling in Western Europe: A Social History*. Albany, NY: State University of New York Press.

McGregor, G. P. (1978) *The History of Bishop Otter College, Chichester in Relation to the Development of Teacher Education in England and Wales, 1836–1976*. Unpublished Ph.D. Thesis, University of Sussex.

MacNaughton, K. F. C. (1947) *The Development of the Theory and Practice of Education in New Brunswick 1874–1900*. Fredericton, University of New Brunswick.

Miller, P. (1989) 'Historiography of compulsory schooling: What is the problem?', *History of Education*, 18(2), 123–44.

Monroe, W. S. (1952) *Teaching-Learning Theory and Teacher Education 1890 to 1950*. New York, Greenwood Press.

More, C. (1992a) *'A Splendid College' an Illustrated History of Teacher Training in Cheltenham 1847–1990*. Cheltenham, Gloucestershire, Cheltenham and Gloucester College of Higher Education.

More, C. (1992b) *The Training of Teachers, 1847–1947: A History of the Church Colleges at Cheltenham*. London, Hambeldon Press.

Morell, J. D. (1853) *Elements of Psychology*. London, William Pickering.

Morrison, B. H. (1971) *An Historical Overview of the Development of the Canadian Educational System with Special Reference to Ontario*. Toronto, Public Archives of Ontario.

Morton, W. L. (1964) *The Critical Years: The Union of British North America 1857–1873*. Toronto, McClelland and Stewart.

National Society (1838–47) *Minutes of Meetings of the General Committee*. London, Church of England Record Centre.

National Society (1847–49) *Monthly Papers, vols. I–XXXVI*. London, Deposition of the Society.

National Society (1849–55) *Monthly Papers, vols. XXXVII–XLVIII*. London, Deposition of the Society.

National Society (1853) *Annual Report*. London, Deposition of the Society.

Naylor, R. T. (1987) *Canada in the European Age: 1453–1919*. Vancouver, New Star Books.

Newcastle Commission (1861a) 'Answers to circular questions'. *Parliamentary Papers*, XXI, v.

Newcastle Commission (1861b) 'Report'. *Parliamentary Papers*, XXI, i.

Newcastle Commission (1861c) 'Reports of the assistant commissioners on popular education (England)'. *Parliamentary Papers*, XXI, ii.

Newcastle Commission (1861d) 'Reports of the assistant commissioners to inquire into the state of popular education in England'. *Parliamentary Papers*, XXI, iii.

Newnham, W. T. and Nease, A. S. (1965) *The Professional Teacher in Ontario: The Heritage, Responsibilities, and Practices*. Toronto, Ryerson Press.

Novick, P. (1988) *That Noble Dream: The "Objectivity Question" and the American Historical Profession*. Cambridge, Cambridge University Press.

Omricon (1853) 'Letter to the editor'. *The Educational Expositor*, I.

Perkin, H. (1990) *The Rise of the Professional Society: England Since 1880*. London, Routledge.

Pestalozzi, J. H. (1801) *Leonard and Gertrude: A Popular Story*. Philadelphia, Josephy Groff.

Pestalozzi, J. H. (1894) *How Gertrude Teaches Her Children* (Trans. L. Holland and F. Turner). London, Swan Sonnenschein.

Pillans, J. (1829) *Principles of Elementary Teaching, Chiefly in Reference to the Parochial Schools of Scotland: In Two Letters to T.F. Kennedy*. Edinburgh, Adam Black.

Popkewitz, T. S. (2001) 'The production of reason and power', in T. S. Popkewitz, B. M. Franklin and M. A. Pereyra (eds) *Cultural History and Education*, pp. 151–83. New York, Routledge Falmer.

Popkewitz, T. S., Franklin, M. B. and Pereyra, M. A. (eds) (2001) *Cultural History and Education*. New York, Routledge Falmer.

Porter, R. (2000) *Enlightenment: Britain and the Creation of the Modern World*. London, Penguin.

Poster, M. (1997) *Cultural History and Postmodernity: Disciplinary Readings and Challenges*. New York, Columbia University Press.

Prentice, A. (1990) '"Friendly atoms in chemistry": Women and men at normal school in mid-nineteenth century Toronto', in D. Keane and C. Read (eds) *Old Ontario: Essays in Honour of J. M. S. Careless*, pp. 285–317. Toronto, Dundurn Press.

Public Schools (1859) *Report of the Past History, and Present Condition, of the Common or Public Schools of the City of Toronto*. Toronto, City of Toronto.

Purvis, J. (1984) 'The experience of schooling for working-class boys and girls in nineteenth-century England', in I. F. Goodson and S. J. Ball (eds) *Defining the Curriculum: Histories & Ethnographies*, pp. 89–116. London, Falmer Press.

Putnam, J. H. (1912) *Egerton Ryerson and Education in Upper Canada*. Toronto, William Briggs.

Reid, T. (1810) *An Inquiry Into the Human Mind*. Edinburgh, Bell & Bradfute.

Rich, R. W. (1933) *The Training of Teachers in England and Wales During the Nineteenth Century*. Cambridge, Cambridge at the University Press.

Richardson, W. (1999a) 'Historians and educationists: The history of education as a field of study in post-war England, Part I: 1945–72'. *History of Education*, 28(1), 1–30.

Richardson, W. (1999b) 'Historians and educationists: The history of education as a field of study in post-war England, Part II: 1972–96'. *History of Education*, 28(2) 109–41.

Roberts, M. (ed.) (1946) *Notes on College History: 1840–1865*. London, George White for the College of St. Mark and St. John.

Rolph, T. (1836) *A Brief Account, Together With Observations, Made During the Visit in the West Indies, and a Tour Through the United States of American in Parts of the Years 1832–33; Together With a Statistical Account of Upper Canada*. Dundas, U. C., G. Heyworth Hackstaff.

Rolph, T. (1839) *Canada v. Australia*. London, Smith, Elder and Co.

Rose, M. (1981) *A History of King Alfred's College, Winchester 1840–1980*. London, Phillimore.

Rose, N. (1989) *Governing the Soul: The Shaping of the Private Self*. London, Routledge.

Rose, N. (1999) *Powers of Freedom, Reframing Political Thought*. Cambridge, Cambridge University Press.

Rosenkratz, J. K. F. (1887) *The Philosophy of Education* (Trans. A. Brackett). New York, D. Appleton and Company.

Ross, W. (1849) 'Moral qualifications of the schoolmaster'. *English Journal of Education*, III, 17.

Rousmaniere, K. (1997a) *City Teachers: Teaching and School Reform in Historical Perspective*. New York, Teachers College Press.

Rousmaniere, K. (1997b) 'Good teachers are born, not made: Self-regulation in the work of nineteenth century American women teachers', in K. Rousmaniere, K. Dehli and N. de Coninck-Smith (eds) *Discipline, Moral Regulation, and Schooling: A Social History*, pp. 117–33. New York, Garland Publishing.

Rousmaniere, K., Dehli, K. and de Coninck-Smith, N. (eds) (1997) *Discipline, Moral Regulation, and Schooling: A Social History*. New York, Garland Publishing.

Rousseau, J. J. (1762) *Emile*. Amsterdam, Jean Neaulme.

Rowe, F. W. (1964) *The Development of Education in Newfoundland*. Toronto, The Ryerson Press.

Ryan, P. (1995) 'The day Mr. Snobelen let the cat out of the bag'. *The Globe and Mail*, October 10 1995, A19.

Ryerson, E. (1846a) 'Circular addressed to District Superintendents of Schools by the Chief Superintendent of Education', in J. G. Hodgins (ed.) *DHE*, vol. 6, p. 269. Toronto, Warwick Bros. & Rutter.

Ryerson, E. (1846b) 'Report on a system of public elementary instruction for upper Canada, 1846', in J. G. Hodgins (ed.) *DHE*, vol. 6, pp. 138–213. Toronto, Warwick Bros. & Rutter.

Ryerson, E. (1848) 'The importance of education to a manufacturing and a free people'. *Journal of Education for Upper Canada*, 1 (October), 300–6.

Ryerson, E. (1850a) *Annual Report of the Normal, Model, and Common Schools in Upper Canada, for the Year 1849*. Toronto, Lowell and Gibson.

Ryerson, E. (1850b) 'A lecture on the social advancement of Canada (Being the introductory lecture of the season, before the Mechanics Institute of Niagara and Toronto)'. *The Niagara Mail*, February 6 1850.

Ryerson, E. (1851) *Annual Report of the Normal, Model, and Common Schools in Upper Canada, for the Year 1850*. Toronto, Lowell and Gibson.

Ryerson, E. (1853) 'Reasons given by the Chief Superintendent of Education for the regulations relating to the intercourse of male and female students in the normal school', in J. G. Hodgins (ed.) *DHE*, pp. 23–4 vol. 11. Toronto, Warwick Bros. & Rutter.

Ryerson, E. (1870) 'Annual report on the normal, model, grammar and common schools in Ontario, for the year 1870', in J. G. Hodgins (ed.) *DHE*, vol. 23, p. 181. Toronto, Warwick Bros. & Rutter.

Salzmann, C. G. (1852) 'Extracts from the Ant's book, or a guide to rational education of teaching'. *English Journal of Education*, II, 210–11. (Originally published in 1805).

Sanderson, M. (1962) 'The grammar school and the education of the poor, 1786–1840'. *British Journal of Educational Studies*, 11(1), 28–43.

Sangster, J. H. (1871) *The Normal School for Ontario: Its Design and Functions (Chiefly Taken from the Report of the Chief Superintendent of Education for Ontario, for the Year 1869)*. Toronto, Hunter, Rose & Co.

Select Committee of the House of Lords (1847) 'First and second reports from the Select Committee of the House of Lords on juvenile offenders'. *Parliamentary Papers XLV*. Shannon, Irish University Press.

Select Committee on Education (1816) 'Reports on the education of the lower orders of the metropolis with the minutes of evidence'. *Parliamentary Papers*, I & II.

Select Committee on Education (1834) 'Report from the Select Committee appointed to inquire into the present state of education of the people of England and Wales'. *Parliamentary Papers*, IX.

Select Committee on Education (1835) 'Report from the Select Committee appointed to inquire into the present state of education of the people of England and Wales'. *Parliamentary Papers*, VII.

Select Committee on Education (1837) 'Education of poorer classes in England and Wales'. *Parliamentary Papers*, VII.

Select Committee on Education (1838) 'Report from the Select Committee on education of the poorer classes in England and Wales; together with the minutes of evidence and index'. *Parliamentary Papers*, VII, 157–344.

Select Committee on Education (1852) 'Report from the Select Committee on Manchester and Salford education'. *Parliamentary Papers*, XI, 3–612.

Shultz, S.K. (1973) *The Culture Factory: Boston Public Schools, 1789–1860*. New York: Oxford Press.

Silber, K. (1960) *Pestalozzi: The Man and His Work*. London, Routledge and Kegan Paul.

Simon, B. (1960) *Studies in the History of Education, 1780–1870*. London, Lawrence and Wishart.

Simon, B. (1966) 'The history of education', in J. W. Tibble (ed.) *The Study of Education*, pp. 91–131. London, Routledge Kegan Paul.

Sissons, C. B. (1937–47) *Egerton Ryerson: His Life and Letters*. Toronto, Clarke, Irwin.

Smaller, H. (1997) 'Regulating the regulators: The disciplining of teachers in nineteenth-century Ontario', in K. Rousaniere, K. Dehli and N. de Coninck-Smith (eds) *Discipline, Moral Regulation, and Schooling: A Social History*, pp. 97–115. New York, Garland Publishing.

Smith, F. (1974) *The Life and Work of Sir James Kay-Shuttleworth*. Bath, Chivers.

Smith, J. (1835) 'Letter to the editor'. *Educational Magazine (Old Series)*, II (November), 432.

Solo (1848) 'Pleasures of school teaching'. *Journal of Education for Upper Canada,* 1 (August), 237–8.

Spence, B. (1972) *Teacher Training in England and Wales During the Period 1846 to 1854.* Unpublished M.Ed. Thesis, Education, Hull, University of Hull.

Spring, J. (1990) *The American School, 1642–1990.* New York, Longman.

St. Mark's College Committee (1845–54) *Minute Book, 1845–54.* Plymouth, College of St. Mark and St. John Archives.

Steedman, C. (1985) '"The mother made conscious": The historical development of a primary school pedagogy'. *History Workshop,* 20, 149–63.

Stephens, W. B. (1998) *Education in Britain, 1750–1914.* London, Macmillan Press.

Stewart, D. (1792–1827) *Elements of the Philosophy of the Human Mind.* Albany, Websters and Skinners.

Stewart, W. A. C. (1972) *Progressives and Radicals in English Education, 1750–1970.* London, Macmillan.

Stow, D. (1853) *The Training System, Moral Training School, and Normal Seminary or College.* London, Longman, Brown, Green, and Longmans.

Sturt, M. (1967) *The Education of the People: A History of Primary Education in England and Wales in the Nineteenth Century.* London, Routledge and Kegan Paul.

Sullivan, R. (1842) *Lectures and Letters on Public Education.* Dublin, William Curry, Jun. and Co.

Symons, J. (1854) 'Hints to teachers: Circular to workhouse masters'. *Educational Record,* III, 207.

Tannoch-Bland, J. M. (2000) *The Primacy of Moral Philosophy: Dugald Stewart and the Scottish Enlightenment.* Unpublished PhD Thesis, School of Humanities, Faculty of Arts, Griffith University, Brisbane.

Tate, T. (1854) 'Method as applied to education'. *The Educational Expositer,* 1, 116.

Tate, T. (1857) *The Philosophy of Education; or, the Principles and Practice of Teaching.* London, Longman, Brown, Green, Longmans, & Roberts.

Thompson, E. P. (1980) *The Making of the English Working Class.* Harmondsworth, Penguin.

Thornburg, L. D. (2004) *Faithful Labor: The Life Work of Julia Anne King, 1838–1919.* Unpublished PhD Dissertation, Michigan State University.

Thorpe, S. (2003) *On the Emergence of 'Crisis' Discourse as a Mode of 'Truth'-telling in Public Education.* Paper Presentation: American Educational Research Association Annual Meeting, New Orleans.

Tomlinson, S. (1997) 'Phrenology, education and the politics of human nature: The thought and influence of George Combe'. *History of Education,* 26, 1–22.

Troman, G. and Woods, P. (2001) *Primary Teachers' Stress.* London, Routledge/Falmer.

Tropp, A. (1957) *The School Teachers: The Growth of the Teaching Profession in England and Wales from 1800 to the Present Day.* London, William Heinemann.

Tyack, D. (1967) 'Bureaucracy and the common school: The example of Portland, Oregon, 1851–1913'. *American Quarterly,* 19, 475–98.

Tyack, D. (1974) *The One Best System: A History of American Urban Education.* Cambridge, MA, Harvard University Press.

Varga, D. (1991) 'Neutral and timeless truths: A historical analysis of observation and evaluation in teacher training'. *The Journal of Educational Thought*, 25(1), 12–26.

Vick, M. (1997) *The Body of the Teacher*. Paper Presentation: Australian Association for Research in Education Annual Meeting, Brisbane, AARE.

Viney, R. J. (1854) 'Aptness to teach'. *The Educator; or, Home, the School, and the Teacher. The Quarterly Journal of the Congregational Board of Education – New Series*, 1(3), 220–9.

Wardle, D. (1976) *English Popular Education, 1780–1975*. London, Cambridge University Press.

Warne, J. (1843) *Phrenology in the Family, or the Utility of Phrenology in Early Domestic Education*. Edinburgh, Maclachlan, Stewart, & Co.

Warwick, D. W. (1966) *The Colleges of S. Mark and S. John: Their History as Illustrating the Development of Teacher-Training in this Country to 1926*. Unpublished M.A. Thesis, Education, London, University of London.

Weinburg, M. (1978) 'The social analysis of three early 19th century French liberals: Say, Comte, and Dunoyer'. *Journal of Libertarian Studies*, 2(3), 45–63.

Welter, B. (1969) 'The cult of true womanhood'. *American Quarterly*, 18, 151–74.

West, E. G. (1975) *Education and the Industrial Revolution*. London, Institute of Economic Affairs.

White, H. (1973) *Metahistory: The Historical Imagination in Nineteenth-Century Europe*. Baltimore, Johns Hopkins University Press.

Whitelands Training Institution (1855) 'A record of certain prizes for common things offered for competition and awarded by Miss Burdett Coutts'. *Education Pamphlets*, XVII, 1–16.

Wilson, J. D. (1974) 'The teacher in early Ontario', in F. H. Armstrong, H. A. Stevenson and J. D. Wilson (eds) *Aspects of Nineteenth-Century Ontario*, pp. 218–36. Toronto, University of Toronto Press.

Windshuttle, K. (1998) 'Foucault as historian'. *Critical Review of International Social and Political Philosophy*, 1(2), 5–35.

Workman, J. (1840) 'Discourse on education', in E. Strong (ed.) *The York Pioneer and Historical Society*, pp. 39–42. Toronto, Dudley & Burns.

W. R. (1861) 'The conduct of Our Saviour towards St. Peter: A model for teachers'. *Journal of Education for Upper Canada*, XIV (March), 42.

Young, J. (1880) *Early History of Galt and the Settlement of Dumfries in the Province of Ontario*. Toronto, Hunter, Rose and Company.

Index